# FOR A CRITIQUE OF THE POLITICAL ECONOMY OF THE SIGN

BY
## JEAN BAUDRILLARD

TRANSLATED WITH AN INTRODUCTION
BY
CHARLES LEVIN

TELOS PRESS
ST. LOUIS, MO.

ISBN: 0-914386-23-9 cloth
        0-914386-24-7 paper

Manufactured in the United States of America

Cover design by Don Powley

Table of Contents

# TRANSLATOR'S INTRODUCTION

## I

The essays in this volume span a period, the late 1960s and early 1970s, when Jean Baudrillard was preparing three other books for publication. In the first, *Système des objets* (1968),[1] he took literally and developed at length Lukacs' observation, at the beginning of his famous essay on reification, that the "problem of commodities...[is] the central, structural problem of capitalist society in all its aspects." For Baudrillard, as for his predecessor, this meant that the commodity was not just a problem in economics, but the nucleus of a semantic crisis which reticulated throughout the entire social system.

Lukacs had gone on to say that "only in this case can the structure of commodity-relations be made to yield a model of all the objective forms of bourgeois society together with all the subjective forms corresponding to them."[2] Baudrillard pursued this line of reasoning further in *La Société de consommation* (1970).[3] Here, he elaborated on the conclusion of his previous book that "consumption" has become a kind of labor, "an active manipulation of signs," a sort of *bricolage* in which the individual desperately attempts to organize his privatized existence and invest it with meaning. But the consumer proceeds through this strange world metonymically, as it were. What is consumed is not the object itself, but the *system* of objects, "the idea of a relation" that is actually "no longer lived, but abolished, abstracted and consumed" by the signifying system itself, of which the commodity is only one kind of differential term. It is this very condition of semiosis, engendered by the universalization of commodity relations, which privatizes experience in the first place. As we "consume" the code, in effect, we "reproduce" the system.

Thus, the alleged "consumer society" surrounds itself with signs of abundance, but abolishes wealth itself, annihilates the *experience* of abundance, by aborting the "concrete, relational dialectic" of social interchange through which real abundance comes into existence, and wealth can be lived. Here, Baudrillard takes issue with

---

1.  *Le Système des objets* (Paris: Denöel-Gonthier, 1968). Henceforth referred to as S.O. in the text.

2.  György Lukacs, *History and Class Consciousness*, trans. Rodney Livingstone (Cambridge, Mass.: MIT Press, 1971), p. 83.

3.  *La Société de consommation* (Paris: Gallimard, 1970). Henceforth referred to as S.C. in the text.

Sartre. Scarcity is not an objective, quantifiable condition against which lives are acted out in struggle, against which societies erect greater and more (or less) humane barriers. Rather it is this competition, the struggle with necessity itself (a gross ideological "form"), and the mythic odyssey of "growth" with which society exorcises this demon, that actually "produce" scarcity as the very principle of social structure.

In 1972, the essays which appear in this volume were published as *Pour une critique de l'économie politique du signe*.[4] Many of them condense what is elaborated in the earlier books, but rough sketches of the themes which will preoccupy the later works emerge as the sequence progresses.

*The Mirror of Production*,[5] which appeared a year later, seems in a way to stand apart from the others in that it explicitly announces a break with Marxism. But this is misleading. In one sense it is true, as Mark Poster has said, that in *Notes For a Critique* Baudrillard "placed himself squarely within Marxist thought as one who was pursuing further the critique of political economy," whereas in *The Mirror of Production* "there are places where Marx is completely rejected."[6] In fact, however, there is no such clear-cut division. Although in *The Mirror of Production* Baudrillard utterly discards any hope that a robust critique is possible from a legitimately Marxist standpoint, he is still recognizably working through a set of problematics which is common to the tradition of Western Marxism. On the other hand, in *Système des objets*, where Baudrillard is most sanguine about adopting conventional Marxist categories, an attentive reader can hardly escape noticing how they are progressively more volatilized by the emerging frame of reference. And in *Notes For a Critique*, most of the distinctive features of Marxist theory are eventually thought through again as structurally implicated in political economy itself. Indeed, what Baudrillard means, in practical terms, when he claims to "extend the critique of political economy to the sign" is that he wishes to include Marx and positivism (with structuralism as the latter's archetypical modern representative), under the heading of political economy, in order to critique the whole lot in one go. So it would be simplifying matters to refer to a particular "conjuncture" in Baudrillard's work. A much more adequate and challenging term for denoting such a moment of inter-relatedness,

---

4. *Pour une critique de l'economie politique du signe* (Paris: Gallimard, 1972). Further references to this translation will appear in the text.
5. *The Mirror of Production*, trans. and introduction by Mark Poster (St. Louis: Telos Press, 1975). Henceforth referred to as M.P. in the text.
6. "Translator's Introduction" to *The Mirror of Production*, p. 13.

which has the advantage of not implying arbitrary closure, has already been coined: "commotion."[7] *Notes For a Critique of the Political Economy of the Sign* is literally a commotion of ideas, sometimes inconsistent, issuing from a period of intense critical activity in which nothing was resolved. This is why I have chosen to append the word "notes" to the original title and to extend occasionally these introductory remarks to other works and writers subtending Baudrillard's discourse.

## II

> ...the once supposedly autonomous subject [is] emptied of any content, until it finally becomes a mere name with nothing to denominate. The total transformation of each and every realm of being into a field of means leads to the liquidation of the subject who is supposed to use them. This gives modern industrialist society its nihilistic aspect.
> — Max Horkheimer, *Eclipse of Reason*[8]

There is no revolutionary substance inhering in people and things, fermenting liberty and peace, as subject and object, reason and nature traverse the battlegrounds and no man's lands of history. There are no "transcendental guarantees," as Marcuse once said; there is no exogenous dialectic. It has always been very tempting to stop right there, abjuring this religion without actually "giving up the ghost," without abandoning the original — indeed the source — of all "transcendental guarantees." The revolution, after all, must go on, and if it won't by itself, then I, *we*, must make it go on. As Marcuse asked: "Are you ready to take yourself as an autonomous subject, through your own revolutionary choice, independently of any 'historical mission,' independently of all 'transcendental guarantees' which, between you and me, are a lot of rubbish anyway, one of the luxuries dear Marx used to allow himself?"[9]

And so we have the autonomous subject, making free choices, independently. This is an indispensable idea, so fundamental that if we do away with it completely, we explode any recognizable version of "emancipation," as Habermas calls it — not to mention "revolution" — and implicitly, we abandon the possibility of critical theory.

A frequent problem with this notion of an autonomous subject has been that, of the many who have written in its name, not a few have

7. John Fekete, *The Critical Twilight* (London: Routledge and Kegan Paul, 1977), p. 223, note 12.

8. Max Horkheimer, *Eclipse of Reason* (New York: Seabury, 1974), p. 93.

9. Quoted in Michel Bosquet, "Herbert Marcuse, professeur de liberté," *Le Nouvel Observateur*, August 6, 1979, p. 17.

written as if it were their *nom de plume*. Perhaps this fact explains, in part, the tyranny wrought, directly (or indirectly, through his epigones), by Marx himself. But Fichtean or Hegelian *hubris* is not the inevitable consequence of belief in a free and vigorous and creative subjectivity. Sartre did much to publicize the idea that nobody, neither the proletariat nor even he, in spite of his stature, could totalize the entire totality. Marcuse linked the idea of autonomy with a non-aggressive sensibility, rooting freedom in the negation of the split with nature, an "explosion of vital needs," as he called it, which transcends the inculcated needs of neo-capitalism.

But if the needs of a "radical sensibility" are intended to recall a harmonious understanding of nature as subjectivity, they nevertheless take the form of categorical imperatives issuing from an imperious reason. As Marcuse himself insisted: "The primary liberation cannot be 'spontaneous' because such spontaneity would only express the values and goals derived from the established system. Self-liberation is self-education but as such it *pre*supposes education by others.... Those who are educated have a commitment to use their knowledge to help men and women realize and enjoy their truly human capabilities."[10] Now, perhaps this explains the "need" for critical theory (or perhaps it doesn't); but it certainly casts the entire project into the whirl of an intolerable circle — one which is hardly resolved with appeals to the Second Thesis on Feuerbach. It is an intolerable circle not because it is a vicious circle, but because it is growing tiresome, and cannot be sustained indefinitely merely by being dubbed "epistemological."

When we have reached this impasse, which has been growing since the early 1970s to the point where it has turned into a major crisis, it becomes interesting to review what the author of the following group of essays has to say. Not that Jean Baudrillard has done much to stave off the crisis. If anything, he has contributed to it, in his own, somewhat *gauche* way. But this is primarily to his credit. There is too much at stake, and the political catastrophe which seems to be upon us now is too profound, for anyone, in the name of anything, to go on pretending, in prose form, that there is *a* theory, and that it is linked to *a* "praxis." For the ever-faithful, a simple argument will suffice: *solvitur ambulando!* The link between critique and political activity has all but polarized around a few issues, notably nuclear fission. The halls of academe are beset by exhaustion. The significant struggles of peoples all over the world have been swallowed and regurgitated in the form of an ever widening and ever more cynical

10. Herbert Marcuse, *Counterrevolution and Revolt* (Boston: Beacon Press, 1972), p. 47.

geopolitics, not to mention kneecapping. To those who complain that the war in Southeast Asia made the truth plainer to see, that *those* were heady days, one can only reply that nastiness, though now in many ways more subtle, is as easy to spot as ever; it has only grown more difficult to live with formulas that should have been buried in 1914.

So we are probably witnessing the demise of Marxism, not of capitalism (if, in reality, that word still adequately denotes the mess we are in).[11] But it is worth remembering: Marx was only a single individual (or perhaps even just a "decentered" subject!); "capitalism," on the other hand, is a whole system. Historical materialism would surely never have had it any other way.

Jean Baudrillard is not the only person who has faced this situation and come away unsilenced. But it is in the context of the kinds of issues raised here that he is best introduced, especially because it is the problematic of subjectivity and the terrible aporia of intervention-understanding which both link and divide him from the tradition of critical theory to which he owes so much. The reader will discover quickly that he has little rhetorical patience with the humanism to which that tradition, sometimes ambiguously (as in the case of Adorno), laid claim. For Baudrillard, as we shall see, the anthropology which many have partitioned off as Young Hegelian juvenilia, is not only essential to the whole Marxian corpus if it is to be taken seriously, but ultimately self-contradictory — and presently, in strategic terms, a sadly impotent response to a world in which what used to be called with confidence the practico-inert has lost its character as a determination of the real, through sheer animation and intimization. "The object," Baudrillard muses, "is the [castrated] household pet *par excellence*. It is the only 'being' whose qualities exalt my person instead of restricting it. And objects, in the plural, are the only existents whose coexistence is truly possible, since their differences do not pit them against each other, as is the case with the living, but converge docilely towards me, smoothly grafting onto my consciousness. They are what is most easily 'personalized,' while simultaneously remaining accountable" (S.O., p. 108). Further: "We can no longer lay claim to the myth of the Pact with the Devil, or the Sorcerer's Apprentice, which thematized the fatal contradiction between the individual being and his Double. And we have no corresponding myth, thematizing the peaceful coexistence, through paradigmatic declension, of the successive terms which define the

---

11. It certainly fails to conjure up the dimensions of the object domain that Baudrillard has constructed in his critique. Let us call it "neo-capitalism," affixing it to most of the world.

model of the 'personal.' The tragic duality had its great myths (which the Situationists have tried to resurrect again with the concept of the 'spectacle,' the 'society of the spectacle,' and radical alienation). All were linked to the notion of a human essence and the fatality of losing it, to Being and its Spectre. But the ludic ramification of the person into a spectre of signs and objects, nuances and differences, which constitute the basis of the consumption process and redefine the individual not as an alienated substance but as a moving difference — this novel process which is not analyzable in terms of the person and the alterity of the person, has not found an equivalent myth to retrace the Metaphysics of Consumption — a myth equivalent to that of the Double and of Alienation for the order of production. *But this is no accident.* Myths, like the faculties of speech, reflection, transcription, are bound up with transcendence, and disappear along with it" (S.C., pp. 310-311). If Lukacs was the extraordinary individual who literally deduced Marx's anthropology before the publication of the *Paris Manuscripts,* if Marcuse was the only member of the Frankfurt School who remained faithful to the vision of Promethean subjectivity that gave meaning to Marx's immense scholarly digressions, still, Baudrillard's impatience with dialectical synthetics owes more in spirit to their work than that of other, less Hegelian members of the critical tradition. His early books can be read as explorations of the social interior of Lukacs' philosophical categories. And, as we shall see, Baudrillard extends the theory of one-dimensionality to the limit beyond which emerge entirely new cognitive and ontological problematics.

It would be simplistic, of course, to put everything in terms of a cosmic contest between phenomenology and structuralism, however loosely understood; but this is the form in which the French elite has so often chosen to understand much of what goes on in the world (especially the subject-knowledge-action problem), and Baudrillard, on the fringes of this elite, inevitably had to confront it. And so, undoubtedly, it was the bitter pill of structuralism he was forced to swallow — and bitter it must have been after the apparent victory of "invariance" over the 1968 "explosion" (which, in some respects, was detonated by his own sociology students at Nanterre). As John Fekete puts it: In structuralism, "attention is shifted away from the ways in which human beings have altered and do alter and may yet alter their objectifications; in consequence, structuralism finds nothing to investigate but order, the codes of order, reflections upon order, and the experience of order."[12] Though Baudrillard agrees with this

---

12. Fekete, p. 197.

view, there is a sense in which the charge can be laid at his own door.

Before we examine this issue in more detail, however, we must be careful to distinguish Baudrillard from those who have turned to structuralism and its "avatars," not so much in order to explore the crisis of subjectivity itself as to resurrect and recuperate the old dogmas, the "historical mission" (or mystique), and the transcendental guarantees whose collapse fed the crisis in the first place. Althusser, for example, has jettisoned people completely from the scheme of things, and has replaced them with an epistemological prop that theoretically produces the algorithms of historical materialism in such a way that their tranquillity is imperturbable. The difficulty seems to have been that Marxism could try to unite theory and praxis in two ways: either with a theory of the subject, ontologically seminated, as it were, or as dogmatic science. When structuralism, with its then more naive scientistic aura, grew influential in the early 1960s, it naturally appealed to those who would opt for the latter orientation. Such is not the case with Baudrillard, whose appropriation of structuralism (or what he prefers to call semio-linguistics) is often precisely that: an act of aggression that virtually destroys its object.

Perhaps, for the moment, it will suffice to say that in *Système des objets,* Baudrillard initiated a peculiar kind of phenomenology, a phenomenology of reification, which in order to permit a more concrete elucidation of its serial and hierarchical structures, brackets consciousness itself. "We are verging on the point where consumption seizes life entirely, where activities concatenate in the same combinatory mode.... In this phenomenology of consumption, the general climatization of life, of social relations represent the accomplished, the 'consummate' stage in an evolution based on stark abundance, moving through the articulated networks of objects to the total conditioning of acts and of time, in the network of systematic ambience we find in the futuristic cities of drugstores, shopping malls, modern airports" (S.S., pp. 23-24).

"Man is rendered incoherent by the coherence of his structural projection," says Baudrillard (S.O., p. 69). In essence, then, he is proposing a phenomenology, if it is a phenomenology, of structuralism itself, in the form of the social world already analyzed structurally. But however we may choose to label it, the ploy allows him to dissect in minute detail the subterranean play of reification as an objective system in which people are to some extent already integrated in their activities and at the level of everyday life: "The code of political economy (both commodity form *and* sign form) does not operate by alienating consciousness from contents. A parallel confusion arises in the view of primitive myths [where] the pregnant effects of mythic 'contents' are held to bind society together (through the 'cohesion' of 'belief' systems). But actually these myths make up a code of signs that exchange among themselves, integrating the group through the very process of their circulation. Likewise, the code of political economy rationalizes and regulates exchange, makes things communicate, but under the law of the code and through the control of meaning. The division of labor, the functional division of the terms of discourse, do not 'mystify' people, they socialize them and inform their exchange according to a general, abstract model. The very concept of the individual is the *product* of this general system of exchange. . . . And ideology, in its version as a superstructure of contents and consciousness, is, in these terms, itself an alienated concept" (p. 147).

So out the window goes a whole set of terms such as projection, introjection, sublimation, repression and especially their macrological complement, "superstructure." This diction, to be sure, provides everyone, including Baudrillard, with an occasionally useful shorthand. But it is also a language that delineates the shadow of a hidden human substance waiting in the wings to be liberated whole when the masquerade of alienation has ended. One has only to ask what it is that capitalism alienates to get all sorts of curious and primitive (though in fact very modern and occidental) answers. Man is an animal who makes himself. He defines himself through his work — give him back some real work. Man is a talking animal, a tool-making animal, a desiring animal, an unconscious animal, etc. And so the critical critics dance their way nimbly through a kind of essentializing evasion of the practical consequences implicit in their own vocabulary: some kind of compulsory therapy, or social engineering on a massive scale. Man at last becomes what he already was anyway by recovering in pristine form the activity that defines his nature; the social infrastructure is thus cleansed (or the other way around), and all the mucky confusion that normally froths atop is automatically eliminated.

On balance, Baudrillard has done well to spurn this mode of paying lip service to the historical subject. But this always ambiguous achievement depends, as we have already begun to see, on a reconceptualization of what critical theory has normally taken to be its object. Here, at least two imposing layers of congealed thought stand in the way.

To begin with, there is the ambiguous patrimony of Marxian sociology itself, which has always tended to be formal and schematic, uncomfortable with the particular — due, no doubt, to its effort to remain consistent with a heritage of conflicting paradigms. The developed critique of political economy was concerned with dialectically unfolding the movement of the capitalist economy, thus exposing its internal contradictions. Apparently starting from an analysis of the commodity (its axiological formation), Marx derived an account in economic terms of the exploitation of labor by capital, revealing a crucial inequality in exchange. The concentrated accumulation of capital itself thereby threatened the existence of the very labor upon which its continued expansion depended. On the other hand, Marx persisted in understanding the movement of history in terms of a dynamic of class domination and overthrow (or mutual disintegration); or, alternatively, in terms of a dialectic of quantity and quality, in which expanding forces of production exploded their constricting social forms. The various models were never successfully coordinated: domination could not be reduced to the specific form of exploitation that Marx had unveiled in *Capital*, and the wage labor-capital relation projected a grainy image when enlarged to the grander proportions of history as class struggle. Inevitably, in addition to this problem of conflicting *representations*, there was the uncertain location of the subject, revolutionary or not, within the staggered interstices of these juxtaposed schemata. As Castoriadis has pointed out, Marx's various hypotheses about the historical drift of capital (for example, his "immiseration" thesis) never took into account the worker's struggle itself. Consequently, in spite of Marx's prediction, real wages have risen.

Now, it seems to have been the job of the Frankfurt School to inherit this bundle of contradictions in all its rich complexity, and then bequeath it to us. The problem was not that Horkheimer and Adorno failed to see inadequacies in the Marxian system, or that they shrank from admitting its failures, but rather how they chose to deal with these. As Richard Bernstein has pointed out: "We do not find in Horkheimer any systematic attempt to refine and develop a historically relevant critique of political economy. Instead, he simply refers to Marx."[13] True, considerable modifications of Marx seem to be implied in the attempt to addend Frankfurt theory, to mention one example; but there is a sense in which the unorthodoxies of the Frankfurt School amount to an elaborate *post bellum auxilium* that indirectly implies the basic rightness of the original Marxian analysis.

It seems clear that the culmination of the Frankfurt position in a purely "negative dialectics" stems from this paradox. Their attempt

---

13.  Richard Bernstein, *The Restructuring of Social and Political Theory* (Philadelphia: University of Pennsylvania Press, 1978), p. 182.

to situate Marx within the general framework of the Enlightenment was not inaccurate as a loose explanation of revolutionary authoritarianism, but it was too broad to carry much critical edge. By reducing Marx to a moment in the history of conceptual double-cross that legitimizes the domination of nature, they totally failed to specify, in the immense theoretical apparatus Marx left behind, where his critique had fallen short, thus hypostatizing their own critical stance in the abstract tension of unresolved contradictions left over from the speculative philosophy of a bygone era. Marx was for them alternately the father of critical theory, the implications of whose work had to be fleshed out, especially at the superstructural level (and preserved from crude reductionism), or the apostle of the world as a workhouse. Their ambivalence seems to have led them to shun the possibility of an immanent critique of Marx, preferring purely external interrogations that juxtapose Marx with Nietzsche and Freud, and play them off against each other in the search for a perspective that is basically secure without being dogmatic. Nevertheless, Horkheimer and Adorno developed vigorous new themes for critical theory, generally as a result of their mistrust of mass culture and of instrumental reason. As Mark Poster pointed out, if Baudrillard and Habermas have anything in common, it is that both have found, in these avenues left open, a perspective from which to begin re-examining Marx's understanding of capitalism, and hence, the strengths and limits of his critique.

It is interesting to pursue the comparison with Habermas. Both have an ultimate interest in elucidating the possibility of a critique from which emancipation emerges as "the practical effect of a theory that does not improve the manipulation of things and of reifications."[14] For both, the critique of political economy succumbed to the latter abuse because Marx had effected a premature theoretical closure that forestalled criticism of the premises and values upon which the critique itself had been based. Both argue that Marx failed to theorize the role of culture and language. For Habermas, these new perspectives offer the possibility of reconstructing a philosophical anthropology by supplementing Marx's *homo faber*, and thereby, following Arendt, correcting Marx's tendency at the categorial level to reduce *praxis* to *techne*.

But here, Baudrillard breaks with the Frankfurt School. Like Habermas, he rejects any retreat to cultured subjectivity, with its meager siege ontology, but he is not interested in Habermas' "quasi-transcendental" reconstitution of the epistemological subject, either.

---

14. Jürgen Habermas, *Theory and Practice,* trans. John Viertel (Boston: Beacon Press, 1973), p. 256.

For him, the re-entry of the language-culture orbit into the heart of the Marxian problematic eliminates the possibility of philosophical anthropology *tout court* as a viable standpoint for critical social theory. Rather, an adequate theorization of these dimensions within the framework of political economy produces an object domain that *in principle* generates no privileged standpoint because it itself has no causal center. Thus, what for Habermas offers the possibility of enriching and preserving the Marxian notion of an essential, rational human praxis, constituting history, for Baudrillard brings about the reverse — in fact, it serves only to explain its decompression, reducing history to an "immense genealogy of the forms of domination" (p. 120). Baudrillard's hypothesis of a "generalized political economy" stands on the same basis as Habermas' *Verstand.*

This returns us to the complex and ambiguous mediating role that structuralism plays in the constitution of this new object. Semio-linguistics, according to Baudrillard, describes the repressive mode of value generation, which is the very articulation of social control. In Baudrillard's view, "All the repressive and reductive strategies of power systems are already present in the internal logic of the sign, as well as those of exchange value and political economy." The structural process of signification "is in some ways akin to the notion of reification" (p. 163).

Here, Baudrillard wishes first to show that the analysis of value, which for Marx revealed a specific logic of exploitation, itself conceals a deeper logic of domination. What enabled Marx to discover surplus value was a dialectical play on the binary internal structure of the commodity, which political economy had already established as use value and exchange value. In exchange for the use value of productive labor, capital supplied an exchange value equivalent, under varying conditions, to the cost of the reproduction of labor power, but less than the exchange value of labor's product itself. Thus labor was a commodity constituting one epicenter in a system revolving around two poles, the other being money. Each in its way, labor and money, was an arch commodity. In a system where use values were otherwise exchanged in equivalence expressed in terms of exchange value, labor was the only commodity that did not receive its own equivalent in return for itself — that is, the internal polarity of the commodity labor was somehow alone, of all commodities in the system, staggered — except for money, which also contained a discoordinated polarity. In labor, the component of use value was disproportionate to its exchange value, in money, the reverse. Yet the tension of the two together, through their internal displacement, conferred a kind of delicate equilibrium on the system as a whole. Quantities of labor provided the ultimate source of measurement of equivalencies between commodities, money the standard in terms of which their equivalence could be established. It was precisely these symmetrical imperfections internal to the commodity system that lent such beauty to the symmetry of the system as a whole.

Now the first complication arises in the tautology of the notion of labor and of its appropriation by capital as a use value. The system of commodities depends on the institution of private property. In this case, it must be assumed that the use value of labor power is the private property of the laborer — he is the *owner* of his own labor capacity, but unlike owners of other kinds of commodities, he is unable to fetch a fair price for the property he sells. This paints a nice picture of capital as theft — which it surely is (why not?) — but the idea is deduced somewhat illegitimately by presupposing private property in the labor power of the worker, precisely that which is supposed to be explained by the advent of capitalism, which in turn is explained by the commodification of labor. Either a person is his own private property or he is not. If he is, as Hobbes believed, then Marx's explanation of capitalism is possible, but it is also eternally true of all complex economic systems. Perhaps this lends a little more credence to Baudrillard's assertion, quoted above, that "The division of labor...and of terms of discourse do not 'mystify' people, they socialize them and inform their exchange according to a general abstract model. The very concept of the individual is the *product* of this general system of exchange."

But the problem goes deeper. Where does Marx get this concept of use value and what function does it serve in the model of capitalism he sets up? The answer is not univocal. On the one hand, use value is a kind of given — it is obvious, self-evident, transparent (whereas exchange value is opaque). Use value is a quality that is only arbitrarily commensurable with the quality of use value in other products — through the medium of exchange value (which makes these products commodities). But then all that Marx seems to be saying is that things can be used for various purposes. I can use my shoe to hammer a nail into a board in order to use the board as an umbrella.... In this case, use value for the most part would be a conventional system of signification. But Marx is claiming much more than this. Use value is "motivated." It is, in fact, created out of labor, *the* value-producing activity. It is a metaphysical entity, arising from a human essence, in a teleological schema, arbitrarily overlaid, suppressed and alienated by the conventional system of exchange value that is capitalism. When the latter is overthrown, use value will resurge as a definite, positive value, a transhistorical human objectification.

I have, of course, simplified the picture of Marxian economics here, because Baudrillard is not concerned with refuting the labor theory of value *per se*, or Marx's explanation of the genesis of surplus value. What worries him is that the "dialectical" unfolding of the structure of the commodity (which looks to Baudrillard more like its structural articulation through the manipulation of binary oppositions) tacitly projects a *functional metaphysic*, which is the very foundation of political economy, *beyond* the system, as its anthropological horizon.

Baudrillard's argument boils down to the insight that the articulation of binary terms must always privilege one side of the opposition, as the means of setting the system in motion. Thus, in the commodity system, it is exchange value that is privileged over use value precisely because exchange value is the system's principle of circulation. Thus it is this very *structural* logic that allows Marx to imagine that use value is not itself structurally implicated in the "logic" of political economy. His critique thus stops short at grasping the form of the commodity, failing to seize its cultural implications. For Marx, use value is an independent and transcendent axiological category, repressed by the system of exchange value that has perverted the fundamental institution of social production. His discussion of the fetishism of the commodity points out the systematic privileging of exchange value, and some of its social implications, but fails to grasp the way in which the structure of the commodity as a whole embodies an ideological form that threatens to permeate the entire social world. The axiological centrality of labor is generated by the system of exchange value itself, and the abstraction and reduction of human exchange that this system entails finds its ideological alibi, to use Baudrillard's term, in the internal structure of the commodity, namely, in use value.

Use value conceptually embodies the reduction of activity in labor by abstractly specifying the meaning of that activity, and the forms of social exchange. Activity is increasingly defined as the production of use value required for the satisfaction of human needs. Interaction is then the circulation of use values necessary to bring about this satisfaction. As the methods of making use value grow more complex, a dialectic is set in motion that refines and multiplies needs, producing more complex modes of civilization. (Progress is the double articulation of consumption on production.) As this system ramifies, circulation problems arise, and exchange value as a total system is born. But it is feeble to single out exchange value as the cause of all the resulting alienation, for according to this conceptual system, or anthropology, praxis and exchange have *already been reduced to a logic of abstract equivalence in the system of use value* (its circulation) and its purely functional coordination of this activity to the system of needs. Exchange value almost appears as an afterthought, a mere byproduct of complexity. But in a crucial sense, everything actually works the other way around. The need-utility relation is not a psychological and axiological bedrock upon which the excrescence of commodity fetishism is erected and from which it can simply be removed (through the rationalization of production), leaving everything else as it was. Rather, for Baudrillard, the cart must definitely be leading the horse, in this case at least — or why isn't the horse romping in the field? Thus, it is precisely the play of exchange value that induces the logic of utility and mobilizes the psychology of needs in order to perpetuate itself in its reduction of human activity to one or another articulation of the systemic adequation of production and consumption. Baudrillard is not thereby denying that certain things are needed and that others are useful.

Now the sociality of language immediately suggests itself in analogy to various features of the commodity system. It might occur to someone that commodities, for example, are like signs, signifying the labor put into them; and that, like the "reality" to which language purports ultimately to refer, the *referent* labor poses epistemological and ontological problems for the signifying (or commodity) system, which the latter therefore tries to occlude. In fact, this is precisely the kind of homolog that semioticians such as Julia Kristeva have proffered in order to explain the essence of "Marx's discovery." It is the standard theory of commodity fetishism as a kind of mystification or veiling of reality.

Baudrillard, however, manages to discover a much more intricate connection between the structural semiotic and the commodity system. If we think of words as the unity of sounds and concepts — i.e., as signs made up of a particular signifier and coordinated internally with a particular signified — then it is obvious that it is the signifier, the *form* of the sign, whether phonic or graphic, that makes the circulation of language possible. Thus, within the sign, the signifier attains a certain privilege over the signified, just as the form of the commodity, the exchange value term, tends to lord it over use value, the other side of the commodity. Furthermore, as the commodity form establishes a legitimizing link with real labor through the somewhat ambiguous mediation of utility, likewise the signifier attempts to suture its enigmatic connection with the world (or the referent) through the *signified*. This sets up the signification process, in which meaning is structured through the formal interplay of signifiers, linked to signifieds as signs, and ultimately to the "world." But structuralism posits an arbitrary relation within this signifying chain, either internal to the sign, between signifier and signified, form and "content," or between the sign and reality, externally. The strategy here is to autonomize the formal systemic feature of communication in the way that political economy attempts to isolate the pure movement of exchange value, in order to constitute the object of a new "science." The arbitrary relation, whether inside or outside the sign, permits the signified or referent to stand in, as it were, for "meaning," while the signifier plays; to serve as a guarantee, backing up the reality that underlies the movement of the signifying form. In other words, like use value, the nether side of the structural equation of the sign functions as the alibi for its privileged term, revealing what for Baudrillard is the basic form of the ideological process: a binary reduction establishing a complementary (i.e., asymmetrical) relation between arbitrarily isolated terms, which institutionalizes a linear, non-reciprocal exchange. This is a pattern of domination that can be found inscribed everywhere: in production-consumption systems, or their ideologies, which strive to reduce all forms of social interchange to a univocal mediation of providing and surviving, where the act of giving and the act of receiving are separated and irreversible instances, like the presence-absence of the penis, the crudest articulation of desire. "It is because *the structure of the sign is at the very heart of the commodity form* that the commodity can take on, immediately, the effect of signification — not epiphenomenally, in excess of itself, as 'message' or connotation — but because its very form establishes it as a total *medium*, as a *system of communication* administering all social exchange. Like the sign-form, the commodity is a *code* managing the exchange of values. It makes little difference whether the contents of material production or the immaterial contents of significations are involved; it is the code that is determinant: the rules of the interplay of signifiers and exchange value" (p. 146).

Thus, as the formal, theoretical articulation of the repressive mode of value production, "structuralism" appears to Baudrillard as a kind of *pis-aller* of positivism. The latter, having failed to preserve the fact-value distinction against the demand for intellectual progress, has in effect resorted, via structuralism, to objectifying the arbitrary mechanism of value formation itself into a "scientific" methodology. The structures that it subsequently examines become a sophisticated substitute for positivism's original, naively conceived plane of the Facts and the "given." The object and its domain must now be constituted, and objectivity once again becomes synonymous with a controlled strategy of projective penetration behind the perceived, the immediate. But the brittle mediations of structuralism retain the positivist maneuver of autonomizing and reifying partial systems, thus limiting its attempt to reintegrate object and value to an epistemological exercise that avoids their meaningful contextualization. In effect, structuralism seems to involve a cautious and somewhat static attempt to force a dialectic onto the contemplative stance of the old, "pure" positivism. For Baudrillard, it is precisely this mutation that allows structuralism, as a conceptual problematic with definite themes, to penetrate and fuse with those of political economy-Marxism to constitute the passive theoretical formalization of the "generalized political economy": "This economy of values is a *political* economy. It goes well beyond economic calculation and concerns all the processes of the transmutation of values, all those socially produced transitions from one value to another, from one logic to another logic of value that may be noted in determinate places and institutions — and so it also concerns the connection and implication of different systems of exchange and modes of production. The critique of this general political economy of value is today the only one that can recapture the spirit of Marx's analysis on a global level" (p. 122).

So it is the interpenetration and mutual reinforcement of these two major problematics that Baudrillard calls "the political economy of the sign." Generally speaking, each appeared to have adopted a rationalist model of the social structure. If Marx bequeathed in spite of himself the dualism of base and superstructure, structuralism tended to play into this by proclaiming, on the one hand, the materiality of culture, and on the other, the sometimes relative "autonomy of the superstructure." Each had a built-in affinity for one side of the infra-superstructure model that, in pursuing its own logic to the end, symptomatically reflected the general polarization of understanding in social theory. Of course, this problem was recognized before Baudrillard, and has been identified over and over again. What is peculiar and fruitful in his approach to this syndrome in critical theory is his discovery that the major conceptual limitations of political economy and its critique can only be sustained by borrowing from the limiting or circular dynamic of the other — cultural theory (which today is what Baudrillard broadly refers to as semio-linguistics); and vice versa. Thus, if Marxism inevitably reverts to a transhistorical axiology as the standpoint for its analysis of the occlusion of the real in the movement of capitalist production, then it is the structural semiotic that reveals (or *is*: there is a genuine ambiguity here) why the critique of political economy can go on believing that its truth lies simply in the recovery of an essence that capitalism hides and represses without actually destroying. This nodal link is the "structural law of value." Structuralism describes, without consciously revealing, the logic that allows the social system with which Marx was concerned to harness its critique into a eulogizing apotheosis of its own legitimizing value system.

John Fekete has described the structuralist semiotic as "the theoretical complement to the neo-capitalist cultural semiosis of never-ending signifying practice...a positivism that accepts this semiosis as the eternal ontology of social being."[15] Baudrillard would agree. But what must now be obvious is that he has gone a step further by arguing that what is being described here is not so much the theoretical complement as the actual, *embodied form* of "everyday life in the modern world." In short, Baudrillard attempts to shift the stance of critical theory by understanding the social, in its totality, as emphatically mediated by the predominant forms of its own self-understanding. This conception may be reminiscent of Durkheim in many ways, but Baudrillard, as we have seen, radically denies any representational model of the social system, any theory of "ideology" as "reflection," however displaced or unevenly developed. In other words, his tendency to merge the forms of intellectual objectification with forms of social life utterly dissolves the distinction between base and superstructure.

Now, such an analysis, if carried off successfully, might indeed provide a fresh basis for conceptualizing subjectivity, one much less dependent on the old schema of rational behavior that Habermas has tried to reformulate. But the maneuver also appears to have unfortunate side effects. It constricts the untheorizable dimension, the gap, the preserve of non-identity that the inverted rationalist model of base and superstructure left unresolved even in its determinism as an open space where one could think alternative forms of living. Instead, Baudrillard projects this virtual space outward, into a no man's land of pure otherness, a hypothetical primitivism rooted in the anthropological evidence of a non-utilitarian, transgressive "symbolic exchange," the reciprocity of an unrationalized semantics of "ambivalence," a world before Weber's disenchantment and the coming of the white man.

As Baudrillard gradually fills out his picture of the "generalized

---

15. Fekete, p. 197.

political economy" that pervades the social system of advanced capitalism, he is compelled to counter stress the urgent power of this radical otherness. Dialectical sublation only results in a reiterative sublimation, as in the case of Marx's idealism of use value. Radical *transgression* is the only alternative. Thus, *symbolic exchange* "haunts" the authoritarian structures of the political economy of the sign, while *ambivalence* perpetually threatens to deconstruct the reified processes of signification. But it grows increasingly difficult to locate anything within this world dominated by the movements of the general system or code, which consistently realizes and embodies them: "Parallel to the concepts of necessity, scarcity and need in the (vulgar or dialectical) materialist code, the psychoanalytic concepts of law, prohibition and repression are also rooted in the objectification of nature.... All the myths of a vengeful, bad, *castrating* nature take root here.... For only then does nature appear as an implacable necessity, 'the alienation of man's own body.' Marx adopted this law of necessity along with the Promethean and Faustian vision of its perpetual transcendence, just as psychoanalysis adopted the principle of castration and repression, prohibition and law (in the Lacanian version, by inscription in the order of the signifier). But in no sense is it a fundamental structure. Neither law nor necessity exists at the level of reciprocity and symbolic exchange, where the break with nature that leads to the irreversibility of castration — and consequently to the entire becoming of history (the operational violence of man against nature) and of the unconscious (the redemption of the symbolic debt owed for this operational violence) — has not occurred. In this sense law, which is called the foundation of the symbolic order and of exchange, results instead from the rupture of exchange and the loss of the symbolic. This is why there is properly neither necessity nor scarcity nor repression nor the unconscious in the primitive order, whose entire symbolic strategy aims at exorcising the apparition of the law" (M.P., pp. 60-61).

Marx had always assumed, as Baudrillard interprets him, that wherever the capitalist weed spread, the symbolic foliage of "backward" societies would be crowded out. The superstructure, so to speak, would be eviscerated in good time, leaving behind it a single level of determinations that led — or could be led — with relative logical clarity to a thoroughly rational future. Perhaps this was why Marx was never bothered by the manifest dualism of his own model: the trenchant rationality of the logic of production would simply rule out irrational social forms and expressions like so many meaningless, metaphysical propositions. Now there are strong echoes of Horkheimer and Adorno's *Dialectic of Enlightenment* in the passage quoted above; but it is clear that Baudrillard's aim, especially in the attack on psychoanalysis, is to discredit their attempt to enrich the withered Marxist account of cultural mediations.

Thus Baudrillard radically confirms the theory of one-dimensionality in his vision of the potential reduction of all social, political, cultural, and economic mediations in a bi-univocal correspondence with the code (which becomes a kind of incarnation of a grandiose tautology — for the code is only the tendency toward this serial reduction itself). In effect, the latter is a principle of absolute translatability without loss of meaning, from one level of determinations to the next. It is this growing correspondence of one institutionally embodied convention with another, *ad infinitum* — as if all social existence were being rearticulated according to a single, crude recursive rule — that evokes bewilderingly the penetration of the signification process of commodities and the commodification of signification into the most intimate texture of social life, virtually "abstracting" it, as Baudrillard says. The possibilities for collective experience are progressively attenuated to the contemplative seizure of coded differences from a serial environment of sign-objects enveloping the consumer. The code is no longer that quaint collection of referents, like God, the Free World, the Father, the Family, the work ethic — increasingly less so, at any rate. It is more like an operationalization at the level of everyday life of that positivist ethos that Marcuse described in *One-Dimensional Man*: "Orienting itself on the reified universe of everyday discourse, and exposing and clarifying this discourse in terms of this reified universe, the analysis abstracts from the negative, from that which is alien and antagonistic and cannot be understood in terms of the established usage. By classifying and distinguishing meanings, and keeping them apart, it purges thought and speech of contradictions, illusions, and transgressions."[16]

## III

"The shadow is in the end
no better than the substance."
— Samuel Beckett, *Molloy*

An obvious and pertinent reaction to all this is to charge that the hypothesis of a generalized political economy has led Baudrillard to *reduce everything to ideology*, in a manner reminiscent of Rousseau in *The Discourse on Inequality*. There is clearly substance to this, especially given the way Baudrillard begins to resort to a version of

16. Herbert Marcuse, *One-Dimensional Man: Studies in the Ideology of Advanced Industrial Society* (Boston: Beacon Press, 1964), p. 182.

the noble savage theme. Mikel Dufrenne, for one, has accused him of getting carried away with his argument in precisely this way.[17] But there is a sense in which this objection eventually turns against itself; for hidden behind the accusation that "everything has been reduced to ideology" lurks the assumption that "ideology" is something real that is also somehow *not* real, an isolatable feature in a larger field, which can be marked out as a distortion in relation to the rest; or conversely, that *within* the misty domain of the ideological there exists an enclave from whose vantage point clarity emanates, like a gifted light. Here, one can perhaps only make a choice, for, as Paul Piccone has pointed out: "If we once and for all get rid of the assumption that we have some direct pipeline to reality through science, revelation or metaphysics, then everything is ideological and the word itself, having no polar otherness, loses its meaning."[18]

This is precisely the point. And as Baudrillard's analysis progresses through the later essays in this book, one begins to sense that when the word "ideology" arises, it does so *faute de mieux*. Concurrently, he gradually abandons the metaphor of an elemental social "primary process" — a version of the unconscious heavily mediated by Lévi-Strauss, which he introduces early on in his studies of objects and consumption in order to convey his notion of a basic, "differential" logic underlying the exchange of signs and commodities. (This "logic" is of course derived from Mauss and Lévi-Strauss also, but with its center of gravity situated more in an imaginative counter-reading of Veblen and Bataille.) The overall shift away from split-level models is consistent with the fact that Baudrillard, though he dabbled with semiological approaches from the beginning, never subscribed to their more naive theory of ideology, which Roland Barthes had originally proposed.[19] Here, ideology was conceived as a sort of non-falsifiable myth, like Freud's unconscious, which is sharply demarcated from "reality" in that it is not susceptible to propositional truth testing or the principle of non-contradiction. (Thus, "reality" is the realm of the true and the false, — or even more radically, "everything that is the case;" whereas ideology is the a-logical dimension of dreams, myths, and even of ethics, if we follow the early Wittgenstein.)

Other sources of terminological confusion arise in the unfolding

17.    Mikel Dufrenne, *Art et Politique* (Paris: Une Générale d'Editions, 1974), p. 59.

18.    Paul Piccone, *Telos*, No. 31 (Spring 1977), p. 195.

19.    Roland Barthes, *Mythologies*, trans. Annette Lavers (Frogmore, St. Albans: Paladin, 1972). For his own reconsideration, see "Change the Object Itself: Mythology Today," in Stephen Heath, trans., *Image-Music-Text* (Glasgow: Fontana, 1977), pp. 165-169.

commotion of these essays — mostly deriving from a certain indigestion in Baudrillard's consumption of anthropology, in particular Lévi-Strauss's. In deference to Marx, there is a temporary and unconvincing effort to coordinate the role of the sign as social discriminant in the production of status and hierarchy with a conventional class analysis, which soon breaks down, and is abandoned. More crucially, Baudrillard has difficulty disengaging the category of symbolic exchange (as opposed to functional, economic and differential forms of activity and exchange) from its original Maussian and Lévi-Straussian context. Thus, the principle of reciprocity which for Baudrillard ruptures and transgresses the axiological determination and abstract finality of social exchange confronts us at the outset as that signification process most popularly associated with the alleged "exchange of women" in kinship structures. In "The Ideological Genesis of Needs," Baudrillard continues to refer to symbolic exchange as a *value*, but he has already begun to distinguish it from the "logic of signification" (sign value) and "consumption." For clarity's sake, the radical exclusion of symbolic, reciprocal, ambivalent, playful potentialities in the institution of the other forms is outlined schematically in "For A General Theory."

The "symbolic debt" owed Lévi-Strauss by Jean Baudrillard is large, but it is most profound in the way he takes inspiration from Lévi-Strauss' evident genius for reconceptualizing social institutions and structures as communication systems. Lévi-Strauss' habit of autonomizing static networks and then demonstrating their apparently endless capacity for internal variation provides Baudrillard with just the counter-model he needs to locate the socially passive, self-reproducing aspects hidden in the intricate, centerless web of the neo-capitalist world. Indeed, in a sense, it is Lévi-Strauss' communication model which gives Baudrillard an initial grip on the Marxian problematic, by providing a means of desituating the more ensconced critical perspectives of Lukacs and Marcuse. But while the status of the structuralist paradigm is often ambiguous in Baudrillard, it is always mediated with Bataille's excessiveness, his stress on *open* systems.

Indeed, in spite of the almost oppressive, seamless texture of the generalized political economy of the sign, the "world" is almost too open in Baudrillard: the potential for alternatives is massively posited, yet thoroughly and intentionally indeterminate. He abjures the quest for a *theorizable* Utopia — a possible subject and a possible world "demarcated" forever on the page. The question here is of a gaping lacuna in Baudrillard's discourse: "It is the symbolic which . . . never ceases to dismantle the formal correlation of signifier and signified. But the symbolic, whose virtuality of meaning is so subversive of the sign, cannot, for this very reason, be named except by allusion, by infraction (*effraction*). For signification, which names everything in terms of itself, can only speak the language of values and of the *positivity* of the sign" (p. 161).

The originality of Baudrillard's work lies perhaps in the way it creates this hiatus, this gap, which is faithful to his own ambivalent "allusions" to the symbolic relation, and which opens up, beyond the field in which his work appears as an effect of discourse, in an intuition, as it were, of a transformative praxis with no instrumental relation to the world. Baudrillard utterly volatilizes the subject's *representational* link to "reality." We are confronted with the terrible internal bind of semiological criticism, over which Roland Barthes has recently mused: "Language, as performance of the language system (*langage*), is neither reactionary nor progressive. It is quite simply fascist: for fascism is not the prohibition of saying things, it is the *obligation* to say them. . . . The Utopia of language is recuperated by the Utopian language — which is just one genre among others. One might say that no writer who has taken up that solitary battle against the power of language has successfully avoided being recuperated by it, whether in the posthumous form of an inscription in the official culture, or in the present form of a fashion which imposes its image and proscribes his living up to what one awaits of him. There is no other alternative for such a writer than to displace himself — or to be stubborn — or to do both at the same time."[20]

Thus, through the sheer vigor of his attack on the sign and its amplified systems, Baudrillard has only reiterated for himself the dilemma posed by the historicity of all critique. But the problem he poses is not merely that the tools of critical theory must ultimately derive from what it takes as its object. What his work begins to call into question is the system-independence of critical theory as such. There are two aspects to this.

To begin with, critical theory is always threatened by the temptation to puff itself up into a kind of gigantic version of the sign, replete with its strategy of abstraction and reduction. This pitfall is implicit in the very activity of constructing a critical model of the "object," which in its claim to avoid passivity, must paradoxically stress its adequacy and therefore its identity with what it claims to transcend. But even the most aggressive model must in principle fall short of its object.

20.  Roland Barthes, *Leçon* (Paris: Seuil, 1977), pp. 14, 25.

Now it is here that *praxis* has traditionally rushed in to the rescue. Unfortunately, what it brings with it, in its "dialectical unity" with theory, is the tacit assumption that critically informed intervention in the object will reduce the object in the image of the theory. The only hope is that this action can be made reciprocal — that *praxis* will be able to return to theory as an enlarging and enriching influence. There is certainly truth to be found in this formulation, but there is not enough of it to herald "the end of philosophy," as Marx had gambled. For what is also involved here is a circle of representations (what Baudrillard calls a "specular relation," or the "Imaginary") in which theory attempts to reduce reality through practice, and practice returns the complement by reducing theory to the terms of its own contingent field of possibilities. Furthermore, critical theory has failed to take into account its own role in system maintenance as a regulative feedback loop — a feature that does not usually appear in its model of the object precisely because it *constitutes* that feature in its distance from, or negation of, the object. In this view, the only difference between "critical" theory and systems theory is that the latter transforms the whole dilemma into a powerful operational principle (like Diamat).

It should be no surprise, then, that Baudrillard moves straight from his critique of the sign to a reality problematic in which he begins to take cybernetics, systems theory, communication theory and (as their archetype) McLuhanism ("the medium is the message") at their face value. Critical theory appeared to have started life lagging a step behind capitalism, because Marx and others had brilliant hallucinations of an otherness which was, in effect, only the projection of the system itself, through the medium of critique. As early as *Système des objets,* Baudrillard was alluding to this possibility as the "energist Imaginary," predicting that "perhaps. . .it will prove necessary to examine the structures of a cybernetic Imaginary, whose focal myth would be neither an absolute organicism nor an absolute functionalism, but the absolute interrelationality of the world" (S.O., p. 142).

In his articles on the media and the environment in this volume, Baudrillard begins to articulate this eventuality by playing with the metaphor of operational simulation models as the potential successor to the critical theory of ideology. For "ideology" has already surpassed itself, in its revolutionary bid for the social totality, by announcing that it has nothing to lose but its disguise, which it is quite willing to risk. A new era dawns in which the scandal of appearances appears to function for its own sake — in which at best it may be claimed that if something lies behind the cycle of simulacra, its character is formally undecipherable. Baudrillard evokes the disturbing possibility that capitalism has triggered a dynamic in which society begins to understand itself *critically*, to be sure, but only from the standpoint of the repressive system itself as it moves operationally to a "higher logical level," thus permitting detection of the simulation model which it is already leaving in its wake. It is no wonder, then, that in *L'échange symbolique et la mort,*  where he seriously begins to advance these hypotheses, he characterizes his own posture in terms of Alfred Jarry's proto-surrealist contestation — "in short, theoretical violence," as he puts it, somewhat facetiously — alluding to Dr. Faustroll's "pataphysics," and comparing the ultimately self-defeating yet impenetrably tautological structure of neo-capitalism to the curious, galactic spiral on the bloated spherical belly of Ubu Roi.

*Charles Levin*

---

21.   Jean Baudrillard, *L'échange symbolique et la mort* (Paris: Gallimard, 1976).

# CHAPTER ONE

## SIGN-FUNCTION AND CLASS LOGIC [1]

### 1. Social Function of the Sign-Object

*The Empiricist Hypothesis: Needs and Use Value*

An analysis of the social logic which regulates the practice[2] (*pratique*) of objects according to diverse classes or categories[3] cannot help but be at the same time a critical analysis of the ideology of "consumption" that today underlies all practice relative to objects. This double analysis — that of the distinctive social function of objects and of the political function of the ideology that is attached to it — must be based upon an absolute precondition: the surpassing of a spontaneous vision of objects in terms of needs and the hypothesis of the priority of their use value.

This hypothesis, which is supported by lived evidence, assigns a functional status to objects, an instrumentality bound up with technical operations upon the world, and by the same token posits a mediating status for the "natural" anthropological needs of the individual. From this perspective objects are primarily a function of needs and take on their meaning in the economic relation of man to the environment.

This empiricist hypothesis is false. Far from the primary status of the object being a pragmatic one which would subsequently come to overdetermine a social value of the sign, it is the sign exchange value (*valeur d'échange signe*) which is fundamental — use value is often no more than a practical guarantee (or even a rationalization pure and simple). Such, in its paradoxical form, is the only correct sociological hypothesis. Below their concrete visibility (*évidence*),

---

1. Appeared in *Communications*, No. 13 (1969).

2. "Pratique," with certain exceptions that should be clear to the reader and are often indicated by *pratique* in parentheses, has generally been translated "practice." This distinguishes it from "praxis," a term regularly used in *Système des objects* (Paris: Gallimard, 1968) but apparently later abandoned. Nevertheless, pratique does retain overtones of praxis and is not the same as usage in the simple utilitarian sense. Rather, it refers to a sort of operative mode, one of the various stances, or practical attitudes that may be reflected in one's use of objects. That there are various pratiques that may be focused simultaneously upon a single object should be made amply clear in the sections later in this chapter concerning the TV-object (see especially Ritual and Rational Practices). — *Translator's note*.

3. Baudrillard seems to use "catégorie" for "classe" (especially catégorie sociale-classe sociale) more often than would be usual in English. We have, however, used category quite strictly as a translation of catégorie because the latter has become a common term in structuralist writing. We cite from Piaget, *Le Structuralisme* (PUF), pp. 24 ; 25: "Il s'agit de l'invention des 'catégories' (MacLane, Eilenberg, etc.), c'est-à-dire d'une classe d'éléments y compris les fonctions qu'ils comportent, donc accompagnée de morphismes." A rough translation: "It involves the invention of 'categories' (MacLane, Eilenberg, etc.), that is to say, a class of elements including the functions they bear with them, thus a class accompanied by morphisms." — *Trans*.

needs and functions basically describe only an abstract level, a manifest discourse of objects, in regard to which the largely unconscious social discourse appears fundamental. An accurate theory of objects will not be established upon a theory of needs and their satisfaction, but upon a theory of *social prestations*[4] and *signification*.

### Symbolic Exchange: the "Kula" and the "Potlatch"

Alluding to primitive societies is undoubtedly dangerous — it is nonetheless necessary to recall that originally the consumption of goods (alimentary or sumptuary) does not answer to an individual economy of needs but is a social function of prestige and hierarchical distribution. It does not derive primarily from vital necessity or from "natural law," but rather from a cultural constraint. In summary, it is an institution. Goods and objects must necessarily be produced and exchanged (sometimes in the form of violent destruction) in order that the social hierarchy be manifest. Among the Trobriand Islanders (Malinowski) the distinction between economic function and sign function (signification ⚌ fonction/signe) is radical: there are two classes of objects upon which two parallel systems are articulated — the *Kula*, a system of symbolic exchange founded upon the circulation, the progressive presentation (*le don en chaîne*) of bracelets, collars, finery, etc., about which a social system of values and status is organized — and the *Gimwali*, the commerce of primary goods.

In our societies this segregation has disappeared (with exceptions: dowries, gifts, etc.). Yet behind all the superstructures of purchase, market, and private property, there is always the mechanism of social prestation which must be recognized in our choice, our accumulation, our manipulation and our consumption of objects. This mechanism of discrimination and prestige is at the very basis of the system of values and of integration into the hierarchical order of society. The *Kula* and the *Potlatch* have disappeared, but not their principle, which we will retain as the basis of a sociological theory of objects — and this is undoubtedly all the more true to the extent that objects multiply and differentiate themselves. The fundamental conceptual hypothesis for a sociological analysis of "consumption" is *not* use value, the relation to needs, but *symbolic exchange* value,[5]

---

4.   "Prestation" is rare in English or French. Baudrillard develops and uses it so extensively that it almost becomes a term. The sense is most succinctly expressed when he refers to "the mechanism of social prestation...a mechanism of discrimination and prestige." The word indicates a feeling of obligation to an irrational code of social behavior.   — *Trans.*

5.   It will later be made clear (cf. *For a General Theory*) that symbolic exchange is radically separate from all values.   — *Trans.*

the value of social prestation, of rivalry and, at the limit, of class discriminants.

## Conspicuous Consumption

The echo of this primordial function of objects is found enlarged in the notion of *conspicuous waste* (ostentatious prodigality, honorific consumption or expenditure) in the analysis of Thorstein Veblen.[6] Veblen shows that even if the primary function of the subservient classes is working and producing, they simultaneously have the function (and when they are kept unemployed, it is their only function) of displaying the *standing* of the Master. Women, the "people," servants are thus the exhibitors of status. These categories also consume, but in the name of the Master (vicarious consumption); their indolence and their superfluousness testify to his wealth and grandeur. Thus their function is no more economic than that of the objects in the *Kula* or the *Potlatch*, but is one of institution or preservation of a hierarchical order of values. From this perspective Veblen analyzes the condition of women in patriarchal society: just as the slave is not fed in order that he eat, but in order that he work, so one does not dress a woman luxuriously in order that she be beautiful, but in order that her luxury testify to the legitimacy or the social privilege of her master (such is also the case of "culture" which often functions for women as a social attribute: in the leisure classes especially, the culture of women is part of the group patrimony). This notion of *vicarious consumption* is crucial: it leads us back to the fundamental theorem of consumption, which is that the latter has nothing to do with personal enjoyment (although the woman is pleased to be beautiful), but that rather it is a restrictive *social institution* that determines behavior before even being considered in the consciousness of the social actors.

Going further, it may lead us to consider consumption, not as it presents itself — as generalized individual gratification — but as a social *destiny* affecting certain groups or social classes rather than others, or as opposed to others. If today, in modern democratic society, there no longer exist categories devoted *de jure* to prestigious, vicarious consumption, it might be asked whether behind the apparent social generalization of the process there are not classes devoted *in fact* to these mechanisms of prodigality — and which in that way re-establish the *timeless* function of the institution of value and social discrimination which belonged to consumption in preindustrial society under the apparent total availability of individual behaviors.

---

6. Thorstein Veblen, *Theory of the Leisure Class* (Mentor, 1953).

According to Veblen, one of the major indications of prestige, apart from wealth and wasteful expenditure (dilapidation), is *waste of time*, exercised directly or by proxy (vicarious leisure). The world of objects does not escape this rule, this constraint of superfluousness. It is always present in their uselessness, their futility, their superfluousness, their decorativeness, and their non-functionality, in entire categories of objects (trinkets, gadgets, accessories) or for every object, in all its connotations and metabolism of forms, e.g., in the game of fashion, etc. In short, objects never exhaust themselves in the function they serve, and in this excess of presence they take on their signification of prestige. They no longer "designate" the world, but rather the being and social rank of their possessor.

## The Functional Simulacrum

Today, however, this constraint of leisure, of non-instrumentality as the source of values, collides so markedly everywhere with an antagonistic imperative, that the current status of the everyday object results from the conflict, or rather, compromise, between two opposed moralities: an aristocratic morality of "*otium*" and a puritan work ethic. In fact, when one makes the object's function into its immanent rationale, one largely forgets to what degree this functional value is itself controlled by a social morality that no more wants the object to be unemployed than the individual. It must dedicate itself to "laboring," to "functioning" and to excusing itself, democratically so to speak, for its previous aristocratic status as a pure sign of prestige. This bygone status, founded upon ostentation and expenditure, is always present, but while clearly imprinted upon the effects of fashion and décor, it is most often doubled — to a variable degree — by a functional discourse that can serve as *alibi* for the function of *invidious distinction*. Thus objects lead a perpetual game which in fact results from a moral conflict, from a disparity of social imperatives: the functional object pretends to be decorative, it disguises itself with non-utility or with transvestite fashion — the futile and indolent object is charged with a practical reason.[7] At the limit is the gadget: pure gratuitousness under a cover of functionality, pure waste under cover of an ethic of practicality. In any case, all objects, even futile ones, are objects of labor: housekeeping, organizing, tinkering, repairing — everywhere *homo faber* is the double of *homo otiosus*. More generally, we would be dealing with (and this not only in the world of objects) a functional *simulacrum*

---

7.  Thus, in the centrally heated country villa, the peasant bed-warming pan disguises its anachronistic "folklore" character: it is said to be "useful in winter all the same."

(*make-believe*), behind which objects would continue to enact their role of social discriminants. In yet another manner of speaking, objects are caught in the fundamental compromise[8] of having to signify, that is, of having to confer social meaning and prestige in the mode of *otium* and the game (an aristocratic and archaic mode with which the hedonist ideology of consumption tries to reestablish ties) and of having incidentally to submit to the powerful consensus of the democratic morality of effort, of doing and of merit.

One can imagine a state of society where this would result in two disjointed classes of objects: prestige/use or sign exchange value/use value — a disjunction bound to a strong hierarchical integration (a primitive society or ritual and caste). Once again, in our societies this most often results in an ambivalence on the level of each object.

It is important to read social obligation, the ethos of "conspicuous" consumption (direct or vicarious)[9] everywhere, beyond the practical evidence of objects and through the apparent spontaneity of behaviors, and so to grasp a permanent dimension of social hierarchy in the context of consumption, and today, in "standing," a morality which is still imperative.

So, under this paradoxical determination, objects are not the locus of the satisfaction of needs, but of a symbolic labor, of a "production" in both senses of the term: *pro-ducers* — they are fabricated, but they are also produced as a *proof*. They are the locus of consecration of an effort, of an uninterrupted performance, of a *stress for achievement*, aiming always at providing the continual and tangible proof of social value. They are a sort of secular *Bewährung,* probation, or prestation, which, under the inverse influences, is the heir of the principles that were the foundation of the Protestant ethic and which, according to Weber, motivated the capitalist spirit of production. The morality of consumption relays that of production, or is entangled with it in the same social logic of salvation.

## 2. Sociological Perspectives

*Chapin: The Living-room Ladder*

Various authors have tried to integrate objects as elements of a

---

8. It is a contradiction in every logic, for the two systems of value are incompatible. Only the "functionalist" industrial aesthetic can imagine a harmonious reconciliation of function and form, because it is unaware of the social contradictions of its employment (*exercise*). Cf. below, Luxury and the Ephemeral.

9. Here it is not a question of individual vanity that wishes to possess more beautiful objects than others: the latter derives from psychological living, from the conscious relation of rivalry. The social goal of ostentation and all the social mechanism of value are largely unconscious, and are exercised by the subjects without their own knowledge. The conscious games of prestige and rivalry are only the refraction of these finalities and constraints in consciousness.

social logic. As a general rule, however, they have only a walk-on role in sociological research. For the analysts of "consumption," objects are one of the preferred themes of the sociological para-literature, the alternative to advertising discourse. Nonetheless there is one systematic attempt to be noted, that of Chapin.[10] He defines status as "the position occupied by an individual or family according to the dominant standards of cultural goods, of net revenues, of material goods and of participation in group activities of the collectivity." Thus he has four scales. Then it was realized that the four components were in such close relation with the independent measure of the living-room furniture that the latter alone was sufficient for the statistical measurement of class. This "living-room scale" involves twenty-three items, in which the various objects are inventoried and accounted (so also are certain aspects relating to the ensemble: cleanliness, order, maintenance). This first exploration towards sociological goals is thus characterized by the most naive empiricism: the social strata are simply indexed upon a balance-sheet of objects. Now, this procedure is not strictly valid (its conclusions are imprecise in any case) except in a society of relative penury where buying power alone clearly separates the classes. Nor is it really valid except for the extremes. Furthermore, such fixed correlations would be unable to contain either the logic or the dynamic of stratification.

### Rhetorical and Syntactic Analysis of the Environment

Having said this, if Chapin's scale were based on a more subtle analysis which inventoried the quality of objects, their material, their form, their stylistic nuance, etc., it could still be of some use, for, notwithstanding the objections made against Chapin, it is still not true that today everyone possesses virtually the same things. The study of models and series [11] shows a complex progression of differences and nuances, which means that the same category of objects (armchairs, shelving units, cars, etc.) can still reconstitute all the social disparities. But it is also clear that with the increase in standard of living, discrimination today has passed from possession, pure and simple, to the organization and the social usage (*pratique*) of objects. Thus a social classification must eventually be founded upon a more subtle semiology of the environment and of everyday practices. An analysis of interiors and of domestic spaces which was founded, not upon the inventory but upon the distribution of objects (centrality-eccentricity; symmetry-asymmetry; hierarchy-

10.  F. Stuart Chapin, *Contemporary American Institutions* (New York: Harper, 1935), Ch. XIX: A Measurement of Social Status. Cf. also Dennis Chapman, *The Home and Social Status* (London: Routledge and Kegan Paul, 1955).

11.  Cf. Jean Baudrillard, *Le Système des objects*.

deviance; promiscuity-distance), upon formal or functional syntagma, in short, an analysis of the syntax of objects, which endeavoured to bring out the organizational constants with reference to
the type of habitation and the social category, as well as the coherence or contradictions of the discourse, would be a preparatory level
for an interpretation in terms of social logic (on the condition that
this "horizontal" topoanalysis was accompanied by a "vertical"
semiology that would explore the hierarchical scale of each category of
objects    from the series to the model through all the significant
differences).

The problem then will be on the one hand to make a coherence
emerge between the relative position of a given object, or ensemble of
objects on the vertical scale, and on the other hand the type of
organization of the context in which it is found and the type of practices connected with it. The hypothesis of coherence will not necessarily be justified: there are barbarisms, lapses not only in the formal
discourse but in the social discourse of objects. It is not only a
question then, of noting them in the structural analysis, but of interpreting them in terms of logic and of social *contradictions*.

In summary: to what may a sociological analysis in this domain
look forward? If it is to bring out a specular [13] or mechanical relation
between a given configuration of objects and a given position on the
social scale, as Chapin does, it is devoid of interest. It is well known
that objects tell a great deal about the social status of their owner,
but there we have a vicious circle: in the objects, one identifies a
social category which has, in the final analysis, already been
described on the basis of these objects (among other criteria). The
recurring induction hides a circular deduction. The specific social
practice, and thus sociology's true object, cannot be brought out by
this operation.

### Strategic Analysis of the Practice of Objects

Undoubtedly, in a preliminary phase one can consider objects
themselves and their summation as indices of *social* membership. But
it is much more important to consider them, as regards their choice,
organization and practice, as the scaffolding for a *global structure* of
the environment, which is simultaneously an active structure of behavior. This structure, then, will no longer be directly bound to a
more or less pre-assigned, pre-inventoried status, but analyzed as an

---

12.   For certain categories the differential scale is relatively impoverished (electric
household gadgets, TV, etc.). For others (seats, wall units), the hierarchical paradigm
of models and series will be rich.

13.   "Spéculaire"; cf. note about Lacan below in "Toward a Political Economy of
the Sign."   — *Trans.*

element of the *social tactic* of individuals and groups, as the living element of their aspirations, which in a larger structure may then coincide with other aspects of this social practice (professional trajectory, education of children, place of residence, network of relations, etc.), but which may also be partly contradictory to them.[14]

What is evident in any case is that one can only speak of objects in terms other than themselves, in terms of social logic and strategy. Simultaneously, however, the analysis must be maintained upon a specific terrain, by determining what specific position is occupied by objects with respect to other systems of signs and what specific field of practices they constitute in the general structure of social behavior.

## Is the Discourse of Objects Specific?

It seems that the norm of consumption attitudes is simultaneously distinction and conformity.[15]   As a general rule it seems that there would be predominance of the membership group over the ideal reference group: one has "conformist" objects, peer objects.[16]   But the problem remains posed: what is the specific position of objects (is there one?) with respect to this very general norm of consumption attitudes (*attitudes de consommation*)? Is there an iso-functionality, a redundance of various systems of signs and behavior, relative to consumption? Clothes, objects, habitations, recreation, cultural activities? Or relative autonomy? Thus today the sectors of clothing, household appliances, automobiles, and apartments all obey norms of accelerated renewal, but each according to its own rhythm — their relative obsolescence varying, moreover, depending on the social categories. But it may also be admitted that all other sectors together are opposed to "inhabiting" — the latter, though integral in the general process, nevertheless constitute a specific function which cannot be assimilated, either brutally or ideally, into the other aspects of consumption and fashion.[17]   Reducing all sectors of distinctive signs to a synchronic and univocal relationship with the position on the social scale (or with the trajectory) would undoubtedly liquidate a whole rich field of contrasts, of ambiguities and of disparities. In other words, is the social practice of objects

14.   Thus at every social level, giving education to children is an essential tactical element: but on certain levels this form of fulfillment conflicts with fulfillment through the possession of objects.

15.   This is also the paradox of fashion: everyone outfits himself in distinctive signs that end up belonging to everyone. Riesman evaluates the paradox in successive types of civilizations: the *other-directed*, which is conformist, succeeds the *inner-directed*, which endeavors to distinguish itself.

16.   Cf. on this point George Katona, *The Powerful Consumer* (New York: McGraw Hill, 1960), and the notion of *inconspicuous consumption*.

17.   See below, Luxury and the Ephemeral.

specific? Is it through these objects, rather than through one's children, friends, clothing, that one indicates a demand for conformity, for security, or rather, what sort of ambition, and through what category of objects? For at the heart of the objects themselves, from one category to another, one can hypothesize their relative autonomy and that of their practice, in the context of social attitudes. In apartments one often notices that from the point of view of status the configuration of the ensemble is not homogeneous — rarely are all objects of a single interior on the same wave-length. Do not certain objects connote a social membership, a factual status, while others a presumed status, a level of aspirations? Are there "unrealistic" objects, that is to say those which falsely register a contradiction of the real status, desperately testifying to an inaccessible standing (all else remaining equal, they are analogous to "escapist" behavior or to the utopian behaviors characteristic of critical phases of acculturation)? Conversely, are there witness-objects that, despite a mobile status, attest a fidelity to the original class and a tenacious acculturation?

## The Formal Code and Social Practice

Thus there is never a place for listing an inventory of objects and the social significances (*significations*) attached to them: a code in such a case would hardly be more valuable than a "clef des songes." It is certain that objects are the carriers of indexed social significations, of a social and cultural hierarchy — and this in the very least of their details: form, material, colors, durability, arrangement in space — in short, it is certain that they constitute a code. But precisely for that reason there is every occasion to think that far from following the injunctions of this code undeviatingly, individuals and groups use it to their advantage, together with its imperative and distinctive repertory of objects, as is the case with any other institutional or moral code. That is to say, they use it in their own way: they play with it, they break its rules, they speak it with their class dialect.

This discourse must then be read in its class grammar, in its class inflections, in the contradictions with its own social situation which the individual or group directs its discourse of objects. A correct sociological analysis must be exercised in the concrete syntax of object ensembles (equivalent to a story and liable to interpretation in terms of social destiny, just like the story of a dream in terms of unconscious conflicts) and in the lapses, incoherencies and contradictions of this discourse, which is never reconciled with itself (possible only in an ideally stable society — a near impossibility in our societies). On the contrary, this discourse always expresses in this very syntax a neurosis of mobility, of inertia or of social regression. And finally, the object of sociological analysis lies in the ultimately disparate or contradictory relationship of this discourse of objects to other social conducts (professional, economic, cultural). That is to say that it must avoid a "phenomenological" reading (the "pictures" of objects brought back to characteristics or social types), and the merely formal reconstitution of a code of objects, which is never spoken as such in any case (although it hides a strict social logic), but is always restored and manipulated according to a logic peculiar to each social situation.

Thus objects, their syntax, and their rhetoric refer to social objectives and to a social logic. They speak to us not so much of the user and of technical practices, as of social pretension and resignation, of social mobility and inertia, of acculturation and enculturation, of stratification and of social classification. Through objects, each individual and each group searches out his-her place in an order, all the while trying to jostle this order according to a personal trajectory. Through objects a stratified society speaks[18] and, if like the mass media, objects seem to speak to everyone (there are no longer by right any caste objects), it is in order to keep everyone in a certain place. In short, under the rubric of objects, under the seal of private property, it is always a continual social process of value which leads the way. And everywhere and always, objects, in addition to utensils, are the terms and the avowal of the social process of value.

### 3. The Differential Practice of Objects

For all these reasons, because social stratification, mobility and aspirations are the keys to a sociological investigation of the "world" of objects, we would prefer to focus on the configuration of these latter in the rising, mobile, or "advanceable" classes that have a critical and uncertain status, in the so-called middle classes, the floating hinge of a stratified society, classes on the way to integration or acculturation, that is to say, which escape the destiny of social exclusion of the industrial proletariat or that of rural isolation, without however enjoying the advantage of inheriting an already acquired social situation. What interests us is the practice (and the psychological aspects ratifying it) that objects play in these social categories.

*Mobility and Social Inertia*

It is known that an essential problem in these mobile strata is the disparity between intentional mobility (aspirations) and real mobility (objective chances of social promotion). It is known also that these

---

18.   Undoubtedly even a class society, as we will see later.

aspirations are not free, that they are a function of social inheritance and acquired position.[19]   Past a certain threshold of mobility they do not even exist: there is absolute resignation. As a general rule they are relatively unrealistic: much more is hoped than it is possible to attain — *and* relatively realistic: the ambitious imagination is not given free rein (except in pathological cases). This complex psychological image itself rests upon the social actors' implicit interpretation of the objective sociological data. Industrial societies offer chances of mobility to the middle classes, but relative chances; in all but exceptional cases, the trajectory is short, social inertia is strong, and regression is always possible. Under these conditions it seems that:

—the motivation to ascend the social scale translates the interiorization of the norms and general schemes of a society of growth;

—but excessive aspirations in relation to real possibilities translate the disequilibrium, the profound contradiction of a society in which the "democratic" *ideology* of social progress often comes to compensate and overdetermine the relative inertia of social mechanisms. In other words, individuals *hope* because they "know" they can hope — they *do not hope too much* because they "know" that in fact this society opposes unconquerable barriers to free ascent — they *hope however a little too much* because they also live by a diffuse ideology of mobility and growth. Thus the level of their aspirations results exactly from a compromise between a realism nourished on facts and an unrealism sustained by an ambient ideology — a compromise which in turn reflects the internal contradiction of global society.

Now this compromise which the social actors realize in their future projects and in those respecting their children is first expressed in their objects.

*Domestic Order and Public Verdict*

Here we must raise a possible objection, which is that private property would create a special jurisdiction for objects which would absolutely distinguish the conduct relative to these private objects from all other conduct regulated by social constraints. "Private" and "social" are not mutually exclusive except in the everyday imagination, and if objects are apparently part of the domestic order, still we have seen that their meaning is only clarified by their relationship to the social constraint of conformity and mobility. More profoundly, the jurisdiction of the system of social values is imma-

---

19.   Thus the proportion of workers who want their children to complete higher education is much lower than that of individuals belonging to the privileged classes.

nent in the domestic order. The private relationship hides a profound recognition and acceptance of the public *verdict*. At bottom individuals know themselves (if they do not feel themselves), to be judged by their objects, to be judged according to their objects, and each at bottom submits to this judgment, though it be by disavowal. Here it is a question of more than the imperative of conformity issuing from a limited group, or that of upward mobility issuing from global society: it is a question of an order in which each group or individual can only come to locate itself in the very movement which makes it exist socially. In the "private," in the "domestic" sphere (and so also in the environment of objects) in which the individual lives as a refuge zone, as an autonomous field of needs and satisfactions, below or beyond social constraints, the individual nevertheless always continues to evince or to claim a legitimacy and to assure it by signs. In the least of behaviors, through the least of objects, he or she translates the immanence of a jurisdiction which in appearance is rejected.

### Ambiguous Rhetoric — Triumph and Resignation

Now, for the categories that interest us, this verdict is never positive: their progress on the social scale is always relative and often ludicrous. Above all, legitimacy, that is to say, the possibility of establishing their acquired situation as an intrinsic value, escapes them. It is this thwarted legitimacy (with respect to cultural, political, and professional life) which makes the middle classes invest in the private universe, in private property and the accumulation of objects with a dedication all the more fierce, autonomizing it all by default in trying to celebrate a victory, a true social recognition which escapes them.

That is what gives objects in this "milieu" a fundamentally ambiguous status: behind their triumph as signs of social promotion they secretly proclaim (or avow) social defeat. Their proliferation, their "stylization," their organization is anchored there in a rhetoric which, in the terms of P. Bourdieu, is quite fittingly a "rhetoric of despair."

The way in which objects present themselves to vision and wish to forestall the objections of value, the way in which they submit to the latent jurisdiction of social hierarchies, all the while repudiating them — this whole discourse of objects, which constitutes the lived drama of private property — also represents a *social* passion and feeds social emotionalism (*le pathétique*). Let us not forget that, *mutatis mutandis* the exhibition of the harvest, piled in heaps in their gardens by the Trobriand Islanders is always a provocation, a competition, a challenge. But it is also a rite, destined to evince an order of values, a rule of the game, in order to be integrated by it. In the *Potlatch*, it is the insolent destruction of objects and wealth which is "the proof." In the private consumption and property which we know, and which are apparently established upon the individual order, this antagonistic social aspect of *prestation* seems to be exorcised, resolved. But such is not the case at all; it may even be that the processes of a society of "consumption" powerfully reactivate this function of objects as "displays of antagonism" (*exposants antagoniques*). In any case, something of these primitive practices still haunts contemporary objects and always makes their presence vehement, powerfully expressive, never neutral.

## Stylistic Modalities

On the level of objects this "rhetoric of despair" is indicated by various stylistic modalities. They all derive from a logic (and an aesthetic) of simulation, a simulation of the bourgeois models of domestic organization. On the other hand, it must be pointed out that the reference models are not the contemporary upper classes insofar as these classes are part of a greater fiction. The reference model of the "mobile" classes is the traditional bourgeois order as it has been recognized since the Empire and Restoration, and which is itself an adaptation of earlier aristocratic models.

This "petty bourgeois" rhetorical order is governed by two essential modes: on the one hand, *saturation and redundance*; on the other, *symmetry and hierarchy*. Obviously there are numerous overlappings (thus symmetry is also redundancy, but it includes centrality). Nonetheless the two modes are quite distinct, the one (saturation-redundancy) expressing the inorganic, the other (symmetry-hierarchy) expressing the organic structure of this order. Let us point out that these modes of organization are not bound in essence to the bourgeois or the petty bourgeois order: they derive also from a more general anthropological or aesthetic analysis. But here they only interest us in a social definition, as the specific rhetoric of a given social category.

With respect to saturation, one knows that the bourgeois house is closed upon itself and full like an egg. Inheritance and accumulation are the signs of "status" and of ease. Along the same line, the petty bourgeois interior is indicated by congestion. True, it often lacks space but this shortage of space in turn gives rise to a compensating reaction: the less space one has, the more one accumulates (a little like the criterion of quantitative memory which is active in radio games in the absence of any "noble" cultural motivations).

Sometimes, on the other hand, it is certain rooms, certain corners of the house that are "full." What would have to be understood, then, is rather the various aspects of a play upon the full and the empty, a logistic which makes certain places into reserves, hoardings, or storehouses — formerly the attic and the cellar had an analogous role. A house or a room can thus be analyzed topographically, according to whether it displays stockpiling pure and simple, or aggregates of objects, residual and partial syntagma or syntactic conceptions of the ensemble. To reiterate, this method is uninteresting if it is not taken up again in a social logic: in the gamut from accumulation, despite penury, to planned architecture, each class has its modes of organization.

## The Tactic of the Pot and Its Saucer

Here we consider redundancy, the whole baroque and theatrical covering of domestic property. The table is covered with a table cloth which itself is protected by a plastic table cloth. Drapes and double drapes are at the windows. We have carpets, slipcovers, coasters, wainscoting, lampshades. Each trinket sits on a doily, each flower in its pot, and each pot in its saucer. Everything is protected and surrounded. Even in the garden each cluster is encircled with wire-netting, each path is outlined by bricks, mosaics or flagstones. This could be analyzed as an anxious compulsion to sequestration, as an obsessional symbolism: the obsession of the cottage owner and small capitalist is not merely to possess, but to underline what he possesses two or three times. There, as other places, the unconscious speaks in the redundancy of signs, in their connotations and their overworking (*surcharge*).

But something else speaks there as well and it is important to draw other conclusions:

(1) The overworking of signs of possession, which here act as demonstration, can be analyzed as not only the intention to possess, but to show how *well*[20] one possesses. Now this demonstration, this over-determination "of style" is always relative to the group: it not only has the psychological function of reassuring the owner of his possession, but also the sociological function of affiliating him with the whole class of individuals who possess in the same way. Thus the very signs of privacy act as signs of social adherence. Through this or that symbolic behavior (*comportement*), it is still the cultural imperative of class which speaks (this of course has nothing to do with political class consciousness).

---

20.   Cf. Sartre's café waiter whose oversignificant actions are intended not so much to do something as to show how well it is done.

(2) On that basis it is interesting to refer the simultaneously anxious and triumphant character of the conduct of possession to the specific position of the middle class(es) on the social trajectory. How is it to be defined? It is a class which has gone far enough to interiorize the models of social success, but not far enough to avoid simultaneously interiorizing the defeat. It is distinguished from the proletariat by the connotation of what it possesses, by the over-valuing of its relative position, by excess. But at the same time it is distinguished from the upper classes by default, by emphasizing the *limits* of what it has attained and by the implicit consciousness that this is all it will ever be able to attain. Hence the double movement of triumph and resignation in this dark line, encircling all its objects as if to frame them and to ennoble them, the ensemble of which is a laborious challenge to inaccessible forms of possession. In a stratified society the middle class has been subjected to a compromise; this compromise is its true social class destiny and it is this sociologically definable compromise that is reflected in the simultaneously resigned and victorious ritual with which it surrounds its objects.

## The "Taste" for the Bygone (l'Ancien)[21]

One can thus do a whole psychology or even psychoanalysis of bygone objects (obsession with authenticity, mystique of the past, of origins, "symbolic" density and other more or less conscious lived aspects). But what concerns us is the distinctive social function, which is indissociable on all levels from the lived psychological "substance" of the bygone.

The bygone object derives from the cultural baroque. Its "aesthetic" value is always a derived value: in it the stigmata of industrial production and primary functions are eliminated. For all these reasons the taste for the bygone is characterized by the desire to transcend the dimension of economic success, to consecrate a social success or a privileged position in a redundant, culturalized, symbolic sign. The bygone is, among other things, social success that seeks a legitimacy, a heredity, a "noble" sanction.

It will thus be characteristic of the privileged classes for whom it is important to transmute their economic status into inherited grace. But it is quite as characteristic of the salaried middle strata who also

---

21.   "Bygone" is used as a translation of "l'Ancien" because there are major objections to the obvious choices of antique, old, prior, etc. It refers to an article that is sanctified because of belonging to another era, yet which exists in the present. Antique is close, but would exclude the pseudo-antique, the bourgeois kitsch of Louis XV or XVI bedsteads actually produced in Plattsburg (or Paris, for that matter). The simultaneous incarnation of petty bourgeois cravings for both old and new in the same object is too juicy to be missed. Baudrillard himself refers to it (note below).   — *Trans.*

wish to consecrate their relative status as an absolute promotion (in relation to the lower classes) via the purchase of rustic furniture (mass-produced, but so what?). It will also be characteristic of the marginal sectors — intellectual and artistic — where a taste for the bygone will instead translate the refusal (or ashamed affiliation) of economic status and of the social dimension, a will to situate themselves outside all classes and in order to do so, a digging about in the stockpile of signs which are emblematic of a past prior to industrial production.[22]

Thus there would be no interest in noting a certain class with Haute Epoque, another with Industrial Rustic, yet another with authentic 18th-century peasant furniture, in order to build up a social stratification in terms of taste. This would still only reflect cultural constraints and laws of the market. The important thing is to see the specific social postulate expressed by the taste for the bygone at each level. From which social class is one being demarcated? What social position is being sanctioned? What class or class model is being aspired to? Beyond descriptive relations which simply expose a social level and a type of object or behaviors (*conduites*), one must perceive a cultural logic of mobility.[23]

*Varnish and Lacquer*

Other aspects come to confirm this cultural class compromise at the level of environment. There is a triumph of conditioning, of envelopment by an all-powerful puritan morality, of ritual hygiene; the triumph of varnish, polish, veneer, plating, wax, encaustic, lacquer, glaze, glass, plastic. It is a whole ethic of protection, care and cleanliness which converges with the disciplinary ritual of framing that we have already discussed (concentric circles and property: shutters, drapes, double drapes, wainscoting, plinths, wallpaper, table cloths, doilies, bedspreads, blotters). It is of the same order as the symmetrical arrangements, where things are duplicated in order to be reflected: yet another redundancy. An

22. Alternatively, in a whole panoply of fashionably "deviant" objects — monstrous, astonishing, bizarre, vicious — such as flourish today in the shop windows on the Left Bank. There is an entire hell of "unique" objects (or objects with limited distribution) in their usefulness or eccentricity, an entire hell of the luxury object that at heart dreams of the Faubourg St. Honoré. That is to say that its forced originality must be interpreted as the challenge of the marginal intellectual classes to all "legitimate" spheres privileged by industrial society.

23. The only ones to remain refractory — provisionally — to the baroque of the bygone are the peasants, whose aspirations pass toward the functional modern serial object via the rejection of signs of the past, and the workers because they still escape cultural mobility and have no worthwhile status to defend or to legitimize. On the 'bygone,' cf. *Système des objets.*

object does not exist literally unless it is thus repeated in itself, and if one can read the fundamental equation of property in this specular redundancy: A is A. The economic principle is sanctioned by symbolic appropriation (mirrors and looking-glasses): it is the formal logic of the "(petty) bourgeois"[24] environment. Of course this formal ordering has ideological value: as a Euclidean and Aristotelian logic, it tends to conjure social development into an order, to abolish its contradiction in a tautological ritual.

Symmetry (together with hygiene and morality) is the "spontaneous" middle class representation of culture. The game with asymmetry only consecrates this representation.

## The Moral Fanaticism of Housekeeping

In this perspective, polish and varnish (like framing and symmetry) are the exaltation of a "trivial" cultural mode which is not that of beauty and ornamentation but the moral one of cleanliness and correction. The objects here are entirely equivalent to children in whom one must first instill good manners, who must be "civilized" by submitting them to the formal imperatives of politeness. Now, that is a *class* compromise: an obsession with the impeccable, a fanatic housekeeping, corresponds to the demand to surpass the strict necessity of use towards an appearance — an imperative of cultural promotion. But given the very strong work and merit ethos, this appearance cannot have an allure of gratuitousness or of pure prodigality. It will thus be the object of a continual doing, of a laborious domestic ritual, of a daily domestic *sacrifice*. The varnished object is satisfying for a vast socio-cultural category because it appears as the synthesis of a *conspicuous morality*, summarizing the two imperatives of the *prestation* of prestige (sign exchange value) and of the *prestation* of merit (productivity and use value), inconsistently on the formal level but according to a closely knit social logic.

This cultural status of the object enters into direct contradiction with its practical status. The housekeeping consciousness deactivates this contradiction in every way: "The varnished object is more beautiful; it lasts longer," and at the limit of the paradox: "The waxed, plasticized object stands up better; it requires less effort," when this solicitude is precisely that of effort, having the effect of making objects fragile and complicating their manipulation. In fact, housekeeping has only secondarily a practical objective (keeping objects ready for use): it is a manipulation of another order — sym-

---

24. It is a tendency that, in its principles of "discreteness" (objects are individual, distinct unities in their form and function) and redundancy, is opposed to the modern principles of the environment: fluidity, polyvalence, combinatory and mobile integration of elements.

bolic — that sometimes totally eclipses practical use (silverware that has to be regularly polished without ever appearing on the table). If the immense work of housewives (children and objects) never appears in the national accounts, it is undoubtedly because these accounts are too abstract to take into consideration anything other than formal social revenue production. But it is also because, in its profound intention, this labor does not emerge from an economic calculus but from a symbolic and statutory calculus dictated by the relative social class configurations.[25]

On the other hand, beyond the ethic of accomplishment that has just been analyzed, there is a true pathos in this fiercely dedicated solicitude: unlike the concrete use one has for objects and which is always defined (by their function), this solicitude is unlimited — it nourishes and devours itself according to the processes of an unhappy consciousness. In its perfectionist formalism it mimics art for art's sake precisely because it is neither true labor nor culture. It is a rhetoric, an outbidding of the signs of civilization, cut off from their cultural finality. It is the rhetoric of domestic salvation and not a rational domestic economy. Triumphant and suffering, unchangeable in its dogma and its ritual, alienated in its meaning, it is the veritable culture of everydayness.

### The Prestige of the "Natural"

The logic of cultural differentiation is going to impose negation at a privileged level, the disavowal of these values of polish and varnish, of care in favor of the values of "frankness" (*franchise*), and of the "natural": the raw, matte, savage and neglected. This "frankness" of the object sanctioned by taste has nothing "natural" about it. On the contrary, it is deduced from lower-class devotion to the artificial, to the baroque affectation of decorum, to the moral values of the veiled, the clothed, the cared for, the preened, to the moral values of effort. Here "preparation" is a cultural fault. Propriety (repressive conditioning) and manners in the matter of objects, which in another age were the cultural signs of the bourgeoisie, are stigmatized as the distinctive marks of the petty bourgeois classes who have outfitted themselves with them. The essential function of the values of "sincerity," "authenticity," "starkness," — inner walls of bare concrete, unfinished timbers — is thus a function of discrimination (*distinction*), and their definition is first social.

Here again one is rationalizing, but less in terms of immediate practicality ("it is more practical," "that washes better") than in

---

25. The employment of domestic personnel for this purpose (maid, cleaning woman, housekeeper, etc.) is an essential social criterion. To have a maid is to leave the middle class.

terms of secondary functions ("direct contact," "warmer atmosphere"), and especially in terms of functional aesthetics ("abolition of décor," "truth of the object," "promotion of form," etc.). One allows it to be understood that, according to a continuous progress, objects would obey an internal aesthetic logic which would ultimately lead them to appear in their "truth," in the harmonious synthesis of their function and their form. This is the fundamental theory of design.[26] Now the hypothesis of a progressive advancement from model to model toward an ideal state of the environment — a hypothesis which secretly rests upon the representation of technological progress — implies a whole ideology, for it masks the social function of formal innovation, which is a function of cultural discrimination. Formal innovation materialized in objects does not have an ideal world of objects as its goal but rather, a social ideal, that of the privileged classes, which is the perpetual reassertion of their cultural privilege.

## Formal Innovation and Social Discrimination

The priority of this social function of discrimination over the "aesthetic" function is visible in fashion, where at any moment the most aesthetically aberrant and arbitrary forms may be reactivated simply for the purpose of providing distinctive signs for a material which is always new.

So, the *paradigmatic oppositions* —varnished-matte, enveloped-stark, polished-rough — are not only the instruments of a semiological analysis of the world of objects, but are also *social discriminants*, characteristics which are not only formally distinct but socially distinctive. Of course their contextual value is relative, because the bareness of a wall may sometimes indicate poverty, unrefined misery, and other times evince a "savage" luxury.

To explain it another way, that which, at the level of a rational logic of models, is given as "universal," as completed beauty, as absolute truth of form and function, has at bottom no truth other than the relative and ephemeral one of its position in the social logic it imposes. This "universal" is still nothing more than a particular sign, an exhibitor of class. The effect of "beauty," of "naturalness," of "functionality" (in the ideal sense of functionalism) is registered in this class relationship and cannot be dissociated from it.

At a later stage, aesthetic privilege is no longer attached to varnish or rawness but to the liberty of freely combining all the terms: the lacquered coffer close beside the rough wood or smooth marble

---

26. Cf. below, Design and Environment. — *Trans.*

together with naked concrete.[27]  At this avant-garde level, the exclusiveness, which pledged the petty bourgeois to artificial luster and the cultivated to "natural" starkness, is apparently lifted, so that here everything is salvaged, all combinations are possible. But once again, that which at the level of form appears to be a surpassing towards a universal position, takes on its true value in an inverse social signification: the universal term (synthesis of difference) once again becomes an effective factor of discrimination because only a few elect will be able to accede to this stage of the *aesthetic* combinatory. The others find themselves relegated to the *moral* manipulation of domestic objects. With respect to objects and their calculus (as other places), the universal once again is the title of nobility held by a specific category.

The aesthetic calculus is always submerged in social logic. In order to avoid taking this ideological process into account, designers exhaust themselves in popularizing audacious, "rational," "functional" forms, being all the while surprised that these forms do not spontaneously seduce the mass public. Yet behind their pious litany (educating public taste), these "popular" creators direct their unconscious strategy: beautiful, stylized, modern objects are subtly created (despite all reversed good faith) *in order not to be understood by the majority* — at least not straight away. Their social function is first to be distinctive signs, to be objects which will distinguish those who distinguish them. Others will not even see them.[28]

---

27.  The mixture that today is in fashion everywhere, in advertising, decoration, clothing, testifies to the same "liberty": Mondrian-like geometricism coexists peacefully with the psychedelic version of art nouveau.

28.  The same analysis can be made with respect to furniture (no longer according to the material, but to the function). The last word in functional furniture is the mobile element, which, stacked with a few cushions, can turn into a bed, seats, wall units, bookshelves, or anything at all (a pure object) at the whim of its owner. It is the Arch-furnishing, the totally polyvalent manifestation of an audacious, incontestably "rational" analytic formula. And this formula paradoxically revives those of the Middle Ages or of poor peasant living, where the same element — the trunk — would also serve as table, bench, cupboard, etc. The meaning, however, is evidently reversed; far from being a solution to poverty, the contemporary mobile element is the synthesis of all these differentiated functions and of all luxurious distinctions. It is the culmination of simplicity and upon the (bad) faith of this apparent simplicity its designers make of it the "popular" and economical solution of the future! The prices, which are always realistic, unpityingly translate the social logic: these simple forms are a costly refinement. Here again formal innovation is justified in terms of severity, economy, "structure," sometimes even in terms of penury and urgency: "If necessary, your bed can be turned into a dresser," etc. Why bother? It is only a game, and one that only plays upon necessity: fashion is pre-eminent here. Technical — real — innovation does not have at heart the goal of genuine economy, but the game of social distinction.

*The Flux and Reflux of Distinctive Signs*

This contradiction between rational economic logic and cultural class logic affects another essential aspect of objects: their status in time, their cycle of erosion and renewal.

The diverse categories of objects have a variable longevity: residence, furniture, electrical appliances, TV, linens, clothing, gadgets, wear out at different rates. But two distinct variables play upon the whole span of objects in calculating their lifetime and durability: one is their real rate of wearing out, registered in their technical structure and their material; the other, the value they take on as patrimony or inversely, the accelerated obsolescence due to fashion. What is important for us here is this second value and its relation to the respective situation of groups in a stratified and mobile industrial society. How does a given group distinguish itself by a more or less strong adhesion to the ephemeral or to the durable? What are the various responses of different groups on the social scale to fashion's demands for accelerated renewal of objects?

In effect fashion does not reflect a natural need of change: the pleasure of changing clothes, objects, cars, comes to sanction the constraints of another order psychologically, constraints of social differentiation and prestige. The effects of fashion only appear in socially mobile societies (and beyond a certain threshold of available money). Ascending or descending social status must be registered in the continual flux and reflux of distinctive signs. A given class is not lastingly assigned to a given category of objects (or to a given style of clothing): on the contrary, all classes are assigned to change, all assume the necessity of fashion as a value, just as they participate (more or less) in the universal imperative of social mobility. In other words, since objects play the role of exhibitors of social status, and since this status has become potentially mobile, the objects will always simultaneously give evidence not only of an acquired situation (this they have always done), but also of the potential mobility of this social status as such objects are registered in the distinctive cycle of fashion.

One might think that on account of their material presence, objects first have the function of enduring, of registering social status "in solidity."[29] This was the case in traditional society, where hereditary décor was evidence of social accomplishment and, at the limit, of the social eternity of an acquired situation. Then the description and social semantics of the environment could be relatively simple. And in a sense it is always thus: at whatever social level one is situated, there is always the tendency to perpetuate an

---

29. "...fonction de durer...'en dur.' " — *Trans.*

acquired situation in objects (and children). The objects with which one surrounds oneself first constitute a balance sheet, a testament (eventually resigned) to social destiny. On the other hand, they often appear to be symbolically framed and fixed on the wall, such as was once the case with school diplomas. A position and a destiny, thus the contrary of social mobility — this is what objects first present. Chosen, bought and arranged, they are part of the completed fulfillment, not of ascending performance. They encircle with their ascriptive dimension. Even when (only too frequently) they outbid social success, even when they seem to take an option on the future, still, it is never through his objects that social man accomplishes himself or is mobile. He falls back upon them, and objects often translate, at the very most, *his* frustrated social aspirations.

This function of the inertia of objects that results in a durable, sometimes hereditary status, is combatted today by that of having to signify social change. As one is elevated on the social scale, objects multiply, diversify and are renewed. Their accelerated traffic (circulation) in the name of fashion quickly comes to signify and to present a social mobility that does not really exist. This is already the meaning of certain mechanisms of substitution: unable to change the apartment, one changes the car. It is even clearer that the accelerated renewal of objects often compensates a disappointed aspiration to cultural and social progress. This is what makes the "reading" of objects complex: sometimes their mobility reflects the rising standing of a given social category by signifying it positively; sometimes, on the contrary, it comes to compensate the social inertia of a certain group or individual whose disappointed and thwarted desire for mobility comes to register itself in the artificial mobility of decor.

Here the whole ideology of fashion is in question. The formal logic of fashion imposes an increased mobility on all the distinctive social signs. Does this formal mobility of signs correspond to a real mobility in social structures (professional, political, cultural)? Certainly not. Fashion — and more broadly, consumption, which is inseparable from fashion — masks a profound social inertia. It itself is a *factor* of social inertia, insofar as the demand for real social mobility frolics and loses itself in fashion, in the sudden and often cyclical changes of objects, clothes and ideas. And to the illusion of change is added the illusion of democracy (which is similar but under another aspect). The constraint of the transitoriness of fashion is claimed to eliminate the possibility of *inheriting* distinctive signs; it is reputed to return the whole world to a position of equal opportunities at each instant of the cycle. In the face of the demands of fashion all objects can be recalled: this would suffice to create the equality of all in the face of objects. Now, this is quite obviously false: fashion, like mass culture, speaks to all in order to better return each one to his place. It is one of those institutions that best restores cultural inequality and social discrimination, establishing it under the pretense of abolishing it. It wishes to be beyond social logic, a kind of second nature: in fact, it is entirely governed by the social strategy of class. "Modern" transitoriness of objects (and other signs) is in fact the luxury of heirs.[30]

## The Luxury of the Ephemeral

Here we will go a little outside the domain of objects, towards architecture, to illustrate what has just been said about fashion and social class distinction. Architecture is in fact a domain where the opposition ephemeral-durable is very evident to the imagination.

For a certain architectural avant-garde, the truth of the dwelling of the future is in ephemeral construction, in detachable, variable and mobile structures. A mobile society ought to have a mobile dwelling. And it is undoubtedly true that this is inscribed in the economic and social demands of modernity. It is true that the social deficit represented today (and increasingly in the future) by hard and durable lot construction is colossal: it contradicts the economic rationality and that of social exchanges, and the irreversible tendency toward more social mobility, flexibility of infrastructures, etc.[31] But if for all these reasons ephemeral architecture must one day be the collective solution, for the moment it is the monopoly of a privileged fraction whose cultural and economic standing permits it to question the myth of durability.

It is because generations of the bourgeoisie were able to enjoy the fixed secular decor of property that their heirs today can give

30. Fashion embodies a compromise between the need to innovate and the other need to change nothing in the fundamental order. It is this that characterizes "modern" societies. Thus it results in a game of change. In this game, the new and the old are functionally equivalent. If one adheres to lived psychology, one would see there two inverse tendencies: the need to change and the nostalgic need for old things. In fact, the function of the *new look* and of the *old fashion* is the alteration: at all levels, it is the result of a logical constraint of the system — old and new are not relative to contradictory needs: they are the "cyclical" paradigm of fashion. "Modern" is the new *and* the old, which no longer have temporal value. For the same reason, "modern" has nothing to do with actual practicality, with a real change, with a structural innovation. New and old, neologism and archaism are homogeneous in the game of changes.

31. Nevertheless, one would have to take into account the latent, psycho-collective functions of the "hard" and the solid — powerful functions of integration that also are included in the social budget.

themselves the luxury of renouncing uncut stone and exalting the ephemeral: this fashion belongs to them. By contrast, consider all the generations of lower classes whose chances in the past of acceding to cultural models and at the same time to durable property were null. To what would one wish them to aspire if not also to live the bourgeois model and to establish a derisory dynasty in turn, for themselves and their children, in the concrete of apartments or the rough-hewn stone of suburban houses? How can one today require that these "advanceable" classes not deify real estate and that they first accept the ideal character of these mobile structures? They are dedicated to desiring that which lasts and this desire only translates their cultural class destiny.

Reciprocally, the cult of the ephemeral is ideologically connoted by the privilege of the avant-garde: according to the eternal logic of cultural distinction, a privileged fraction savors the instantaneous and mobile character of architectural structures at the moment when others just gain access to the square between their walls. Only the privileged classes have the right to the reality (*actualité*) of models. The others will have the right to them when these models have already changed.

So if the ephemeral represents the truth of modernity in the logic of forms, if it represents the "formula of the future" for a harmonious and rational society, its meaning in the present cultural system is quite different. If, in its *logical* foundation, culture acts upon two terms: ephemeral-durable, neither of which can be autonomized (architecture will always be a game moving from one to the other) — in the *cultural class system*, on the contrary, this relation breaks out in two distinctive poles, one of which, the ephemeral, is autonomized as a superior cultural mode referring the other (the durable) to its obsolescence and to the aspirations of a naive majority.[32]

### 4. A Logic of Segregation

Those are only some elements of a logical analysis of social mechanisms that are articulated upon the distinctive function of objects (and of their practice). We base ourselves upon the *tactical* cultural elements of the middle class, opposing them to those of a privileged stratum. This is obviously an undue simplification, and a more penetrating analysis ought to tend towards establishing a more differentiated hierarchical classification, a more subtle stratification of the social pyramid.

---

32.  Of course, there is also a question of price: the most audacious and thus the most ephemeral fashion is also the most costly in all domains. But the price only comes to sanction a *logical* process of discrimination.

However, all efforts in this direction, in the direction of a logical analysis in terms of stratification, risk making us forget a fundamental truth, which is that the sociological analysis cannot be merely a logical analysis, but is also an ideological, or political, analysis. In other words, the *distinguishing function* (*distinctive*) of objects (as well as of other systems of signs relevant to consumption) is fundamentally registered within (or flows into) a *discriminating function:* thus the logical analysis (in tactical terms of stratification) must also open onto a political analysis (in terms of class strategy).

Before generalizing these conclusions at the level of consumption, we wish to show how, at a simpler level — that of the very practice of the object — these differences are far from punctuating a progressive social hierarchy, and result instead in a radical discrimination, in a de facto segregation that consecrates certain "classes" to certain signs and practices, and not others, guiding them in this vocation and destiny according to a whole social systematic. Then in consumption, in that dimension of generalized sign exchange, we will have a basis for seeing the locus of an intense political manipulation.

*Objective Practice and Ritual Practice — The TV Object*

We will take television for an example, but from a particular viewpoint, that of the TV object. On an early level, the studies of television in fact deliver some truths respecting the various correlations between rates of possession and amount of listening, on the one hand, and, on the other, socio-professional categories, income and levels of education.

On a more involved level, the studies incline toward the mode of listening (family, collective, individual, mixed) and the quality of attention (fascinated, curious, diffuse, passive, selective, distracted, etc.), always in relation to broadly defined social categories. All these studies deal with the relation of the user to the televised message, to the TV discourse, that is, to the images as mass medium. They largely omit the dimension of the object itself, of the television *set*. Now it is obvious that before being the vehicle of images, a transmitter addressing a receiver, the TV is first a "set" sold by a manufacturer to an individual. It is an object, bought and possessed. Undoubtedly its status is never just that, at any level of the social scale, but this primary status secretly induces a great number of ambiguous cultural behaviors in image reception. In other words, the demand is divided between that of an object (producer of images) and that of images (vehicles of meaning). These two exigencies are logically incompatible, although practice inextricably confuses them. According to whether the TV is there as a TV object or as a means of communication, the TV discourse will itself be received as an object or as meaning. The *object (sign) status* is opposed to the *objective (rational and practical) status*. This distinction revives that of sign exchange value and use value. The whole social logic of culture is registered in this radical divergence. And it is the social theory of the sign-object that we wish to dwell on here, in the perspective of consumption.

The evidence according to which the television is bought for the purpose of cultural edification or for the simple pleasure of images (that is, as a function of a deliberated personal objective) is undoubtedly increasingly deceptive as one descends the social scale. More profoundly than interest or pleasure, which often merely ratify the social constraint, the index of conformity and prestige (and the term "index" must retain all its value as a moral injunction) is active, imposing the acquisition of the TV (like that of the refrigerator, car, or washing machine). As in John Stuart Mill, the possession of such and such an object is in itself a social service: as a certificate of citizenship the TV is a token of recognition, of integration, of social legitimacy. At this level of almost unconscious response it is the object that is in question, not its objective function — and it no longer has an objective function, but a *proof* function. It is a social exhibitor and is given value as such: it is exposed and overexposed. This can be seen in middle (and lower) class interiors, where the TV is enthroned on a sort of pedestal, focusing attention on it as an object.

One will be less astonished by the "passivity" experienced by the average TV viewer with respect to the content of TV messages if one considers that implicitly all his social activity is concentrated upon the effort of economic accumulation and especially upon the effort of performance, upon the symbolic payment, as of a toll, constituted by the acquisition of the object itself. It is because according to a naive evaluation, the purchase is considered as a satisfaction, and thus as a passive procedure, that a cultural "activity" is subsequently required of the user. This may be valid for the educated upper classes, but the contrary is true at a lower level: all the activity is invested in the appropriation of the object as sign and token on the one hand, as capital on the other — the use itself is then logically transformed into passive satisfaction, real usufruct, profit and benefit, and reward (*récompense*) for a completed social duty. Because the object has value conferred upon it as a token, it can only occasion a magical economy (cf. Mauss and the value of symbolic exchange). Because the object is considered as capital, it can only occasion a quantitative profitability (*rentabilité*); in neither case can it give rise to an autonomous cultural activity, which derives from another system of values.

Because it is a token, the appropriation of the object is not prolonged by a rational practice, but logically, by its continual demonstration according to a quasi-religious process of ostentation. Because it is capital, the object must be able to produce revenue. In our modern industrial societies the object is rarely a pure fetish;[33] in general, the technical imperative of functionality is imposed. It is necessary to witness objects that are operating, or which serve some purpose. This does not so much resemble an objective rationale as a supplementary *mana*: if it does not work, the object loses its prestige potential. Once again use value is fundamentally an alibi for sign exchange value. The thing must serve a purpose: revenue production is a moral imperative, not an economic function. Also, it is logically in these same social categories where the TV object is sanctified as such apart from its function as communication, that one indulges in systematic, non-selective viewing. The TV is watched every evening, the disparate and successive programs are followed from beginning to end. Lacking a rational economy of the object, one deliberately submits to an irrational and formal economic norm: the absolute amount of use in hours. The apparent passivity of long hours of viewing thus in fact hides a laborious patience. Lacking qualitative selection, it is expressed by quantitative devotion (as in game shows relying on rote memorization and chance).[34] But this norm is not admitted as such: to do so would be to confront autonomous, superior cultural activities (that is, those that are not made subservient to that latent imperative of revenue production) and to be disqualified in advance. It will thus be preferable to present it as pleasure, interest, "free" distraction; spontaneous decision. But this alleged pleasure is a challenge to the profound objection — that of cultural inferiority — which undoubtedly will never be formulated (save clandestinely in ritual recriminations: "They bore us with this stuff" or, "They always show the same things"

---

33. This pure prestige value of the object as such, a magical prestation independent of its function, emerges in the limiting cases (which we gratuitously burden with the label "prelogical mentality," although it is quite simply a question of social logic), where, for example, a broken TV set, vacuum cleaner or watch, or a car out of gas are still prestige elements in the African bush.

34. This "economic fetishism" or the fetishism of revenue production in fact realizes a compromise between the impossibility — socially defined — of being autonomously culturally defined, and the injunction of an industrial (capitalist) society with a very strong economic imperative.

— simulacra indicating the superior cultural processes of judgment, selection, etc., by default).

"It must necessarily serve a purpose": thus for certain social categories this translates the uselessness of this object with respect to superior cultural ends. As concerns pleasure, it is the ritual rationalization of a procedure that does not wish to admit to itself that, through this object, it first obeys a social injunction of conformist ritual prestation. In summary, the quantification of viewing, linked to its "passivity," refers to a socio-economic imperative of revenue production, to the *object as capital*. But perhaps this "capitalization" still only comes to reinforce a more profound social constraint — that of symbolic prestation, of legitimation, of social credence, of *mana* — which attaches itself to the *object as fetish*.

All this outlines a cultural class configuration — that of a class where the autonomous and rational ends of a culture freely exercised by the mediation of an object are not even suspected, and yet are contradictorily internalized. It is that of a resigned and accultured class whose *demand for culture*, following a relative social promotion, is *conjured in objects and their worship* or at least in a cultural compromise governed by the economic and magical constraints of the collectivity. It is the face and very definition of *consumption*.

Other indices come to be associated with those of the volume and mode of listening, according to the same class determination. Consider the physical situation of the TV object in the house. At the lower level, the most frequent configuration has the set isolated in a corner on a pedestal (table, TV stand, shelf), possibly covered by a dust cover and topped by a knick-knack, outside viewing hours; the room, which was hardly conceived traditionally for this use (radio still did not disturb any aspect of its arrangement), is redistributed more or less as a field of vision: the TV logically condemns high, massive furniture, hanging lamps, etc. But most of the time at this level the TV constitutes an eccentric pole opposing the traditional centrality of the room. At an intermediate level, the set is lowered (at the same time as the furniture) to the height of armchair vision. It is on a low table or built into a cabinet console. It is no longer a pole, and reception no longer demands a posture of collective devotion: the room is less centered and so the set is less eccentric. At the limit, in very modern interiors of high standing, there is an integration into other furnishings or into the wall, a total eclipse of the object as furniture. The TV object ceases to be the object of a rite (simultaneously the room is ventilated by independent spaces, luminous sources are concealed, etc.).

There are other significant aspects: ambient lighting — according to whether one recreates the fascinating vision of cinema in the darkness or whether the light is merely veiled or normal. Also, there is the dimension of behavior; whether there is free movement, or no one moving at all. All these scales of indices can be correlated with that principal one of volume and selectivity of use, to outline a coherent structure for each level of the social scale. But (and for us this is the important point), the process of inquiry and the empirical correlations, however subtle they may be, will never give us the image of a stratified society. The studies will describe to us transitively that whole *differential* gamut from one category to the next, from sanctified ostentation to selective use, from domestic rite to autonomous cultural exercise, without ever marking the *theoretical discrimination that opposes the ritual practices centered on the object to the rational practices centered on function and meaning.* Only a theory of culture can account for this theoretical bifurcation on which an antagonistic social strategy is established. Empirical studies only make, and can only make, apparent a logic of stratification (distinction-inclusion-transition by plateaus — a continuous ascent); theoretical analysis makes a class logic emerge (distinction-exclusion). *There are those for whom TV is an object, there are those for whom it is a cultural exercise:* on this radical opposition a cultural class privilege is established that is registered in an essential social privilege.

It is obvious that neither one of these two antagonistic cultural classes exists in its pure state: but the cultural class strategy does exist in the pure state.[35] *The social reality* (subject to empirical investigation) makes hierarchical dosages appear, respective statuses for each social "category." But the *social logic* (subject to a theoretical analysis of the cultural system) makes two opposed terms appear, not the two "poles" of an evolution, but the two exclusive terms of an opposition; and these are not only the two distinct terms of a formal opposition, but the two distinctive-exclusive terms of a social opposition.

## The Democratic Alibi: The "Universe" of Consumption

Of course, this cultural class logic is never manifest: on the contrary, consumption presents itself as a democratic social

---

35. Just as neither the bourgeoisie nor the proletariat has ever been alone, confronted by the other, nor have they ever existed in the pure state in real society. This does not hinder class logic and strategy from being defined, and from acting concretely according to this antagonistic model.

function; in that way it can act as a class institution. It presents itself as a function of human needs, and thus as a universal empirical function. Objects, goods, services, all this "responds" to the universal motivations of the social and individual anthropos. On this basis one could even argue (the leitmotiv of the ideologues of consumption) that its function is to correct the social inequalities of a stratified society: confronting the hierarchy of power and social origin, there would be a democracy of leisure, of the expressway and the refrigerator.

The cultural class logic in bourgeois society is always rooted in the democratic alibi of universals. Religion was a universal. The humanist ideals of liberty and equality were universals. Today the universal takes on the absolute evidence of concreteness: today the universal is human needs, and all the cultural and material goods that respond. It is the universal of consumption.

This ambiguity of consumption — that it seems to act as a factor of democratization in a society calling itself stratified, and this to function better as a class institution — finds its most vivid illustration in the *Reader's Digest Selection* survey of "the consumers' Europe:"[36] "221,750,000 consumers (Common Market and Great Britain)." Out of this gigantic economic tableau, which includes essential, directly comparable statistics with respect to lifestyles, habits of consumption, opinions, attitudes and goods possessed by the inhabitants of seven countries, Piatier draws a certain number of perspectives: "Thanks to complementary statistical reductions it was possible to systematically isolate the responses of group A (upper groupings) and to compare them to the ensemble of other groups."

"It seems that for the Common Market and Great Britain one can speak of a civilization of A's, or to employ a more picturesque expression, of a civilization of white collars; these latter (and this is one of the most interesting results of the *Selection* study) appear to represent a homogeneous group crossing all borders."

"Thus according to this hypothesis, the inhabitants of the seven countries would have a common model of consumption: in the process of development of consumption, group A could constitute a sort of directing schema towards which the rest of the population would gravitate as its revenues increased."

The indices of the ensemble that divide group A (upper groupings, liberal professions, heads of industry and commerce) from group non-A are: luxury equipment (dishwasher, tape recorder, camera, etc.), luxury foods, comfortable living quarters and automobile,

---

36.   André Piatier, "Structures and Perspectives of European Consumption" (Paris, 1967), published by *Reader's Digest Selection*.

toiletries for women, basic household equipment (television, refrigerator, washing machine, etc.), cleaning products, everyday food, male toiletries and intellectual curiosity (voyages abroad, speaking a foreign language)!

So here it is a question of formalizing social realities (which are already deliberately simplified and reduced to formal indices of consumption) into an artificial scheme of stratification (A's and non-A's). The political, social, economic (structures of production and the market) and cultural — all these aspects are volatilized. At the individual-massified level only the quantifiable remains, the statistical balance sheet of goods of consumption taken as the absolute indicators of social essence.[37] Thus an elite is revealed that is not a bearer of values nor of power, but of objects, of a panoply of deluxe gadgets in which the "idea" of Europe is registered materially beyond ideologies. The European ideal thus defined will permit the systematic orientation and sanctioning of the confused aspirations of consuming masses: to be European will consist in passing from the trinity of television, refrigerator and washing machine to the sublime trinity of sports car, stereo system and country house.

Now in fact behind this group of A's, this directing schema of the European ideal, rests a European reality, which is the more or less forced solidarity of the industrial and technical Western European bourgeoisies in global competition. But this common strategy, this political International is hidden here by an International of standing. This very real solidarity disguises itself in the formal solidarity of the consuming masses (so much the more formal in that its indices, the goods of consumption, are more "concrete"). The Europe of trusts adopts the mask of the Europe of cubic inch displacement, the living room and ice cream.

*The A's and the Non-A's*

In fact this schema of international stratification aims above all towards a political operation of national integration appropriate to each of the countries concerned, under the symbol of "Europe" — and this not only by means of the bias of consumption but also by that of stratification. In fact, one could have schematized it into a complex model, but here the statistical craftiness is to schematize it into a simple and striking binary model: the group of A's and the Others, the non-A's. Thus, the old bogey of the duel between antagonistic classes is conjured away in a statistical dichotomy: there are still two terms, but they are no longer in conflict — they change into the two poles of a social dynamic. The effect (and objective) of

---

37. A much more suspect procedure than Chapin's scale of the living room, cited above.

this tactical division is to neutralize the extremes and hence any contradiction that might result on the social level: there is a model-level (directing schema) and — all the others. These latter, mixed in together by the statistics, no longer appear except as a population, an immense and virtual middle class that is already morally accultured to the displays of the privileged classes. No longer is there a radical distortion between the company president and ordinary salaried employees, because the latter, while statistically lost in the middle classes, see themselves with a "middle" standing and as having been promised that of the upper classes. From top to bottom of the scale, no one is inexorably cut off by distance. There are no more extremes, no more tension: the formal frontier between the A's and the non-A's is there only to better prime the aspiration toward the higher level and the illusion of a general regrouping to take place sooner or later in the paradise of A. For "Europe," it is clearly understood, can only be democratic.

The two groups are in formal opposition and virtual homogeneity: this stratification, simplified to the extreme, is the coronation of a statistically based integrating sociology. The whole logic of social contradiction is volatilized. This binary schema is a magic schema of integration: the arbitrary division of distinctive signs on the same scale allows the suggestion of an international model of distinction (the A's), all the while preserving an international model of democracy; the idea of Europe — which is in fact quite simply that of the virtual homogenization of all social categories under the beneficent constellation of objects.

There is a double mystification. On the one hand, there is the illusion of a "dynamic" of consumption, of an ascending spiral of satisfactions and distinctions toward a paradoxical summit where all would enjoy the same prestigious standing. This false dynamic is in fact entirely permeated by the inertia of a social system that is immutable in its discrimination of real powers. On the other hand, there is an illusion of a "democracy" of consumption. On the balance sheet of objects, one can formally gather together widely separated social categories: the real discrimination is made at the level of selective practices (choice, taste, etc.) and above all, of more or less strong adherence to the very values of consumption. This last point requires commentary.[38]

The study clarifies the disparities appearing between A and non-A in certain sectors: equipment, luxury food, and intellectual curiosity(!). In other sectors the authors note (triumphantly) the weak

---

38.  Regarding "practices" as marks of social destiny, see above.

disparity between lifestyles of A's and non-A's, marked in such indices as regular food, basic equipment and toiletries. The disparity is weakest in the richest countries: Germany, Great Britain and the Netherlands. In Great Britain the average consumption of male toiletries for non-A's is even superior to that of A's! The criterion of "goods consumed" is thus not decisive: the fundamental inequality is elsewhere. Even if the inequality escapes the study, and is made more subtle,[39] one must search beyond figures, statistics and the study itself, for what it does not wish to express, for what it wishes to hide. Its secret is that consumption, with its false social appearance, veils the true political strategy, and is thus one of the essential elements of this strategy.

## A Slave Morality

A whole new conception of class strategy is organized around the possession of cultural and material goods. One only pretends to universalize the criteria and values of consumption in order to better assign the "irresponsible" classes (without the power of decision) to consumption and thus to preserve the exclusive access of the directing classes to their powers. The formal frontier traced by the statisticians between A's and non-A's is quite fundamentally a social barrier, but it does not separate those who enjoy a higher standing from those who will enjoy it later. It distinguishes those who are *in addition* privileged consumers, those for whom the prestige of consumption is in a way the usufruct of their fundamental privilege (cultural and political), from those who are *consecrated* to consumption, triumphantly resigning themselves to it as the very sign of their social relegation, those for whom consumption, the very profusion of goods and objects, marks the limit of their social chances, those for whom the demands for culture, social responsibility, and personal accomplishment are resolved into needs and absolved in the objects that satisfy them. In this perspective, which is not legible at the level of the apparent mechanisms, consumption and the *values* of consumption are defined as the very criterion of a new discrimination: adherence to these values acts as a new morality for the use of slaves.

One must wonder whether social salvation by consumption, whether prodigality and sumptuous expenditure (formerly the appendage of chiefs and notables) is not today *conceded* to the lower and middle classes. For this selective criterion has long ago given way as the foundation of power to the criteria of production,

---

39. Thus the fact of acquiring a certain model a month or a day before others can constitute a radical privilege.

responsibility, and economic and political decision.

It must be asked whether certain classes are not consecrated to finding their salvation in objects, consecrated to a social destiny of consumption and thus assigned to a slave morality (enjoyment, immorality, irresponsibility) as opposed to a master morality (responsibility and power). Such are the heirs of the servile, subaltern classes, or of courtesans dedicated to *paraphernalia*.

In this sense it is absurd to speak of a consumer society as if consumption were a system of universal values appropriate to all men because of being founded upon the satisfaction of individual needs, when really it is an institution and a morality, and in this way an element of the strategy of power in any society, past or future.

Here sociology is most of the time both a dupe and an accomplice: it takes the ideology of consumption for consumption itself. Pretending to believe that objects and consumption (as formerly moral principles or religion) have the same meaning from top to bottom of the social scale, it accredits the universal myth of status and on this basis goes on sociologizing, pondering, stratifying and correlating things at statistics' whim.

Now what must be read and what one must know how to read in *upper class* superiority, in electric household equipment or in luxury food, is precisely *not* its advance on the scale of material benefits, but rather its *absolute privilege*, bound up in the fact that its preeminence is precisely not established in signs of prestige and abundance, but elsewhere, in the real spheres of decision, direction and political and economic power, in the manipulation of signs and of men. And this relegates the Others, the *lower* and *middle* classes, to phantasms of the promised land.

# CHAPTER TWO

# THE IDEOLOGICAL GENESIS OF NEEDS [1]

The rapturous satisfactions of consumption surround us, clinging to objects as if to the sensory residues of the previous day in the delirious excursion of a dream. As to the logic that regulates this strange discourse — surely it compares to what Freud uncovered in *The Interpretation of Dreams*? But we have scarcely advanced beyond the explanatory level of naive psychology and the medieval dreambook. We believe in "Consumption": we believe in a real subject, motivated by needs and confronted by real objects as sources of satisfaction. It is a thoroughly vulgar metaphysic. And contemporary psychology, sociology and economic science are all complicit in the fiasco. So the time has come to deconstruct all the assumptive notions involved — object, need, aspiration, *consumption* itself — for it would make as little sense to theorize the quotidian from surface evidence as to interpret the manifest discourse of a dream: it is rather the dream-work and the dream-processes that must be analyzed in order to recover the unconscious logic of a more profound discourse. And it is the workings and processes of an unconscious social logic that must be retrieved beneath the consecrated ideology of consumption.

## 1. Consumption as a Logic of Significations

The empirical "object," given in its contingency of form, color, material, function and discourse (or, if it is a cultural object, in its aesthetic finality) is a myth. How often it has been wished away! But the object is *nothing*. It is nothing but the different types of relations and significations that converge, contradict themselves, and twist around it, as such — the hidden logic that not only arranges this bundle of relations, but directs the manifest discourse that overlays and occludes it.

## The Logical Status of Objects

Insofar as I make use of a refrigerator as a machine, it is not an object. It is a refrigerator. Talking about refrigerators or automobiles in terms of "objects" is something else. That is, it has nothing to do with them in their "objective" relation to keeping things cold or transportation. It is to speak of the object as functionally decontextualized:

1. Either as an object of psychic investment [2] and fascination, of

---



1.  This piece first appeared in *Cahiers Internationaux de Sociologie*, 1969.

2.  *Investissement:* this is the standard, and literal, French equivalent of Freud's *Besetzung*, which also means investment in ordinary German. The English, however,

passion and projection — qualified by its exclusive relation with the subject, who then cathects it as if it were his own body (a borderline case). Useless and sublime, the object then loses its common name, so to speak, and assumes the title of Object as generic proper name. For this reason, the collector never refers to a statuette or a vase as a beautiful statuette, vase, etc., but as "a beautiful Object." This status is opposed to the generic dictionary meaning of the word, that of the "object" plain and simple: "Refrigerator: an object that refrigerates..."

2. Or (between the Object, as proper name and projective equivalent of the subject, and the object, with the status of a common name and implement) as an object specified by its trademark, charged with differential connotations of status, prestige and fashion. *This* is the "object of consumption." It can just as easily be a vase as a refrigerator, or, for that matter, a whoopee cushion. Properly speaking, it has no more existence than a phoneme has an absolute meaning in linguistics. This object does not assume meaning either in a symbolic relation with the subject (the Object) or in an operational relation to the world (object-as-implement): it finds meaning with other objects, in difference, according to a hierarchical code of significations. This alone, at the risk of the worst confusion, defines the object of consumption.

## Of Symbolic Exchange "Value"

In symbolic exchange, of which the gift is our most proximate illustration, the object is not an object: it is inseparable from the concrete relation in which it is exchanged, the transferential pact that it seals between two persons: it is thus not independent as such. It has, properly speaking, neither use value nor (economic) exchange value. The object given has symbolic exchange value. This is the paradox of the gift: it is on the one hand (relatively) arbitrary: it matters little what object is involved. Provided it is given,[3] it can fully signify the relation. On the other hand, once it has been given — and *because* of this — it is *this* object and not another. The gift is unique, specified by the people exchanging and the unique moment of the exchange. It is arbitrary, and yet absolutely singular.

As distinct from language, whose material can be dissassociated from the subjects speaking it, the material of symbolic exchange, the

have insisted on rendering this concept by coining a word that sounds more technical: cathexis, to cathect, etc. The term has been used here mainly to draw attention to the psychoanalytic sense, which varies in intensity and precision, of Baudrillard's *investissement, investir*. Loosely, Freud's concept involves the quantitative transfer of psychic energy to parts of the psyche, images, objects, etc. — *Trans.*

3. *Not* epistemologically given! — *Trans.*

objects given, are not autonomous, hence not codifiable as signs. Since they do not depend on economic exchange, they are not amenable to systematization as commodities and exchange value.

What constitutes the object as value in symbolic exchange is that one separates himself from it in order to give it, to throw it at the feet of the other, under the gaze of the other (*ob-jicere*); one divests himself as if of a part of himself — an act which is significant in itself as the basis, simultaneously, of both the mutual presence of the terms of the relationship, and their mutual absence (their distance). The ambivalence of all symbolic exchange material (looks, objects, dreams, excrement) derives from this: the gift is a medium of relation *and* distance; it is always love and aggression.[4]

*From Symbolic Exchange to Sign Value*

It is from the (theoretically isolatable) moment when the exchange is no longer purely transitive, when the object (the material of exchange) is immediately presented as such, that it is reified into a sign. Instead of abolishing itself in the relation that it establishes, and thus assuming symbolic value (as in the example of the gift), the object becomes autonomous, intransitive, opaque, and so begins to signify the abolition of the relationship. Having become a sign object, it is no longer the mobile signifier of a lack between two beings, it is 'of' and 'from' the reified relation (as is the commodity at another level, in relation to reified labor power). Whereas the symbol refers to lack (to absence) as a virtual relation of desire, the sign object only refers to the absence of relation itself, and to isolated individual subjects.

The sign object is neither given nor exchanged: it is appropriated, withheld and manipulated by individual subjects as a sign, that is, as coded difference. Here lies the object of consumption. And it is always of and from a reified, abolished social relationship that is "signified" in a code.

What we perceive in the symbolic object (the gift, and also the traditional, ritual and artisanal object) is not only the concrete manifestation of a total relationship (ambivalent, and total because it is ambivalent) of desire; but also, through the singularity of an object, the transparency of social relations in a dual or integrated group relationship. In the commodity, on the other hand, we perceive the opacity of social relations of production and the reality of the division of labor. What is revealed in the contemporary profusion of sign objects, objects of consumption, is precisely this

---

4.   Thus the structure of exchange (cf. Lévi-Strauss) is never that of simple reciprocity. It is not two simple terms, but two *ambivalent* terms that exchange, and the exchange establishes their relationship as ambivalent.

opacity, the *total constraint of the code* that governs social value: it is the specific weight of *signs* that regulates the social logic of exchange.

The object-become-sign no longer gathers its meaning in the concrete relationship between two people. It assumes its meaning in its differential relation to other signs. Somewhat like Lévi-Strauss' myths, sign-objects exchange among themselves. Thus, only when objects are autonomized as differential signs and thereby rendered systematizable can one speak of consumption and of objects of consumption.

*A Logic of Signification*

So it is necessary to distinguish the logic of consumption, which is a logic of the sign and of difference, from several other logics that habitually get entangled with it in the welter of evidential considerations. (This confusion is echoed by all the naive and authorized literature on the question.) Four logics would be concerned here:

1. A functional logic of use value;
2. An economic logic of exchange value;
3. A logic of symbolic exchange;
4. A logic of sign value.

The first is a logic of practical operations, the second one of equivalence, the third, ambivalence, and the fourth, difference.

Or again: a logic of utility, a logic of the market, a logic of the gift, and a logic of status. Organized in accordance with one of the above groupings, the object assumes respectively the status of an *instrument*, a *commodity*, a *symbol*, or a *sign*.

Only the last of these defines the specific field of consumption. Let us compare two examples:

*The wedding ring:* This is a unique object, symbol of the relationship of the couple. One would neither think of changing it (barring mishap) nor of wearing several. The symbolic object is made to last and to witness in its duration the permanence of the relationship. Fashion plays as negligible a role at the strictly symbolic level as at the level of pure instrumentality.

The ordinary ring is quite different: it does not symbolize a relationship. It is a non-singular object, a personal gratification, a sign in the eyes of others. I can wear several of them. I can substitute them. The ordinary ring takes part in the play of my accessories and the constellation of fashion. It is an object of consumption.

*Living accommodations:* The house, your lodgings, your apartment: these terms involve semantic nuances that are no doubt linked to the advent of industrial production or to social standing. But, whatever one's social level in France today, one's domicile is not necessarily perceived as a "consumption" good. The question of residence is still very closely associated with patrimonial goods in general, and its symbolic scheme remains largely that of the body. Now, for the logic of consumption to penetrate here, the exteriority of the sign is required. The residence must cease to be hereditary, or interiorized as an organic family space. One must avoid the appearance of filiation and identification if one's debut in the world of fashion is to be successful.

In other words, domestic practice is still largely a function of determinations, namely: symbolic (profound emotional investment, etc.), and economic (scarcity).

Moreover, the two are linked: only a certain "discretionary income" permits one to play with objects as status signs — a stage of fashion and the "game" where the symbolic and the utilitarian are both exhausted. Now, as to the question of residence — in France at least — the margin of free play for the mobile combinatory of prestige or for the game of substitution is limited. In the United States, by contrast, one sees living arrangements indexed to social mobility, to trajectories of careers and status. Inserted into the global constellation of status, and subjugated to the same accelerated obsolescence of any other object of luxury, the house truly becomes an object of consumption.

This example has a further interest: it demonstrates the futility of any attempt to define the object empirically. Pencils, books, fabrics, food, the car, curios — are these objects? Is a house an object? Some would contest this. The decisive point is to establish whether the symbolism of the house (sustained by the shortage of housing) is irreducible, or if even this can succumb to the differential and reified connotations of fashion logic: for if this is so, then the home becomes an object of consumption — as any other object will, if it only answers to the same definition: being, cultural trait, ideal, gestural pattern, language, etc. — anything can be made to fit the bill. The definition of an object of consumption is entirely independent of objects themselves and *exclusively a function of the logic of significations*.

An object is not an object of consumption unless it is released from its psychic determinations as *symbol*; from its functional determinations as *instrument*; from its commercial determinations as *product*; and is thus *liberated as a sign* to be recaptured by the formal logic of fashion, i.e., by the logic of differentiation.

*The Order of Signs and Social Order*

There is no object of consumption before the moment of its substitution, and without this substitution having been determined by the social law, which demands not only the renewal of distinctive material, but the obligatory registration of individuals on the scale of status, through the mediation of their group and as a function of their relations with other groups. *This scale is properly the social order,* since the acceptance of this hierarchy of differential signs and the interiorization by the individual of signs in general (i.e., of the norms, values, and social imperatives that signs are) constitutes the fundamental, decisive form of social control — more so even than acquiescence to ideological norms.

It is now clear that there is no autonomous problematic of objects, but rather the much more urgent need for a theory of social logic, and of the codes that it puts into play (sign systems and distinctive material).

*The Common Name, the Proper Name, and the Brand Name*

Let us recapitulate the various types of status of the object according to the specific and (theoretically) exhaustive logics that may penetrate it:

1. The refrigerator is specified by its function and irreplaceable in this respect. There is a necessary relation between the object and its function. The arbitrary nature of the sign is not involved. But all refrigerators are interchangeable in regard to this function (their objective "meaning").

2. By contrast, if the refrigerator is taken as an element of comfort or of luxury (standing), then in principle any other such element can be substituted for it. The object tends to the status of sign, and each social status will be signified by an entire constellation of exchangeable signs. No necessary relation to the subject or the world is involved. There is only a systematic relation obligated to all other signs. And in this combinatory abstraction lie the elements of a code.

3. In their symbolic relationship to the subject (or in reciprocal exchange), all objects are potentially interchangeable. Any object can serve as a doll for the little girl. But once cathected, it is *this* one and not another. The symbolic material is relatively arbitrary, but the subject-object relation is fused. Symbolic discourse is an idiom.

The functional use of the object occurs in relation to its technical structure and its practical manipulation. It relates to the common name: e.g., refrigerator. The use of the symbol-object occurs in the context of its concrete presence and through the proper name proper to it. Possession and passion baptize the object (in the metaphorical name of the subject), affixing their seal to it. The "consumption of the object occurs in the context of its brand name, which is not a proper name, but a sort of generic Christian name.[5]

## 2. Consumption as a Structure of Exchange and Differentiation

*Of the Invalidity of the Notion of the Object and Need*

We can see now that objects have no meaning except in those logical contexts that can mingle, often contradictorily, on the plane of one object alone; and that these various significations depend on the index and modalities of *commutation* possible within the framework of each logic. And so what possible meaning can any classification, definition, or categorization of objects in themselves have when the object (once again taken in the widest sense of the term) is commutable according to many rules (the rules of equivalence in the functional and economic domain; the rules of difference in the domain of signs; the rule of ambivalence in that of the symbolic)? Is it when the discourse of the conscious and the unconscious gets entangled in the object — the full discourse of denotation, the parallel discourse of connotation, the internal discourse of the subject and social discourse of relationship — even the entirely latent discourse, in the object, of the symbolic absence of the subject from himself and the other?[6] And what possible foundation could there be for all the possible theories of needs, more or less indexed as they are to these would-be categories and classifications of objects? In such an area of flux, empirical formalizations are devoid of meaning. The situation is reminiscent of Borges' zoological classification: "Animals are divided into: (a) belonging to the Emperor; (b) embalmed, (c) tame, (d) suckling pigs, (e) sirens, (f) fabulous, (g) stray dogs, (h) included in the present classification, etc., etc.,...."[7] All classifications of objects and needs are neither more logical nor less surrealist than this.

---

5.  In the logic of the commodity, all goods or objects become universally commutable. Their (economic) practice occurs through their price. There is no relationship either to the subject or to the world, but only a relation to the market.

6.  The same goes for food: as a "functional need," hunger is not symbolic. Its objective is satiation. The food object is not substitutable. But it is well known that eating can satisfy an oral drive, being a neurotic substitute for lack of love. In this second function, eating, smoking, collecting objects, obsessive memorization can all be equivalent: the symbolic paradigm is radically different from the functional paradigm. Hunger as such is not signified, it is appeased. Desire, on the other hand, is signified throughout an entire chain of signifiers. And when it happens to be a desire for something experienced as lost, when it is a lack, an absence on which the objects that signify it have come to be inscribed, does it make any sense to treat such objects literally, as if they were merely what they are? And what can the notion of need possibly refer to, in these circumstances?

7.  Borges, cited in Michel Foucault, *The Order of Things* (New York: Vintage, 1970), p. xv.

## Need and Mana

To reduce the conceptual entity "object" is, by the same token, to deconstruct the conceptual entity "need." We could explode that of the subject as well.

Subject, object, need: the mythological structure of these three ideas is identical, triply elaborated in terms of the naive factuality and the schemas of a primary level psychology.

What speaks in terms of need is magical thinking. The subject and the object having been posited as autonomous and separated entities — as specular [8] and distinct myths — it then becomes necessary to establish their relation. This is accomplished, of course, with the concept of need. Incidentally — all else remaining equal — the concept resembles that of *mana*.[9] Conceiving exchange as an operation between two separated terms, each existing in isolation prior to the exchange, one has to establish the existence of the exchange itself in a double obligation: that of giving and that of returning. Thus it is necessary to imagine (as Mauss and the native apparently do) an immanent power in the object, the *hau*, whose force haunts the recipient of the object and incites him to divest himself of it. The insurmountable opposition between the terms of the exchange is thus reduced at the price of a tautological, artificial, magical, supplementary concept, of which Lévi-Strauss, in his critique, has worked out the economics in positing exchange directly as structure. Thus, the psychologist, economist, etc., having provided themselves with a subject and an object, can barely rejoin them but for the grace of need. But this concept can only explain the subject-object relation in terms of adequation, the functional response of subjects to objects, and vice versa. It amounts to a kind of functionalist nominalism, which precipitates the whole psycho-economic ideology of optimality, equilibrium, functional regulation

---

8.   *Speculaire:* The adjective specular and the noun specularity occur often in Baudrillard's analyses of ideology. They deliberately recall the mirror-like relations of the Imaginary order, which is opposed to the Symbolic order in Lacanian psychoanalysis. For the best introduction to Lacan in English, see Anthony Wilden, *The Language of the Self* (New York: 1968) and *System and Structure* (London: 1972). The latter work is less informative with respect to Lacan specifically, but attempts a curious synthesis that may fruitfully be compared with Baudrillard's work. Wilden is more sympathetic toward traditional Marxist assumptions and to mainstream social science in the form of cybernetics, systems theory, etc. With the work of Lévi-Strauss, Lacan and others behind them, both have in common a concern for the apparently special or traditionally unaccountable status of *symbolic* exchange, a critique of the "digital bias" (Wilden) in the Western *epistème* (which, by definition, would include the 19th-century revolutionary critique of or version of political economy); and both attempt to reexamine such basic concepts as need, desire, the subject, object, etc.   — *Trans.*

9.   According to Marcel Mauss in *The Gift* (London: Routledge, 1970).

and adaptation of needs.

In fact, the operation amounts to defining the subject by means of the object and the object in terms of the subject. It is a gigantic tautology of which the concept of need is the consecration. Metaphysics itself has never done anything else and, in Western thought, *metaphysics and economic science* (not to mention traditional psychology) *demonstrate a profound solidarity,* mentally and ideologically, in the way they posit the subject and tautologically resolve its relation to the world. *Mana,* vital force, instincts, needs, choices, preferences, utilities, motivations: it is always a question of the same magical copula, the equal sign in "A = A." Metaphysics and economics jostle each other at the same impasses, over the same aporias, the same contradictions and dysfunctions, condemning each from the start to unlimited circular speculation by positing the autonomy of the subject and its specular reflection in the autonomy of the object.

## The "Circle" of Power

But we know that the tautology is never innocent — no more than the finalism that underlies the entire mythology of needs. Such run-arounds are always the rationalizing ideology of a system of power: the dormant virtue of opium, the refrains of "Que Sera Sera": like Borges' animal categories ("included in the present classification"), or like the theological pronouncement: "When a given subject purchases such and such an object, this behavior is a function of his particular choices and preferences." At bottom, under the umbrella of the logical principle of identity, such admirable metaphors for the void sanction the circular principle of a system of power, the reproductive finality of the order of production. This is why economic science does not dispense with the concept of need. It could easily do so, for its calculations operate at the level of statistical demand. But the notion is urgently required for ideological support.

The *legitimacy* of production rests on a *petitio principii,* i.e., that people discover a posteriori and almost miraculously that they need what is produced and offered at the marketplace (and thus, in order that they should experience this or any particular need, the need must already exist inside people as a virtual postulation). And so it appears that this begging of the question — this forced rationalization — simply masks the *internal finality* of the order of production. To become an end in itself, every system must dispel the question of its real teleology. Through the meretricious legitimacy of needs and satisfactions, the entire question of the social and political finality of productivity is repressed.

One could object that this is not a forced rationalization, since the discourse of needs is the subject's spontaneous form of interpreting his relation to objects and to the world. But this is precisely the problem. In his attempt to recapture this discourse, the analyst of modern society reproduces the misconstruction of naive anthropology: *he naturalizes the processes of exchange and signification.*

Thus social logic itself escapes him. It is true that all magical thinking draws a certain measure of efficacy from the empirical manipulation and theoretical misunderstanding of its own procedures. Thus, speculation on needs converges with the long tradition of speculation on *mana.* It is mythical thought that reflects in the mirror of economic "rationality."

### Interdisciplinary Neo-Humanism, or Psycho-Social Economics

It thus proves necessary to reconstruct social logic entirely. Nothing is more instructive in this regard than the adulterous relations that obtain between the economic and the social sciences. Virtuous thinkers have done their utmost for a generation now to reconcile these estranged disciplines (in the name of Man, their dada). They have striven to attenuate all that is profoundly inadmissible — *obscene* — for their disciplines in the very existence of the others and in the haunting memory of a knowledge that escapes them. Economics in particular can only delay the eruption, in the midst of its calculations, of a psychological logic of the unconscious or of an equally unconscious logic of social structures. The logic of ambivalence on the one hand, of difference on the other, are incompatible with the logic — sacred to economics — of equivalence. To foil their literally destructive influence, "economic science" will throw in its lot with desiccated and inoffensive forms of psychology and sociology, i.e., the latter as traditional disciplines — all in the name of pious interdisciplinary study. One never thinks, from this viewpoint, of introducing social or psychological dimensions of a specific nature: rather, one simply adds to the criteria of individual utility ("rational" economic variables) a pinch of "irrational" *individual* psychology (motivational studies, depth psychology) and some interpersonal social psychology (the individual *need* for prestige and status) — or simply a kind of global socio-culture. In short, one looks for *context.*

Some examples: certain studies (Chombart de Lauwe) reveal in the lower orders an abnormal consumption of meat: too little, or too much. As long as one consumes meat along the mean, one partakes of economic rationality. No problems. Otherwise, one produces the psychological: the need for prestige, conspicuous under- or over-consumption, etc. Hence, the social and the psychological are defined as the "economically pathological"! Another social analyst, Katona, discovers his "discretionary income" and his cultural implications with relish: he explores, beyond purchasing power, a "propensity to buy that reflects the motivations, the tendencies and the expectations of the clientele!"[10] Such are the maudlin illuminations of psycho-economics.

Or sometimes it is observed (when it becomes impossible to ignore) that the individual is never alone, that he is determined by his relation to others. And so Robinsonades are abandoned for micro-sociological *bricolage*. American sociology has somehow been arrested at this point. Even Merton, with his theory of the reference group, always works on groups that in fact are empirically given and with the empirical notion of aspiration as a lubricant of the social dynamic.

Psychologism goes hand in hand with culturalism, another benign version of a sociology that refuses to live dangerously: needs are functions of the particular history and culture of each society. This is the zenith of liberal analysis, beyond which it is congenitally incapable of thinking. The postulate of man endowed with needs and a natural inclination to satisfy them is never questioned. It is simply immersed in a historical and cultural dimension (very often defined in advance, and by other means); and then, by implication, impregnation, interaction, articulation or osmosis, it is recontextualized in a social history or a culture that is understood really as a second nature! All this culminates in overblown "character structures," cultural types writ large that are given as structures, though they are only empirical totalizations of distinctive traits, and — again — basically gigantic tautologies, since the "model" is composed of an admixture of the characteristic traits it is intended to explain.

Tautology is at work everywhere. Thus, in the theory of "consumption models": social situations can be as important as taste in determining the level of consumption (in France, sweets are inseparable from their use by parents as instruments of education). "It would thus be possible, when one got acquainted with the sociological significance of products, to paint the portrait of a society with the aid of the products that correspond to these norms. Reference groups and membership groups could be understood at the level of consumer behavior." Or, again, the concept of "role" in the work of Lazarsfeld and others: the good housekeeper is supposed

10. Chombart de Lauwe, *Pour une Sociologie des Aspirations* (Gonthier) and George Katona, *The Society of Mass Consumption*.

to do the washing herself, use a sewing machine, and refrain from using instant coffee. The "role" plays the same function in the relation of the subject to social norms as need does in relation to objects. The same circle and the same white magic.

In the end, it is discovered that you can break down the purchase of a car into a whole constellation of possible motivations: biographical, technical, utilitarian, psychosymbolic (overcompensation, aggressiveness), sociological (group norms, desire for prestige, conformism or originality). The worst of it all is that every one of these is equally valid. It would be difficult to imagine a case where any one wouldn't apply. Often they formally contradict each other: the need for security versus the need to take risks; the desire to conform versus the need to be distinctive, etc. And which are determinant? How do you structure or rank them? In an ultimate effort, our thinkers strain to make their tautology dialectical: they talk about ongoing interaction (between the individual and the group, from one group to another, from one motivation to another). But the economists, hardly fond of dialectical variables, quickly retreat to their measurable utilities.

The confusion is quite irreparable, in fact. Without entirely lacking in interest, the results obtained at these different levels of abstraction (needs, social aspirations, roles, models of consumption, reference groups, etc.) are partial and misleading. Psycho-social economics is a sort of near-sighted, cross-eyed hydra. But it surveys and defends something, for all that. It exorcises the danger of a radical analysis, whose object would be neither the group nor the individual subject at the conscious level, but social logic itself, for which it is necessary to create a *principle* of analysis.

We have already asserted that this logic is a logic of differentiation. But this is not a question, as should be clear by now, of treating prestige, status, distinction, etc., as motivations, a level that has been largely thematized by contemporary sociology. At any rate, it is little more than a para-sociological extension of the traditional psychological givens. There is no doubt that individuals (or individuated groups) are consciously or subconsciously in quest of social rank and prestige and, of course, this level of the object should be incorporated into the analysis. But the fundamental level is that of *unconscious* structures that organize the social production of differences.

## The Logic of Sign Exchange: The Production of Differences

Even before survival has been assured, every group or individual experiences a vital pressure to produce themselves meaningfully in a system of exchange and relationships. Concurrently with the production of goods, there is a push to elaborate significations, meaning — with the result that the one-for-the-other exists before the one *and* the other exist for themselves.

The logic of exchange is thus primordial. In a way, the individual is non-existent (like the object of which we spoke at the beginning). At any rate, a certain language (of words, women, or goods) is prior to the individual. This language is a social form in relation to which there can properly speaking be no individuals, since it is an exchange structure. This structure amounts to a logic of differentiation on two simultaneous planes:

1. It differentiates the human terms of the exchange into partners, not individuated, but nevertheless distinct, and bound by the rules of exchange.

2. It differentiates the exchange material into distinct and *thus significant* elements.

This is true of language communication. It applies also to goods and products. Consumption is exchange. A consumer is never isolated, any more than a speaker. It is here that total revolution in the analysis of consumption must intervene: *Language cannot be explained by postulating an individual need to speak* (which would pose the insoluble double problem of establishing this need on an individual basis, and then of articulating it in a possible exchange). Before such questions can even be put, there is, simply, language — not as an absolute, autonomous *system*, but as a structure of exchange contemporaneous with meaning itself, and on which is articulated the individual intention of speech. Similarly, consumption does not arise from an objective need of the consumer, a final intention of the subject towards the object; rather, there is social production, in a system of exchange, of a material of differences, a code of significations and invidious (*statuaire*) values. The functionality of goods and individual needs only follows on this, adjusting itself to, rationalizing, and in the same stroke repressing these fundamental structural mechanisms.

The origin of meaning is never found in the relation between a subject (given a priori as autonomous and conscious) and an object produced for rational ends — that is, properly, the *economic* relation, rationalized in terms of choice and calculation. It is to be found, rather, in difference, systematizable in terms of a code (as opposed to private calculation) — a differential structure that establishes the social relation, and not the subject as such.

## Veblen and Invidious Distinction

We should refer at this point to Veblen, who, even if he posited the logic of differentiation more in terms of individuals than of classes, of prestige interaction rather than of exchange structure, nevertheless offers in a way far superior to those who have followed him and who have pretended to surpass him the discovery of a principle of total social analysis, the basis of a radical logic, in the mechanisms of differentiation. This is not a superadded, contextual variable, situationally given, but a relational variable of structure. All of Veblen's work illustrates how the production of a social classification (class distinctions and statutory rivalry) is the fundamental law that arranges and subordinates all the other logics, whether conscious, rational, ideological, moral, etc.

Society regulates itself by means of the production of distinctive material: "The end of acquisition is conveniently held to be the consumption of the goods accumulated... but it is only in a sense far removed from its native meaning that consumption of goods can be said to afford the incentive from which accumulation proceeds.... Possession of wealth confers honors: it is an invidious distinction."[11]

### Leisure

"Conspicuous abstention from labor becomes the conventional index of reputability."[12] Productive labor is degrading: the tradition never dies; it is only reinforced as social differentiation increases in complexity. In the end, it takes on the axiomatic authority of an absolute prescription — even alongside the moral reprobation of idleness and the reactive valorization of labor so strong in the middle classes (and today recuperated ideologically by the ruling class itself): a *président directeur général* works a fifteen-hour day, devotedly — it is his token of *affected* servitude. In fact, this reaction-formation proves, to the contrary, the power of leisure-nobility value as a deep-seated, unconscious representation.

Leisure is thus not a function of a need for leisure in the current sense of enjoying free time and functional repose. It can be invested in activities, provided they do not involve economic necessity. Leisure may be defined as any consumption of unproductive time. Now, this has nothing to do with passivity: it is an *activity*, an *obligatory* social phenomenon. Time is not in this instance "free," it is sacrificed, wasted: it is the moment of a production of value, of an invidious production of status, and the social individual is not free to escape it. No one needs leisure, but everyone is called upon to provide evidence of his availability for *unproductive* labor. The consumption of empty time is a form of potlatch. Here, free time is a material of exchange

---

11.  Thorstein Veblen, *The Theory of the Leisure Class* (New York: Mentor, 1953), p. 35.
12.  *Ibid.,* p. 43.

and signification. Like Bataille's "accursed share,"[13] it assumes value in the exchange itself — or in destruction — and leisure is the locus of this symbolic operation.[14]

The style of contemporary leisure provides a kind of experimental verification: left to himself, the conditions for creative freedom at last realized, the man of leisure looks desperately for a nail to hammer, a motor to dismantle. Outside the competitive sphere, there are no autonomous needs. Spontaneous motivation doesn't exist. But for all that, he can't permit himself to do nothing. At a loss for something to do with his free time, he nevertheless urgently "needs" to do nothing (or nothing useful), since this has distinctive social value.

Even today, what claims the average individual, through the holidays and during his free time, is not the liberty to "fulfill" himself (in terms of what? What hidden essence will surge to the fore?). He must verify the uselessness of his time — temporal surplus as sumptuous capital, as wealth. Leisure time, like consumption time in general, becomes emphatic, trade-marked social time — the dimension of social salvation, productive of value, but not of economic survival.[15]

Veblen pushed the law of distinctive value very far: "the canon of honorific waste may, immediately or remotely, influence the sense of duty, the sense of beauty, the sense of utility, the sense of devotional or ritualistic fitness, and the scientific sense of truth."[16]

## The Law of Distinctive Value and its Paradox

This law of value can play on wealth or on destitution. Conspicuous luxury or conspicuous austerity answer to the same fundamental rule. What appears as an insoluble formal contradiction at the level of the empirical theory of needs falls into place, arranged according to this law, in a general theory of distinctive material.

Thus, churches are traditionally more sumptuous in the fashionable districts, but class imperative can impose a type of

---

13. Georges Bataille, *La Part Maudite* (Les Editions de Minuit, 1967).
14. See the analysis of an analogous type of operation in the chapter below on The Art Auction.
15. "Free" time brings together the "right" to work and the "liberty" to consume in the framework of the same system: *it is necessary* for time to be "liberated" in order to become a sign-function and take on social exchange value, whereas labor time, which is constrained time, possesses only economic exchange value. Cf. Part I of this essay: one could add a definition of symbolic time to that of the object. It would be that which is neither economically constrained nor "free" as sign-function, but *bound*, that is, inseparable from the concrete act of exchange — a rhythm.
16. Veblen, *op.cit.*, p. 88.

ascetic religiosity: Catholic pomp becomes the fact of the lower classes whereas, among Protestants, the spareness of the chapel only testifies to the greater glory of God (and establishes the distinctive sign of the class as well). There are innumerable examples of this paradox of value — of spartan wealth. People manipulate the subtle starkness of modern interiors. You pay through the nose to eat practically nothing. To deny oneself is a luxury! This is the sophistry of consumption, for which the refusal to validate a value is merely a hierarchical nuance in its formal verification.[17]

It is important to grasp that behind all these alleged finalities — functional, moral, aesthetic, religious and their contradictions — a logic of difference and super-difference is at work. But it is always repressed, since it belies the ideal finality of all the corresponding behavior. This is social reason, social logic. It transverses all values, all materials of exchange and communication.

In principle, nothing is immune to this structural logic of value. Objects, ideas, even conduct are not solely practiced as use values, by virtue of their "objective" meaning, in terms of their official discourse — for they can never escape the fact that they may be potentially exchanged as signs, i.e., assume another kind of value entirely in the very act of exchange and in the differential relation to the other that it establishes. The differential function of sign exchange always overdetermines the manifest function of what is exchanged, sometimes entirely contradicting it, repossessing it as an alibi, or *even producing it as an alibi*. This explains how the differential function materializes indifferently in opposite or contradictory terms: the beautiful or the ugly, the moral or the immoral, the good or the bad, the ancient or the new. The logic of difference cuts across all formal distinctions. It is equivalent to the primary process and the dream work: it pays no heed to the principle of identity and non-contradiction.[18]

### Fashion

This deep-seated logic is akin to that of fashion. Fashion is one of the more inexplicable phenomena, so far as these matters go: its

---

17.   Cf. "universal" furniture (or "universal" clothing in Roland Barthes' study of fashion): as the epitome of all functions, it becomes once again opposable to them, and thus simply one more term in the paradigm. Its value isn't universal, but derived from relative distinction. Thus all the "universal" values (ideological, moral, etc.) become again — indeed, perhaps are produced from the outset as — differential values.

18.   In relation to this one, the other functions are secondary processes. They certainly constitute part of the sociological domain. But the logic of difference (like the primary process) constitutes the proper object of genuine social science.

compulsion to innovate signs, its apparently arbitrary and perpetual production of meaning — a kind of meaning drive — and the logical mystery of its cycle are all in fact of the essence of what is sociological. The logical processes of fashion might be extrapolated to the dimension of "culture" in general — to all social production of signs, values and relations.

To take a recent example: neither the long skirt nor the mini-skirt has an absolute value in itself — only their differential relation acts as a criterion of meaning. The mini-skirt has nothing whatsoever to do with sexual liberation; it has no (fashion) value except in opposition to the long skirt. This value is, of course, reversible: the voyage from the mini- to the maxi-skirt will have the same distinctive and selective fashion value as the reverse; and it will precipitate the same effect of "beauty."

But it is obvious that this "beauty" (or any other interpretation in terms of chic, taste, elegance, or even distinctiveness) is nothing but the exponential function — the rationalization — of the fundamental processes of production and reproduction of distinctive material. Beauty ("in itself") has nothing to do with the fashion cycle.[19] In fact, it is inadmissible. Truly beautiful, definitively beautiful clothing would put an end to fashion. The latter can do nothing but deny, repress and efface it — *while conserving, with each new outing, the alibi of beauty*.

Thus fashion continually fabricates the "beautiful" on the basis of a radical denial of beauty, by reducing beauty to the logical equivalent of ugliness. It can impose the most eccentric, dysfunctional, ridiculous traits as eminently distinctive. This is where it triumphs — imposing and legitimizing the irrational according to a logic deeper than that of rationality.

### 3. The System of Needs and of Consumption as a System of Productive Forces

It would appear that a "theory of needs" has no meaning. Only a theory of the *ideological concept* of need would make any sense. Before certain false problems have been overcome and radically reformulated, any reflection on the genesis of needs would have as little foundation as, for example, a history of the will. A form of the chimerical dialectic of being and appearance, soul and body still persists in the subject-object of dialectic of need. Ideological speculation of this sort has always appeared as a "dialectical" game

19.  Any more than originality, the specific value, the objective merit is belonging to the aristocratic or bourgeois class. This is defined by signs, to the exclusion of "authentic" values. See Goblot, *La Barrière et le Niveau* (Presse Universitaire de France, 1967).

of ceaseless interaction in a mirror: when it is impossible to determine which of two terms engenders the other and one is reduced to making them reflect or produce each other reciprocally, it is a sure sign that the terms of the problem itself must be changed.

So it proves necessary to examine how economic science — and behind it, the political order — operates the concept of need.

### The Myth of Primary Needs

The legitimacy of the concept is rooted in the alleged existence of a vital anthropological minimum that would be the dimension of "primary needs" — an irreducible zone where the individual chooses himself, since he knows what he wants: to eat, to drink, to sleep, to make love, to find shelter, etc. At this level, he cannot, it is supposed, be alienated in his need as such: only deprived of the means to satisfy it.

This bio-anthropological postulate directly launches the insoluble dichotomy of primary and secondary needs: beyond the threshold of survival, man no longer knows what he wants. And it is here that he becomes properly "social" for the economist: i.e., vulnerable to alienation, manipulation, mystification. On one side of the imaginary line, the economic subject is prey to the social and the cultural; on the other, he is an autonomous, inalienable essence. Note that this distinction, by conjuring away the socio-cultural in secondary needs, permits the recuperation, behind the functional alibi of survival-need, of a level of individual essence: a human essence grounded in nature. Moreover, this all proves quite versatile as an ideology. It has a spiritualist as well as a rationalist version. Primary and secondary needs can be separated in order to refer the former back to animality, the latter to the immaterial.[20] Or one can simply reverse the whole procedure by positing primary needs as (alone) objectively grounded (thus rational), and treat the others as subjectively variable (hence irrational). But this ideology is quite coherent in its overall features, because it always defines man a priori as an essence (or a rationality) that the social merely obscures.

In fact, the "vital anthropological minimum" doesn't exist: in all societies, it is determined residually by the fundamental urgency of an excess: the divine or sacrificial share, sumptuous discharge, economic profit. It is this pre-dedication of luxury that negatively determines the level of survival, and not the reverse (which is an idealist fiction). Advantages, profits, sacrifice (in the sense of social wealth) and "useless" expenditures are all deducted in advance. And the priority of this claim works everywhere at the expense of the

20. On this point, see Ruyer, *La Nutrition Psychique*.

functional side of the balance sheet — at the expense, where necessary, of minimal subsistence.

There have never been "societies of scarcity" or "societies of abundance," since the expenditures of a society (whatever the objective volume of its resources) are articulated in terms of a structural surplus, and an equally structural deficit. An enormous surplus can coexist with the worst misery. In all cases, a certain surplus coexists with a certain poverty. But the crucial point is that it is always the production of this surplus that regulates the whole. The survival threshold is never determined from below, but from above. Eventually, one might hypothesize, there will be no survival at all, if social imperatives demand it: the newborn will be liquidated (like prisoners of war, before a new constellation of productive forces made slavery profitable). The Siane of New Guinea, enriched through contact with Europeans, squandered everything in feasts, without ceasing to live below the "vital minimum." It is impossible to isolate an abstract, "natural" stage of poverty or to determine absolutely "what men need to survive." It may please one fellow to lose everything at poker and to leave his family starving to death. We know it is often the most disadvantaged who squander in the most "irrational" way. The game flourishes in direct relation to underdevelopment. There is even a narrow correlation between underdevelopment, the size of the poor classes, and the tentacular spread of the church, the military, domestic personnel, and expensive and useless sectors in general.

Conversely, just as survival can fall well below the vital minimum if the production of surplus value requires it, the threshold of *obligatory* consumption can be set well above the strictly necessary — always as a function of the production of surplus value: this is the case in our societies, where no one is free to live on raw roots and fresh water. From which follows the absurdity of the concept of "discretionary income" (the complement of the "vital minimum" concept): "the portion of his income the individual is free to spend as he pleases." In what way am I more free buying clothing or a car than buying my food (itself very sophisticated)? And how am I free *not* to choose? Is the purchase of an automobile or clothing "discretionary" when it is the unconscious substitute for an unrealistic desire for certain living accommodations? The vital minimum today, the minimum of imposed consumption, is the standard package. [21] Beneath this level, you are an outcast. Is loss of status — or social non-existence — less upsetting than hunger?

---

21. English in the original. — *Trans.*

In fact, discretionary income is an idea rationalized at the discretion of entrepreneurs and market analysts. It justifies their manipulation of secondary needs, since, in their view, these don't touch on the essential. The line of demarcation between essential and inessential has quite a precise double function:

1. To establish and preserve a sphere of individual human essence, which is the keystone of the system of ideological values.

2. To obscure behind the anthropological postulate the actual productivist definition of "survival": during the period of (capital) accumulation, what is "essential" is what is strictly necessary for the reproduction of the labor force. In the growth phase, however, it is what is necessary to maintain the rate of growth and surplus value.

## The Emergence of Consummativity:[22] Need-Productive Force

One can generalize this conclusion by saying that needs — such as they are — can no longer be defined adequately in terms of the naturalist-idealist thesis — as innate, instinctive power, spontaneous craving, anthropological potentiality. Rather, they are better defined as a *function* induced (in the individual) by the internal logic of the system: more precisely, *not as a consummative force liberated* by the affluent society, but *as a productive force* required by the functioning of the system itself, by its process of reproduction and survival. In other words, there are only needs because the system needs them.

And the needs invested by the individual consumer today are just as essential to the order of production as the capital invested by the capitalist entrepreneur and the labor power invested by the wage laborer. It is *all* capital.

Hence, there is a compulsion to need and a compulsion to consume. One can imagine laws sanctioning such constraint one day (an obligation to change cars every two years).[23]

To be sure, this systematic constraint has been placed under the sign of choice and "liberty," and hence appears as entirely opposed to the labor process as the pleasure principle is to the reality principle. In fact, the "liberty" to consume is of the same order as the freedom offered by the labor market. The capitalist system was erected on this liberty — on the formal emancipation of the labor force (and not on the concrete autonomy of work, which it abolishes). Similarly, consumption is only possible in the abstraction of a system based on

---

22. *Consommativité:* Baudrillard's neologism obviously suggests a parallel with the term "productivity," and all that connotes. — *Trans.*

23. It is so true that consumption is a productive force that, by significant analogy, it is often subsumed under the notion of profit: "Borrowing makes money." "Buy, and you will be rich." It is exalted not as expenditure, but as investment and profitability.

the "liberty" of the consumer. It is *necessary* that the individual user have a choice, and become through his choice free at last to enter as a productive force in a production calculus, exactly as the capitalist system frees the laborer to sell, at last, his labor power.

And just as the fundamental concept of this system is not, strictly speaking, that of production, but of *productivity* (labor and production disengage themselves from all ritual, religious, and subjective connotations to enter the historical process of rationalization); so, one must speak not of consumption, but of *consummativity*: even if the process is far from being as rationalized as that of production, the parallel tendency is to move from subjective, contingent, concrete enjoyment to an indefinite calculus of growth rooted in the abstraction of needs, on which the system this time imposes its coherence — a coherence that it literally produces as a by-product of its productivity.[24]

Indeed, just as concrete work is abstracted, little by little, into labor power in order to make it homogeneous with the means of production (machines, energy, etc.) and thus to multiply the homogeneous factors into a growing productivity — so desire is abstracted and atomized into needs, in order to make it homogeneous with the means of satisfaction (products, images, sign-objects, etc.) and thus to multiply consummativity.

The same process of rationalization holds (atomization and unlimited abstraction), but the ideological role of the concept of need is expanded: with all its hedonist illusions, *need-pleasure* masks the objective reality of *need-productive force*. Needs and labor[25] are therefore two modalities of the same exploitation[26] of productive forces. The saturated consumer appears as the spellbound avatar of the wage laborer.

---

24.  Hence, it is vain to oppose consumption and production, as is so often done, in order to subordinate one to the other, or vice versa, in terms of causality or influence. For in fact we are comparing two heterogeneous sectors: productivity, that is, and abstract and generalized exchange value system where labor and concrete production are occluded in laws — the modes and relations of production; secondly, a logic, and a sector, that of consumption, which is entirely conceived in terms of motivations and individual, contingent, concrete satisfactions. So, properly speaking, it is illegitimate to confront the two. On the other hand, if one conceives of consumption as production, the production of signs, which is also in the process of systematization on the basis of a generalization of exchange value (of signs), then the two spheres are homogeneous — though, at the same time, not comparable in terms of causal priority, but homologous from the viewpoint of structural modalities. The structure is that of the mode of production.

25.  Cf. *besoin* and *besogne*. Baudrillard here draws attention to the etymological connection between the French term for need and the archaic word *besogne*, which commonly referred to labor, a heavy burden, etc., as well as meaning to need. — *Trans.*

26.  In both senses of the term: technical and social.

Thus it should not be said that "consumption is entirely a function of production": rather, *it is consummativity that is a structural mode of productivity*. On this point, nothing has really changed in the historical passage from an emphasis on "vital" needs to "cultural" needs, or "primary" needs to "secondary" ones. The slave's only assurance that he would eat was that the system needed slaves to work. The only chance that the modern citizen may have to see his "cultural" needs satisfied lies in the fact that the system needs his needs, and that the individual is no longer content just to eat. In other words, if there had been, for the order of production, any means whatever of assuring the survival of the anterior mode of brutal exploitation, there would never have been much question of needs.[27] Needs are curbed as much as possible. But when it proves necessary, they are instigated as a means of repression.[28]

*Controlled Desublimation*

The capitalist system has never ceased to make women and children work *first* (to whatever extent possible). Under absolute constraint, it eventually "discovered" the great humanitarian and democratic principles. Schooling was only conceded piece by piece, and it was not generalized until it had imposed itself on the system — like universal suffrage — as a powerful means of social control and integration (or as a means of acculturation to industrial society). During the phase of industrialization, the last pennyworth of labor power was extorted without compunction. To extract surplus value, it was hardly necessary to prime the pump with needs. Then capital, confronted by its own contradictions (over-production, falling rate of profit), tried at first to surmount them by totally restructuring its accumulation through destruction, deficit budgeting and bank-ruptcy. It thus averted a redistribution of wealth, which would have placed the existing relations of production and structures of power seriously in question. But as soon as the threshold of rupture had been reached, capital was already unearthing the individual *qua* consumer. He was no longer simply the slave as labor power. This

27.   A hypothesis: labor itself did not appear as a productive force until the social order (the structure of privilege and domination) absolutely needed it to survive, since the power based on personal and hierarchical relations was no longer sufficient by itself. The exploitation of labor is a last resort for the social order. Access to work is still refused to women as socially subversive.

28.   Nonetheless, this emergence of needs, however formal and subdued, is never without danger for the social order — as is the liberation of any productive force. Apart from being the dimension of exploitation, it is also the origin of the most violent social contradictions, of class struggle. Who can say what historical contradictions the emergence and exploitation of this new productive force — that of needs — holds in store for us?

was truly a "production." And in bringing it off, capital was only delivering up a new kind of serf: the individual as consumption power.[29]

This is the point of departure for an analysis of consumption at the political level: it is necessary to overcome the ideological understanding of consumption as a process of craving and pleasure, as an extended metaphor on the digestive functions — where the whole issue is naturalized according to the primary scheme of the oral drive. It is necessary to surpass this powerful imaginary preconception in order to define consumption *not only structurally as a system of exchange and of signs, but strategically as a mechanism of power*. Now, the question of consumption is not clarified by the concept of needs, nor by theories of their qualitative transformation, or their massive extension: these phenomena are no more than the characteristic effect, at the individual level, of a certain monopolistic productivity, of a totalitarian economy (capitalist or socialist) driven to conjuring up leisure, comfort, luxury, etc.; briefly, they are the ultimate realization of the private individual as a productive force. The system of needs must wring liberty and pleasure from him as so many functional elements of the reproduction of the system of production and the relations of power that sanction it. It gives rise to these private functions according to the same principle of abstraction and radical "alienation" that was formerly (and still today) the case for his labor power. In this system, the "liberation" of needs, of consumers, of women, of the young, the body, etc., is always really the *mobilization* of needs, consumers, the body.... It is never an explosive liberation, but a controlled emancipation, a mobilization whose end is competitive exploitation.

It would appear that even the most deep-seated forces, the unconscious instincts, can be mobilized in this way by the "strategy of desire." We are now at the very heart of the concept of controlled desublimation (or "repressive desublimation," as Marcuse would say). At the limit, retranscribed in this primary psychoanalysis, the consumer appears as a knot of drives (future productive forces) repressed by the system of ego defense functions. These functions must be "desublimated" — hence, the deconstruction of the *ego* functions, the conscious moral and individual functions, to the benefit of a "liberation" of the id and the super-ego as factors of integration, participation and consumption — to the benefit of a kind of total consuming immorality in which the individual finally submerges himself in a pleasure principle entirely controlled by production planning.

29.  There is no other basis for aid to underdeveloped countries.

To sum up: man is not simply *there* first, equipped with his needs, and designated by nature to fulfill and finalize himself *qua* Man. This proposition, which smacks of spiritualist teleology, in fact defines the individual function in our society — the functional myth of productivist society. The whole system of individual values — this religion of spontaneity, liberty, creativity, etc. — is bloated with the productivist option. Even the vital functions are immediately "functions" of the system.

We must reverse the terms of the analysis, and abolish the cardinal reference to the individual, for even that is the product of this social logic. We must abandon the constitutive social structure of the individual, and even his lived perception of himself: for man never really does come face to face with his own needs. This is not only true of "secondary" needs (where the individual is reproduced according to the finalities of production considered as consumption power). It applies equally well to "survival" needs. In this instance, man is not reproduced as man: he is simply regenerated as a survivor (a surviving productive force). If he eats, drinks, lives somewhere, reproduces himself, it is because the system requires his self-production in order to reproduce itself: it needs men. If it could function with slaves, there would be no "free" workers. If it could function with asexual mechanical robots, there would be no sexual reproduction.[30] If the system could function without feeding its workers, there would be no bread. It is in this sense that we are all, in the framework of this system, survivors. Not even the instinct of self-preservation is fundamental: it is a social tolerance or a social imperative. When the system requires it, it cancels this instinct and people get excited about dying (for a sublime cause, evidently).

We do not wish to say that "the individual is a product of society" at all. For, as it is currently understood, this culturalist platitude only masks the much more radical truth that, in its totalitarian logic, a system of productivist growth (capitalist, but not exclusively) can only produce and reproduce men — even in their deepest determinations: in their liberty, in their needs, in their very unconscious — as productive forces. The system can only produce and reproduce individuals as elements of the system. It cannot tolerate exceptions.

---

30.   Robots remain the ultimate and ideal phantasm of a total productivist system. Still better, there is integrated automation. However, cybernetic rationality is devouring itself, for men are necessary for any system of social order and domination. Now, in the final analysis, this amounts nonetheless to the aim of all productivity, which is a *political* goal.

*Generalized Sign Exchange and the Twilight of "Values"*

So today everything is "recuperable."[31] But it is too simple to argue that first there are needs, authentic values, etc., and then they are alienated, mystified, recuperated, or what have you. This humanitarian Manicheanism explains nothing. If everything is "recuperable," it is because everything in monopoly capitalist society[32] — goods, knowledge, technique, culture, men, their relations and their aspirations — everything is reproduced, from the outset, immediately, as an element of the system, as an integrated variable.

The truth is — and this has been recognized for a long time in the area of economic production — that use value no longer appears anywhere in the system. The determining logic of exchange value is, however, as ubiquitous as ever. This must be recognized today as the truth of the sphere of "consumption" and the cultural system in general. In other words, everything, even artistic, intellectual, and scientific production, even innovation and transgression, is immediately produced as sign and exchange value (relational value of the sign).

A structural analysis of consumption is possible to the extent that "needs," consumption behavior and cultural behavior are not only recuperated, but systematically induced and produced as productive forces. Given this abstraction and this tendency toward total systematization, such an analysis is entirely possible, if it in turn is based on an analysis of the social logic of production and the *generalized exchange* of signs.

---

31. The term itself has been "recuperated," for it presupposes an original purity and delineates the capitalist system as a maleficent instance of perversion, revealing yet another moralizing vision.
32. Or, more simply, in a system of generalized exchange.

# CHAPTER THREE

## FETISHISM AND IDEOLOGY:
## THE SEMIOLOGICAL REDUCTION [1]

The concepts of commodity fetishism and money fetishism sketched, for Marx, the lived ideology of capitalist society — the mode of sanctification, fascination and psychological subjection by which individuals internalize the generalized system of exchange value. These concepts outline the whole process whereby the concrete social values of labor and exchange, which the capitalist system denies, abstracts and "alienates," are erected into transcendent ideological values — into a moral agency that regulates all alienated behavior. What is being described here is the successor to a more archaic fetishism and religious mystification ("the opium of the people"). And this theory of a new fetishism has become the icing on the cake of contemporary analysis. While Marx still attached it (though very ambiguously) to a *form* (the commodity, money), and thus located it at a theoretically comprehensive level, today the concept of fetishism is exploited in a summary and empirical fashion: object fetishism, automobile fetishism, sex fetishism, vacation fetishism, etc. The whole exercise is precipitated by nothing more sophisticated than a diffuse, exploded and idolatrous vision of the consumption environment; it is the conceptual fetish of vulgar social thought, working assiduously towards the expanded reproduction of ideology in the guise of a disturbing attack on the system. The term fetishism is dangerous not only because it short-circuits analysis, but because since the 18th century it has conducted the whole repertoire of occidental Christian and humanist ideology, as orchestrated by colonists, ethnologists and missionaries. The Christian connotation has been present from the beginning in the condemnation of primitive cults by a religion that claimed to be abstract and spiritual; "the worship of certain earthly and material objects called fetishes...for which reason I will call it fetishism." [2] Never having really shed this moral and rationalistic connotation, the great *fetishist metaphor* has since been the recurrent leitmotiv of the analysis of "magical thinking," whether that of the Bantu tribes or that of modern metropolitan hordes submerged in their objects and their signs.

---

1. This article first appeared in *Nouvelle Revue de Psychanalyse* Vol. II (Autumn 1970).
2. De Brosses, *Du Culte des dieux fetiches* (1760).

As an eclecticism derived from various primitive representations, the fetishist metaphor consists of analyzing myths, rites and practices in terms of *energy*, a magical transcendent power, a *mana* (whose latest avatar would possibly be the libido). As a power that is transferred to beings, objects and agencies, it is universal and diffuse, but it crystallizes at strategic points so that its flux can be regulated and diverted by certain groups or individuals for their own benefit. In the light of the "theory," this would be the major objective of all primitive practices, even· eating. Thus, in the animist vision, everything happens between the hypostasis of a force, its dangerous transcendence and the capture of this force, which then becomes beneficent. Aborigines apparently rationalized their experience of the group and of the world in these terms. But anthropologists themselves have rationalized their experience of the aborigines in these same terms, thus exorcising the crucial interrogation that these societies inevitably brought to bear on their own civilization.[3]

Here we are interested in the extension of this *fetishist metaphor* in modern industrial society, insofar as it enmeshes critical analysis (liberal or Marxist) within the subtle trap of a rationalistic anthropology. What else is intended by the concept of "commodity fetishism" if not the notion of a false consciousness devoted to the worship of exchange value (or, more recently, the fetishism of gadgets or objects, in which individuals are supposed to worship artificial libidinal or prestige values incorporated in the object)? All of this presupposes the existence, somewhere, of a non-alienated consciousness of an object in some "true," objective state: its ·use value?

The metaphor of fetishism, wherever it appears, involves a fetishization of the conscious subject or of a human essence, a rationalist metaphysic that is at the root of the whole system of occidental Christian values. Where Marxist theory seems to prop itself up with this same anthropology, it ideologically countersigns the very system of values that it otherwise dislocates via objective historical analysis. By referring all the problems of "fetishism" back to superstructural mechanisms of false consciousness, Marxism eliminates any real chance it has of analyzing the *actual process of ideological labor*. By refusing to analyze the structures and the mode of ideological production inherent in its own logic, Marxism is condemned (behind the façade of "dialectical" discourse in terms of

---

3. Being *de facto* rationalists, they have often gone so far as to saturate with logical and mythological rationalizations a system of representations that the aborigines knew how to reconcile with more supple objective practices.

class struggle) to expanding the reproduction of ideology, and thus of the capitalist system itself.

Thus, the problem of the generalized "fetishization" of real life forces us to reconsider the problem of the reproduction of ideology. The *fetishistic* theory of infrastructure and superstructure must be exploded, and replaced by a more comprehensive theory of productive forces, since these are *all structurally* implicated in the capitalist system — and not only in some cases (i.e., material production), while merely superstructurally in others (i.e., ideological production).

The term "fetishism" almost has a life of its own. Instead of functioning as a metalanguage for the magical thinking of others, it turns against those who use it, and surreptitiously exposes their own magical thinking. Apparently only psychoanalysis has escaped this vicious circle, by returning fetishism to its context within a perverse *structure* that perhaps underlies all desire. Thus circumscribed by its structural definition (articulated through the clinical reality of the fetish object and its manipulation) as a refusal of sex differences, the term no longer shores up magical thinking; it becomes an analytic concept for a theory of perversion. But if in the social sciences, we cannot find the equivalent — and not merely an analogical one — of this strict use of the term, *the equivalent of the psychoanalytic process of perverse structure at the level of the process of ideological production* — that is, if it proves impossible to articulate the celebrated formula of "commodity fetishism" as anything other than a mere neologism (where "fetishism" refers to this alleged magical thinking, and "commodity" to a structural analysis of capital), then it would be preferable to drop the term entirely (including its cognate and derivative ideas). For in order to reconstitute the *process of fetishization* in terms of structure, we would have to abandon the fetishist metaphor of the worship of the golden calf — even as it has been reworded by Marxists in the phrase "the opium of the people" — and develop instead an articulation that avoids any projection of magical or transcendental animism, and thus the rationalist position of positing a false consciousness and a transcendental subject. After Lévi-Strauss' analysis, the "totem" was overthrown, so that only the analysis of the totemic system and its dynamic integration retained any meaning. This was a radical breakthrough that should be developed, theoretically and clinically, and extended to social analysis in general. So, we started by meddling with received ideas about fetishism, only to discover that the whole theory of ideology may be in doubt.

If objects are not these reified agencies, endowed with force and *mana* in which the subject projects himself and is alienated — if fetishism designates something other than this metaphysic of alienated essence — what is its real process?

We would not make a habit of this, but here an appeal to etymology may help us sort through the confusion. The term "fetish" has undergone a curious semantic distortion. Today it refers to a force, a supernatural property of the object and hence to a similar magical potential in the subject, through schemas of projection and capture, alienation and reappropriation. But originally it signified exactly the opposite: a *fabrication*, an artifact, a labor of appearances and signs. It appeared in France in the 17th century, coming from the Portuguese *feitiço*, meaning "artificial," which itself derives from the Latin *factitius*. The primary sense is "to do (to make," *faire*), the sense of "to imitate by signs" ("act as a devotee," etc.; this sense is also found in "makeup" [*maquillage*], which comes from *maken*, related to *machen* and to make). From the same root (*facio, facticius*) as *feitiço* comes the Spanish *afeitar*: "to paint, to adorn, to embellish," and *afeite*: "preparation, ornamentation, cosmetics," as well as the French *feint* and the Spanish *hechar*, "to do, to make" (whence *hechizo*: "artificial, feigned, dummy").

What quickly becomes apparent is the aspect of faking, of artificial registering — in short, of a cultural sign labor — and that this is at the origin of the status of fetish object, and thus also plays some part in the fascination it exercises. This aspect is increasingly repressed by the inverse representation (the two still exist in the Portuguese *feitiço*, which as an adjective means artificial and as a noun an enchanted object, or sorcery), which *substitutes a manipulation of forces for a manipulation of signs* and a magical economy of transfer of signifieds for a regulated play of signifiers.

The "talisman" also is lived and represented in the animist mode as a receptacle of forces: one forgets that it is first an object marked by signs — signs of the hand, of the face, or characters of the cabal, or the figure of some celestial body that, registered in the object, makes it a talisman. Thus, in the "fetishist" theory of consumption, in the view of marketing strategists as well as of consumers, objects are given and received everywhere as force dispensers (happiness, health, security, prestige, etc.). This magical substance having been spread about so liberally, one forgets that what we are dealing with first is signs: a generalized code of signs, a totally arbitrary code of differences, *and that it is on this basis, and not at all on account of their use values or their innate "virtues," that objects exercise their fascination.*

If fetishism exists it is thus not a fetishism of the signified, a fetishism of substances and values (called ideological), which the fetish object would incarnate for the alienated subject. Behind this reinterpretation (which is truly ideological) it is a *fetishism of the signifier*. That is to say that the subject is trapped in the factitious, differential, encoded, systematized aspect of the object. It is not the passion (whether of objects or subjects) for substances that speaks in fetishism, it is the *passion for the code*, which, by governing both objects and subjects, and by subordinating them to itself, delivers them up to abstract manipulation. This is the fundamental articulation of the ideological process: not in the projection of alienated consciousness into various superstructures, but in the generalization at all levels of a structural code.

So it appears that "commodity fetishism" may no longer fruitfully be interpreted according to the paleo-Marxist dramaturgy of the instance, in such and such an object, of a force that returns to haunt the individual severed from the product of his labor, and from all the marvels of his misappropriated investment (labor and effectiveness). It is rather the (ambivalent) fascination for a form (logic of the commodity or system of exchange value), a state of absorption, for better or for worse, in the restrictive logic of a system of abstraction. Something like a desire, a perverse desire, the desire of the code is brought to light here: it is a desire that is related to the systematic nature of signs, drawn towards it, precisely through what this system-like nature negates and bars, by exorcising the contradictions spawned by the process of real labor — just as the perverse psychological structure of the fetishist is organized, in the fetish object, around a mark, around the abstraction of a mark that negates, bars and exorcises the difference of the sexes.

In this sense, fetishism is not the sanctification of a certain object, or value (in which case one might hope to see it disappear in our age, when the liberalization of values and the abundance of objects would "normally" tend to desanctify them). It is the sanctification of the system as such, of the commodity as system: it is thus contemporaneous with the generalization of exchange value and is propagated with it. The more the system is systematized, the more the fetishist fascination is reinforced; and if it is always invading new territories, further and further removed from the domain of economic exchange value strictly understood (i.e., the areas of sexuality, recreation, etc.), this is not owing to an obsession with pleasure, or a substantial desire for pleasure or free time, but to a progressive (and even quite brutal) systematization of these sectors, that is to say their reduction to commutable sign values within the framework of a system of exchange value that is now almost total.[4]

Thus the fetishization of the commodity is the fetishization of a product emptied of its concrete substance of labor [5] and subjected to another type of labor, a labor of signification, that is, of coded abstraction (the production of differences and of sign values). It is an active, collective process of production and reproduction of a code, a system, invested with all the diverted, unbound desire separated out from the process of real labor and transferred onto precisely that which denies the process of real labor. Thus, fetishism is actually attached to the sign object, the object eviscerated of its substance and history, and reduced to the state of marking a difference, epitomizing a whole system of differences.

That the fascination, worship, and cathexis (*investissement*) of desire and, finally, even pleasure (perverse) devolve upon the system and not upon a substance (or *mana*) is clarified in the phenomenon, no less celebrated, of "money fetishism." What is fascinating about money is neither its materiality, nor even that it might be the intercepted equivalent of a certain force (e.g., of labor) or of a certain potential power: it is its *systematic nature*, the potential enclosed in the material for total commutability of all values, thanks to their definitive abstraction. It is the abstraction, the total artificiality of the sign that one "adores" in money. What is fetishized is the closed perfection of a system, not the "golden calf," or the treasure. This specifies the difference between the pathology of the miser who is attached to the fecal materiality of gold, and the fetishism we are attempting to define here as an ideological process. Elsewhere we have seen[6] how, in the *collection*, it is neither the nature of objects nor even their symbolic value that is important; but precisely the sense in which they negate all this, and deny the reality of castration for the subject through the systematic nature of the collective cycle, whose continual shifting from one term to another helps the subject to weave around himself a closed and invulnerable world that dissolves all obstacles to the realization of desire (perverse, of course).

Today there is an area where this fetishist logic of the commodity

4.   In this system, use value becomes obscure and almost unintelligible, though not as an original value which has been lost, but more precisely as a *function derived from exchange value*. Henceforth, it is exchange value that induces use value (i.e., needs and satisfactions) to work in common with it (ideologically), within the framework of political economy.

5.   In this way labor power as a commodity is itself "fetishized."

6.   In my *Le Système des objects* (Paris: Gallimard, 1968), pp. 103ff.

can be illustrated very clearly, permitting us to indicate more precisely what we call the process of ideological labor: the body and beauty. We do not speak of either as an absolute value (speaking of which, what is an absolute value?), but of the current obsession with "liberating the body" and with beauty.

This fetish-beauty has nothing (any longer) to do with an effect of the soul (the spiritualist vision), a natural grace of movement or countenance; with the transparency of truth (the idealist vision); or with an "inspired genius" of the body, which can be communicated as effectively by expressive ugliness (the romantic vision). What we are talking about is a kind of anti-nature incarnate, bound up in a general stereotype of *models of beauty*, in a perfectionist vertigo and controlled narcissism. This is the absolute rule with respect to the face and the body, the generalization of sign exchange value to facial and bodily effects. It is the final disqualification of the body, its subjection to a discipline, the total circulation of signs. The body's wildness is veiled by makeup, the drives are assigned to a cycle of fashion. Behind this *moral* perfection, which stresses a valorization of exteriority (and no longer, as in traditional morality, a labor of interior sublimation), it is insurance taken out against the instincts. However, this anti-nature does not exclude desire; we know that this kind of beauty is fascinating precisely because it is trapped in models, because it is closed, systematic, ritualized in the ephemeral, without symbolic value. It is the sign in this beauty, the mark (makeup, symmetry, or calculated asymmetry, etc.), which fascinates; *it is the artifact that is the object of desire*. The signs are there to make the body into a perfect object, a feat that has been accomplished through a long and specific labor of sophistication. Signs perfect the body into an object in which none of its real work (the work of the unconscious or psychic and social labor) can show through. The fascination of this fetishized beauty is the result of this extended process of abstraction, and derives from what it negates and censors through its own character as a system.

Tattoos, stretched lips, the bound feet of Chinese women, eyeshadow, rouge, hair removal, mascara, or bracelets, collars, objects, jewelry, accessories: anything will serve to rewrite the cultural order on the body; and it is this that takes on the effect of beauty. The erotic is thus the reinscription of the erogenous in a homogeneous system of signs (gestures, movements, emblems, body heraldry) whose goal is closure and logical perfection — to be sufficient unto itself. Neither the genital order (placing an external finality in question) nor the symbolic order (putting in question the division of the subject) have this coherence: neither the functional nor the symbolic can weave a body from signs like this — abstract, impeccable, clothed with marks, and thus invulnerable; "made up" (*faict* and *fainct*) in the profound sense of the expression; cut off from external determinations and from the internal reality of its desire, yet offered up in the same turn as an idol, as the *perfect phallus for perverse desire*: that of others, and its own.[7]

Lévi-Strauss has already spoken of this erotic bodily attraction among the Caduvéo and the Maori, of those bodies "completely covered by arabesques of a perverse subtlety," and of "something deliciously provocative."[8] It suffices to think of Baudelaire to know how much sophistication alone conveys charm (in the strong sense), and how much it is always attached to the *mark* (ornamentation, jewelry, perfume) — or to the "cutting up" of the body into partial objects (feet, hair, breasts, buttocks, etc.), which is a profoundly similar exercise. It is always a question of substituting — for an erogenous body, divided in castration, source of an ever-perilous desire — a montage, an artifact of phantasmagorical fragments, an arsenal or a panoply of accessories, or of parts of the body (but the whole body can be reduced by fetishized nudity to the role of a partial object as well). These fetish objects are always caught in a system of assemblage and separation, in a code. Circumscribed in this way, they become the possible objects of a security-giving worship. This is to substitute the line of demarcation between elements-signs for the great dividing line of castration. It substitutes the significant difference, the formal division between signs, for the irreducible ambivalence, for the symbolic split (*écart*).

It would be interesting to compare this perverse fascination to that which, according to Freud, is exercised by the child or the animal, or even by those women "who suffice to themselves, who properly speaking love only themselves" and who for that reason "exercise the greatest charm over men not only for aesthetic reasons... but also on account of interesting psychological constellations." "The charm of a child," he says again, "lies to a great extent in his narcissism, his self-sufficiency and inaccessibility, just as does the charm of certain animals which seem not to concern themselves about us, such as cats and the large beasts of prey."[9] One would have to distinguish

7.  Now this is how the body, re-elaborated by the perverse structure as phallic idol, manages to function simultaneously as the ideological model of socialization and of fulfillment. Perverse desire and the ideological process are articulated on the same "sophisticated" body. We will return to this later.

8.  Claude Lévi-Strauss, *Tristes Tropiques*, trans. John and Doreen Weightman (New York: Atheneum, 1975), p. 188.

9.  Sigmund Freud, "On Narcissism: An Introduction" (1914), in *Collected Papers*

between the seduction associated, in the child, the animal or the women-child, with *polymorphous perversity* (and with the kind of "freedom," of libidinal autonomy that accompanies it), and that linked to the contemporary commercialized erotic system, which precipitates a "fetishistic" perversion that is restricted, static and encompassed by models. Nevertheless, what is sought for and recognized in both types of seduction is another side or "beyond" of castration, which always takes on the aspect either of a harmonious natural state of unity (child, animal) or of a summation and perfect closure effected by signs. What fascinates us is always that which radically excludes us in the name of its internal logic or perfection: a mathematical formula, a paranoic system, a concrete jungle, a useless object, or, again, a smooth body, without orifices, doubled and redoubled by a mirror, devoted to perverse autosatisfaction. It is by caressing herself, by the autoerotic maneuver, that the striptease artist best evokes desire.[10]

What is especially important for us here is to demonstrate the general ideological process by which beauty, as a constellation of signs and work upon signs, functions in the present system simultaneously as the negation of castration (perverse psychic structure) and as the negation of the body that is segmented in its social practice and in the division of labor (ideological social structure). The modern rediscovery of the body and its illusions (*prestiges*) is not innocently contemporary with monopoly capitalism and the discoveries of psychoanalysis:

1. It is because psychoanalysis has brought the fundamental division of the subject to light through the body (but not the same "body"), that it has become so important to ward off this menace (of castration), to restore the individual (the undivided subject of consciousness). This is no longer achieved, however, by endowing the individual with a soul or a mind, but a body properly all his own, from which all negativity of desire is eliminated and which functions only as the exhibitor of beauty and happiness. In this sense, the current myth of the body appears as a process of *phantasmagorical rationalization*, which is close to fetishism in its strict analytical definition. Paradoxically, then, this "discovery of the body," which alleges itself to be simultaneous and in sympathy with psychoanalytic discoveries, is in fact an attempt to conjure away its revolutionary implications. The body is introduced in order to liquidate the

(New York: Basic Books, 1959), Vol. IV, p. 46.
    10.   Ideological discourse is also built up out of a redundancy of signs, and in extreme cases, forms a tautology. It is through this specularity, this "mirage within itself," that it conjures away conflicts and exercises its power.

unconscious and its work, to strengthen the one and homogeneous subject, keystone of the system of values and order.

2. Simultaneously, monopoly capitalism, which is not content to exploit the body as labor power, manages to fragment it, to divide the very expressiveness of the body in labor, in exchange, and in play, recuperating all this as individual needs, hence as productive (*consummative*) forces under its control. This mobilization of cathexes at all levels as productive forces creates, over the long term, profound contradictions. These contradictions are still political in nature, if we accept a radical redefinition of politics that would take into account this totalitarian socialization of all sectors of real life. It is for these reasons that the body, beauty and sexuality are imposed as new universals in the name of the rights of the new man, emancipated by abundance and the cybernetic revolution. The deprivation, manipulation and controlled recycling of the subjective and collective values by the unlimited extension of exchange value and the unlimited rival speculation over sign values renders necessary the sanctification of a glorious agency called the body that will become for each individual an ideological sanctuary, the sanctuary of his own alienation. Around this body, which is entirely positivized as the capital of divine right, the subject of private property is about to be restored.

So ideology goes, always playing upon the two levels according to the same process of labor and desire attached to the organization of signs (process of signification and fetishization). Let us consider this articulation of the semiological and ideological a little more closely.

Take the example of nudity as it is presented in advertising, in the proliferation of erotica, in the mass media's rediscovery of the body and sex. This nudity claims to be rational, progressive: it claims to rediscover the truth of the body, its natural reason, beyond clothing, taboos and fashion. In fact, it is too rationalistic, and bypasses the body, whose symbolic and sexual truth is not in the naive conspicuousness of nudity, but in the *uncovering* of itself (*mise à nu*), insofar as it is the symbolic equivalent of putting to death (*mise à mort*), and thus of the true path of desire, *which is always ambivalent*, love and death simultaneously.[11] Functional modern nudity does not involve this ambivalence at all, nor thus any profound symbolic function, because such nudity reveals a body *entirely positivized by sex* — as a cultural value, as a model of fulfillment, as an emblem, as a morality (or ludic immorality, which is the same thing) — and *not a body divided and split by sex*. The sexualized body, in this case, no

_____

11.   These terms are drawn from Georges Bataille, *L'Erotisme* (Paris: Les Editions de Minuit, 1957).

longer functions, save on its positive side, which is that of:
— need (and not of desire);
— satisfaction (lack, negativity, death, castration are no longer registered in it);
— the *right* to the body and sex (the subversiveness, the social negativity of the body and sex are frozen there in a formal "democratic" lobby: the "right to the body").[12]

Once ambivalence and the symbolic function have been liquidated, nudity again becomes one sign among others, entering into a distinctive opposition to clothing. Despite its "liberationist" velleities, it no longer radically opposes clothing, it is only a variant that can coexist with all the others in the systematic process of fashion: and today one sees it everywhere acting "in alternation." It is this nudity, caught up in the differential play of signs (and not in that of eros and death) that is the object of fetishism: the absolute condition for its ideological functioning is the loss of the symbolic and the passing over to the semiological.

Strictly speaking, it is not even because (as has just been said) "once the symbolic function has been liquidated there is a passage to the semiological." In fact, it is the semiological organization itself, the entrenchment in a system of signs, that has the goal of reducing the symbolic function. *This semiological reduction of the symbolic properly constitutes the ideological process.* Other examples can illustrate this semiological reduction, this fundamental scheme of the process of ideology.

*The Sun:* The vacation sun no longer retains anything of the collective symbolic function it had among the Aztecs, the Egyptians, etc.[13] It no longer has that ambivalence of a natural force — life and death, beneficent and murderous — which it had in primitive cults or still has in peasant labor. The vacation sun is a completely positive sign, the absolute source of happiness and euphoria, and as such it is significantly opposed to non-sun (rain, cold, bad weather). At the same time as it loses all ambivalence, it is registered in a distinctive opposition, which, incidentally, is never innocent: here the

---

12. The whole illusion of the *Sexual Revolution* is here: society could not be split, divided and subverted in the name of a sex and a body whose current presentation has the ideological function of veiling the subject's division and subversion. As usual, everything holds together: the reductive function that this mythical nudity fulfills in relation to the subject divided by sex and castration is performed simultaneously on the macroscopic level of society divided by historical class conflicts. Thus the sexual revolution is a subsidiary of the industrial revolution or of the revolution of abundance (and of so many others): all are decoys and ideological metamorphoses of an unchanged order.

13. Cf. Alain Laurent in *Communications*, No. 10.

opposition functions to the exclusive benefit of the sun (against the other negativized sun). Thenceforth, from the moment it functions as ideology and as a cultural value registered in a system of oppositions, the sun, like sex, is also registered institutionally as the right to the sun, which sanctions its ideological functioning, and morally registered as a fetishist obsession, both individual and collective.

*Masculine-Feminine:* No being is assigned by nature to a sex. Sexual ambivalence (activity-passivity) is at the heart of each subject, sexual differentiation is registered as a difference in the body of each subject and not as an absolute term linked to a particular sexual organ. The question is not "having one or not." But this ambivalence, this profound sexual valence must be reduced, for as such it escapes genital organization and the social order. Once again, the ideological labor consists in semiologically reducing, in dispersing this irreducible reality into a great distinctive structure, masculine-feminine — into sexes that are full, distinct and opposed to one another. This structure leans on the alibi of biological organs (the reduction of sex as a difference to the difference of the sexual organs); and, above all, it is pegged to the grandiose cultural models whose function it is to separate the sexes in order to establish the absolute privilege of one over the other. If everyone is led, by this controlled structuration, to confuse himself with his own sexual status, it is only to resign his sex the more easily (that is, the erogenous differentiation of his own body) to the sexual segregation that is one of the political and ideological foundations of the social order.[14]

*The Unconscious:* The contemporary unconscious is diffused by the mass media, celebrated by semiology, but still given a substance that is individualized and personalized. Today, everyone "has" an unconscious: mine, yours, his. The structure and work of the unconscious is primarily a challenging of the conscious subject. Here, then, the possessive pronoun is itself semiologically reductive and ideologically effective insofar as it reduces this unconscious to a

---

14.   The fact that from the very first this great structural opposition is a functional, hierarchical, logistic difference for the social order, the fact that if there must be two sexes it is so that one may be subjected to the other, makes clear the ambiguity of "sexual liberation." Since this "liberation" is that of everyone's sexual needs as assigned to his sex in the framework of the ideological-structural model of bisexuality, any reinforcement of sexual practices in this sense can only reinforce this structure and the ideological discrimination that it bears. In our "liberal" society of "mixedness," the separation between masculine and feminine models has never ceased to entrench and crystallize itself since the start of the industrial era. Today, in spite of pious, liberal pathos over the question, it is taking on ever more generalized forms.

simple oppositional term *vis-à-vis* consciousness. Together, they operate in the name of the individual (as the possessive case indicates), fundamentally to the advantage of the subject of consciousness. So, the "rediscovered" unconscious, generally exalted from the beginning, runs directly counter to its original meaning: initially structure and labor, it is transformed into a sign function, labor power and object of appropriation by a unified, autonomous subject, the eternal subject of consciousness and of private property. Henceforth, to each his own unconscious, his own symbolic deposit to exploit, his capital! And shortly, there will be the right to the unconscious, the *habeas corpus* of *homo cyberneticus*, that is, the transfer of bourgeois liberties into a domain that everywhere escapes them and which denies them. But the reason is clear: it is the transfer of social control to the domain of the irreducible. The revolution of the unconscious becomes the avatar of a new humanism of the subject of consciousness; and through the individualist ideology of the unconscious, fetishized and reduced by signs such as sex and sun to a calculus of pleasure and consumed satisfaction, each subject itself drains and monitors the movement and the dangerous labor of the unconscious for the benefit of the social order. The myth of the unconscious becomes the ideological solution to the problems of the unconscious.[15]

It is seen that the *semiological reduction* of the unconscious to a simple term opposed to consciousness implies a hierarchical subordination to consciousness, a reductive formalization of the unconscious to the benefit of consciousness, and thus an *ideological reduction* to the (capitalist) system of order and social values.

There is no conclusion to this preliminary analysis of the ideological process. In summary, the schemes that emerge are:

1. Homology, simultaneity of the ideological operation on the level of psychic structure and social structure. Here we find neither cause nor effect, neither super- nor infrastructure, nor the analytical privilege of one field or the other, of one agency or the other — *without risking causal distortion and desperate recourse to analogy*.

2. The process of ideological labor always aims toward reducing the process of real labor (the process of unconscious symbolic labor in the division of the subject, the process of labor of productive forces in the explosion of relations of production). This process is always a

---

15. Also, logically, this "liberation," like that of any other productive force, takes on the force of a moral imperative. Everyone is called upon (be it in the name of hygiene, even) to *become conscious of his unconscious*, not to let this productive potential lie fallow, to make his unconscious emerge in order to "personalize" it. Absurd, perhaps, but coherent with the logic of the ideological system.

process of abstraction by signs, of substituting a system of distinctive oppositions for the process of real labor (the first moment: process of signification). But these oppositions are not neutral; they rank themselves hierarchically, privileging one of the terms (second moment: process of discrimination). Signification does not always carry discrimination with it (phonemic differences at the level of language), but discrimination always presupposes signification — the sign-function that reduces ambivalence and the symbolic.

3. Bifurcation, or marking by signs, is always accompanied by a *totalization via signs* and a formal autonomy of sign systems. Sign logic operates by internal differentiation and by general homogenization. Only labor on the homogeneous formal, abstract material of signs makes possible this closure, this perfection, this logical mirage that is the effectiveness of ideology. It is the abstract coherence, suturing all contradictions and divisions, that gives ideology its power of fascination (fetishism). This coherence is found in the erotic system as well as in the perverse seduction exercised by the system of exchange value, which is entirely present in even the very smallest of commodities.

4. This abstract totalization permits signs to function ideologically, that is, to establish and perpetuate real discriminations and the order of power.

# CHAPTER FOUR

## GESTURE [1] AND SIGNATURE:
## SEMIURGY IN CONTEMPORARY ART

The painting is a signed object as much as it is a painted surface.
The paraph of the creator seems actually to increase its singularity.
What does this signature indicate? The act of painting, the subject
who paints. But it indicates that this subject entrenched at the heart of
an object and the very act of painting is named by a sign. Im-
perceptibly, but radically, the signature introduces the *oeuvre*
which is that of the painting. In certain modern works it is
unique — no longer as an oeuvre, but as an object — until it bears
this signature. Then it becomes a model to which an extraordinary,
differential value is brought by a visible sign. But it is not a meaning
value — the meaning peculiar to the painting is not in question here
— it is a *differential* value, carried by the ambiguity of a sign that
does not cause the work to be seen, but to be recognized and
evaluated in a system of signs, and which, while differentiating it as a
model, already, from another perspective, integrates it in a series,
that of the works of the painter.

---

1. *Le gestuel* is difficult to translate: it is opposed to *geste* as its extension, not
contradiction. Yet it is the latter that is usually translated as "gesture." Briefly, *le
gestuel* refers to a sort of complex, or paradigm, of gestures, and this is the simplest
way to grasp the term. However, constantly referring to "the gestural" is awkward in
English, and various renderings are thus to be found in the text. There is another sense
in which *le gestuel* refers to a congealment, petrifaction or crystallization of gestures,
of single, relatively independent, unsolicited, physical actions into sequences that take
on an almost magical, incantatory aspect. For clarification we have taken a brief
passage from Baudrillard's *Le Système des objects* (Paris: 1968), pp. 57-58: "Still in
the analysis of ambient values, when we broach the study of functional forms (that
may be called forms drawn in profile, dynamic, etc.), we see that their stylization is
inseparable from that of the *gestuel humain* (the complex of human gestures) that
goes with them. Stylization always signifies the elision of muscular energy and of work.
All the processes of the elision of primary functions to the profit of the secondary
functions of relation and calculation, or of the elision of the drives to the profit of
culture (*culturalité*) have for a practical and historical mediation at the level of objects
the fundamental elision of the gestures of effort (*gestuel d'effort*), the passage from a
*universal gestural paradigm of work* to a *universal gestural paradigm of control*. It is
there that a millenarian status of objects, their anthropomorphic status, definitively
comes to an end; in the abstraction of the sources of energy." And further along: "this
profound, gestural relation of man to objects that epitomizes the integration of man
with the world and with social structures...is still a constraint...a complex of
gestures and of forces, of symbols and of functions, illustrated and stylized by human
energy.... The splendor of this relation of conformity remains subordinated to the
relational constraint." — *Trans.*

Thus the painted oeuvre becomes a cultural object by means of the signature. It is no longer simply read, but perceived in its differential value. A single aesthetic emotion often confuses the critical reading and the distinguishing signs of its physical identity.[2]

A certain fact may be of interest here: until the 19th century, the copy of an original work had its own value, it was a legitimate practice. In our time the copy is illegitimate, inauthentic: it is no longer "art." Similarly, the concept of the forgery has changed — or rather, it suddenly appears with the advent of modernity. Formerly painters regularly used collaborators or "negros": one specialized in trees, another in animals. The act of painting, and so the signature as well, did not bear the same mythological insistence upon authenticity — that moral imperative to which modern art is dedicated and by which it becomes modern — which has been evident ever since the relation to illustration and hence the very meaning of the artistic object changed with the act of painting itself.

It is useless to argue that the forgery, the copy or the counterfeit are unacceptable today because photographic technique has disqualified "photocopy" by hand. That sort of explanation is specious. Something else has changed: the conditions of signification of the oeuvre itself.

In a world that is the reflection of an order (that of God, of Nature or, more simply, of discourse) in which all things are representation, endowed with meaning and transparent to the language that describes them, artistic "creation" proposes only to describe. The appearance of things has the keys to the city,[3] being itself the signature of an order that is given there to be recognized and not to be analyzed. The oeuvre wishes to be the perpetual commentary of a given text, and all copies that take their inspiration from it are justified as the multiplied reflection of an order whose original is in any case transcendent. In other words, the question of authenticity does not arise, and the *work of art is not menaced by its double*. The various copies do not constitute a series in the modern sense of the word, whose model would be the original: all else remaining equal, original and copy are equivalent in a single finality, whose "reason" escapes them. In summary, it is impossible to circumvent the true source of values. *The Forgery does not exist*. Nor is the signature there in order to turn the oeuvre into a pure object, which has surged with emotional power from the act of painting. Even if he signs it

---

2. This is not peculiar to painting: this ambiguous apprehension defines the *consumption* of all cultural goods.

3. As is shown by Michel Foucault in *The Order of Things*.

(sometimes with a monogram), the artist does not attest to its truth: he is never more than the one who gives (*donateur*).

Today the conjuncture of values is entirely different: transcendence is abolished, the oeuvre becomes the original. Its meaning passes from the restitution of appearances to the act of inventing them. Value is transferred from an eminent, objective beauty to the singularity of the artist in his gesture.

And this new act is temporalized: it is the irreversible moment of invention to which other irreversible creative moments can only be subsequent. Here modernity begins. The modern oeuvre is no longer a syntax of various fragments of a general tableau of the universe, "in extension," where continuity and reversibility are active; rather, it is a succession of moments. The oeuvres no longer combine with one another to revive the model in its likeness (the world and its order) by means of their contiguity. They are only able to follow one another in order then to refer, by virtue of their difference and their discontinuity in time, to a quite different model, to the *subject-creator himself* in his unlikeness and his repeated absence. We are no longer in space but in time, in the realm of difference and no longer of resemblance, in the series and no longer in the order. This last point is essential. Once legitimacy is transferred to the act of painting, the latter can only prove itself untiringly: by this very fact it constitutes a series. Incidentally, since the final term of this series is no longer the world to be represented by the ever absent subject, it becomes essential to indicate this subject as such, and in the same act to declare the oeuvre as the object of this subject: that is the function of the signature, it is from that necessity that it derives its present privilege.

Otherwise, how could we explain the insistent mythological demand for authenticity in contemporary art — that each painting be the emanation of a unique moment, often sanctioned by the very day and hour of its execution, and by the signature? And how explain the fact that any contemporary oeuvre is constituted as a declension of objects — each painting being a discontinuous term of an indefinite series, and thus legible first, not in its relation to the world but in its relation to the other paintings by the same artist, its meaning being thus tied down to succession and repetition? What paradoxical law, in its very movement, bends authenticity to the constraint of seriality? Once again we can look for *de facto* determinations, the conditions of the market, for example, which chain the artist to his mannerism and to a cadence of production. And once again, this would be too simple.

In fact, *it is precisely because the series has become the constitutive dimension of the modern oeuvre that the inauthenticity of one of the elements of the series becomes catastrophic.* Each term in its specific difference is essential to the functioning of the series as such, and to the convergence of meaning from one term to the other toward the model (here the subject himself). If one defects, it is the rupture of an order. A false Soulages may well be worth another Soulages [4] but it throws suspicion on all Soulages. The code of recognition becomes suspect, and hence the integrity of meaning of the oeuvre itself. If you like, there is no longer a God today to separate out his elect. The work is no longer rooted in God (in the objective order of the world) but in the series itself. *The essential task then is to preserve the authenticity of the sign.*

Hence the mythical value taken on by that guarantee of vintage (*appellation contrôlée*): the signature. It becomes the veritable caption of our oeuvres. In the absence of fable, of the figures of the world and of God, it is that which tells us what the work signifies: the artist's gestures that are materialized in it (as in the other signs of the painting, moreover). For if the signature can fulfill that legible function of meaning, it is because in its allusive singularity as a sign it is fundamentally homogeneous with the combinatory order of signs which is that of the painting. In certain modern worsk it is graphically mixed with the content of the canvas, it becomes a rhythmic element and one may conceive of a painting that realizes and abolishes itself in its signature, which is only a signature. That is a limit, however, for — sign among signs — the signature always retains legendary values. If each sign of the painting retraces the subject in his act, only the signature designates him explicitly, giving us that particle of meaning, that reference and, hence, that security, which, in modern painting, is no longer given by the illegible truth of the world. The social consensus, and beyond that, of course, all the subtle combinations of supply and demand play upon the signature. But one can see that this myth is not purely and simply an effect of commercial orchestration. There is a conjunction of sign and name in the signature — a sign different from the other signs in the painting, but homogeneous with them; a name different from the names of other painters but complicit in the same game. It is through this ambiguous conjunction of a subjective series (authenticity) and an objective series (code, social consensus, commercial value), through this inflected sign, that the system of consumption can operate.

---

4.   In the end, Soulages copies himself well and Fautrier admits he does not always know whether a given canvas is his work.

That is why the slightest attack upon this sign which is both authentic and accepted, unmotivated and codified, is felt as a profound attack upon the cultural system itself — and why today the forgery and the copy are viewed as sacrilege. In our time, moreover, there no longer remains any difference between copy and forgery (the forgery plays upon the signature and presents itself as authentic; the copy plays upon the content and avows itself a copy). If one admits that the value of the painting is established upon the gesture, it is clear that every copy is a forgery because it no longer simulates a content but an irreversible act (*geste*) of pictorial invention.

Today only the artist may copy himself. In a sense, *he is condemned to do so* and to assume, if he is logical, the serial character of creation. At the limit, he reproduces himself literally: "In Factum I and Factum II, Rauschenberg has done the same canvas twice, almost to the last daub, literally.... What seems a brush stroke thrown on as hurriedly as possible and followed by droplets in an entirely accidental fashion is in fact a very studied gesture which Rauschenberg is capable of executing repeatedly at will" (Otto Hahn, *Les Temps Modernes,* March 1964).

Here we find something like a truth of modern art: it is no longer the literality of the world, but the literality of the gestural elaboration of creation — spots, lines, dribbles. At the same time, that which was representation — redoubling the world in space — becomes repetition — an indefinable redoubling of the act in time. Moreover, the performance of Rauschenberg, that tautology of the gesture, marks only the paradoxical limit of a logical evolution. In his case, there is a sort of coquettishness (realist) or obsession (paranoid) in redoing his own canvas stroke for stroke; but in fact that literality is not necessary in order for repetition to take place. In any case, Rauschenberg knows that although his two paintings are identical, they are nonetheless different because they testify to two distinct moments and so retain their own individual value on the market. So this duplication retains nothing of a copy. *Subjectivity triumphs in the mechanical repetition of itself.* That is why this concern can be left to no one else.

What must be clearly understood is that this *formal literality of the gesture* carries a structural constraint of succession and of differentiation from one sign to another of the same canvas, and from one canvas to another. This constraint is at work everywhere in our oeuvres, even when their individual themes and techniques can be specified. In this sense, Rauschenberg's "doubled" canvas (and the analogous procedures of other serial painters) is misguided, insofar as it tries, with photographic literalness, to exorcise, at the level of content, a seriality that is of a profoundly different order.

But then everything comes back to this question: what are the possibilities, for modern art, of retracing the actuality of our world (the everyday reality of objects, social reality and its conflicts)? What can be its critical value? Artists themselves are often divided between the ideology of pure gestural values (values of authenticity) and this other ideology, the critical necessity of regrasping reality. The same dilemma is posed for art critics, moreover, who have great difficulty reconciling a tangled paraphrase of the creative action (*gestuel*) with an analysis of objective significations.

In the light of what has just been said, this velleity of regrasping the world that is still new in contemporary art (recently again in pop art and the new portraiture) appears naive: it seems unaware of that systematic dimension according to which the modern gesture of painting is first organized — beside, or outside, or despite the conscious intentions of the artist. This velleity seems unaware that what is signified (and thus in a way domesticated) in contemporary art is no longer the world as substance and extension, but rather a certain temporality that is that of the subject in its self-indexing (and not the social individual of biographical data). There is a discontinuity and reconstitution of the subject from act to act, of which the signature is the socio-culturally encoded index. Modern art is actual (i.e., contemporary) in the strict sense of being "in the act" (*en acte*), from action to action: not contemporary with the world, but with itself and with itself alone in its own movement.[5] It changes gears according to a formal constraint of succession and plays upon variations and differences ("reading" the work will, most of the time, consist inversely in the decoding of these variations and differences).

Any function that one may wish to assign to art (among others, that of critical realism and of any form of commitment) must be measured with respect to this basic structure, and thus to this limit of meaning. Otherwise, the artist condemns himself to a pious ideology (which, on the other hand, is always the dominant ideology in matters of art): the eternal illusion of the philosophic consciousness, which makes him live his work as an absolute uniqueness that *confronts* the world and is responsible for bearing witness to it (for every philosophic consciousness is necessarily accompanied by a moral conscience).

---

5. Thus, no longer at the level of "creation" this time, but of appropriation, the collection of objects has no other temporality than that of the cycle that it constitutes: it is outside of "real" time.

Having said that, modern art is no less contemporary but its contemporaneity is neither direct nor critical: if it fully describes what we are, it does so by its very ambiguity.

Let us reconstruct this ambiguity. In a technical civilization of operatory abstraction, where neither machines nor domestic objects require much more than a controlling gesture (that gestural abstraction signifying a whole mode of relations and behavior), modern art in all its forms has for its primary function the salvation of the gestural moment, the intervention of the integral subject. It is the part of us, crushed by the technical habitus, that art conjures up in the pure gestural complex of the act of painting and its apparent liberty. Thus art (in its gesture) registers itself negatively as the sign of a lack. But this inscription that nourishes the most current ideology (that art is spontaneity, upsurge, living opposition to a mechanized universe) is not critical: it poses as a challenge confronting the world; but by default, it is stamped with nostalgic values, it compensates. And above all, it is caught up in its subjectivity, in its very act, by that seriality against which it registers itself in the external world. Despite this inscription, despite the sublime instantaneousness which it proclaims (in good faith, however: it seriously believes in it), subjectivity in action can only obey the same formal constraints of organization as the functional world. And here we have the truth of our modern art: if it bears witness to our time, it does so neither by direct allusion nor even in its pure gesture denying a systematized world — it is in testifying to the *systematic* of this full world by means of the inverse and homologous systematic of its empty gesture, a pure gesture marking an absence.

This serial dimension and this absence value are its absolute conditions of signification. Whether it assumes them or not, enacts them or evades them, it is in this that it is the only art possible. It is an art that is neither positive nor critical — contradictory (these are the two sides of the same illusion) but homologous and collusive: and thus, ambiguous. Most artists (and consumers) flee this contradiction. And even the acknowledgement of this systematic dimension may still be a detour to escape it. This is what one perceives in the mannerisms of the literal repetition of Andy Warhol, Rauschenberg, etc., by which they proclaim themselves painters of seriality and thus redirect this fundamental structure, turning it into an effect of fashion.

Before sinking into pure consumption, pop art will have had the merit of exposing these contradictions more clearly in the actual exercise of painting and in the latter's difficulties in deciding upon its true object. Thus we read in Warhol: "The canvas is an absolutely everyday object, on the same plane as this chair or this poster." Let us applaud this democratic conception, but recognize that it is either very naive or in very bad faith. Even if art wishes to signify the "everyday," that is not what it is: that would be to confuse the thing and its meaning. Now, art is constrained to signify, it cannot even commit suicide in the everyday. In that wish to absorb art, there is simultaneously an American pragmatism (terrorism of the useful, blackmail of integration) and something like an echo of a mystique of sacrifice. Warhold adds: "Reality has no need of an intermediary, it is necessary only to isolate it from the surroundings, transfer it to the canvas." The whole question is there: for the "everydayness" of this chair (or of that slice of meat, car fender, or centerfold) is precisely its context, and singularly, the serial context of all similar, or slightly different, chairs, etc. Everydayness is difference in repetition. In isolating the chair on the canvas, I remove all its everydayness from it and at the same time remove from the canvas all the characteristics of an everyday object (which in the theorists' illusion ought to make it absolutely resemble the chair).

This is the stumbling block: art can neither be absorbed into the everyday (canvas equals chair) nor grasp the everyday as such (chair isolated on the canvas equals real chair). Immanence and transcendence are equally impossible: they are two faces of the same dream. In fact, the discourse of modern art is of another order: *it is to signify in the same mode as objects do in their everydayness, that is, in their latent systematic.* It is in this serial and differential organization, with its own temporality punctuated by fashion and the recurrence of behavior models, to which art currently testifies. This by continually proving itself in a gesture that is repeated according to a play of inessential and combinatory variations in turn permits art to be something other than absolute repetition. "I would like to be a machine," Andy Warhol says.

Of course, this formula is paradoxical, because there is no greater affectation for art than for it to pose as mechanical, nor a greater coquettishness for subjectivity than to dedicate itself to serial automatism. But it testifies all the same to a logical exigency and to the limiting condition of modern art: that of a subjectivity fascinated by a technical world that denies it, fascinated by the positivity of that world but which paradoxically can only absorb this world by repeating itself across serial diffractions.

The world in its objective systematic and art in its subjective systematic exchange their significations. This is their homologous situation.[6] Art is assigned there in all lucidity: it can only signify the world on the basis of a structural affinity that simultaneously marks the fatal character of its *integration*.

Only recognition of this structural homology between a systematized world and an art that is itself serial in its most profound exercise[7] permits one to grasp this contradiction of modern art — which is deplored everywhere, even by artists themselves, as a fatality. Modern art wishes to be negative, critical, innovative and a perpetual surpassing, as well as immediately (or almost) assimilated, accepted, integrated, consumed. One must surrender to the evidence: art no longer contests anything, if it ever did. Revolt is isolated, the malediction "consumed." All the more reason there would seem to be, then, to abandon all nostalgia, resign negativity, and admit finally that it is in the very movement of its authenticity, in systematizing itself according to a formal constraint, in constituting itself according to a play of successive differences, that the work of art offers itself of its own initiative as immediately integrable in a global system that conjugates it like any other object or group of objects.

In this sense, modern works have indeed become everyday object: although laden with cultural connotations, they pose no problems to the environment. A modern painting, pop, abstract, a "tachiste," contradicts nothing: it enters into the play of the syntagmatic distribution of objects in space (in the modern interior) just as — and because it issues from the inventory of a circumscribed subjectivity — one sign passes into another, from one moment to another. Two chains cross: the necessary dimension of signification is also the "fatal" dimension of integration and consumption.

Modern art, midway between critical terrorism (ideological) and *de facto* structural integration, is quite exactly an *art of collusion vis-à-vis* this contemporary world. It plays with it, and is included in the game. It can parody this world, illustrate it, simulate it, alter it; it never disturbs the order, which is also its own. We are no longer dealing with the bourgeois art which, in its redundancy, presents beings and objects, reconciled with their image (all "representation" carries this ideology of reconciliation). In modern art it is a subjectivity which, unreconciled with the world, endeavors to

---

6. Moreover, this structural homology not only constitutes art as a series, but also the world itself as "mechanical." The world only really becomes mechanical from the moment it can no longer be evoked save mechanically.

7. And for which the reference to the world becomes secondary — just as the exercise of collection is valued above the thematic of the objects collected.

reconcile itself with its own image: it is a subjectivity whose redundancy, while committed in an implicit seriality, is dedicated to homologically illustrating the seriality of all other objects and the systematic of an increasingly well integrated world through its own withdrawal and defiance.

# CHAPTER FIVE

## THE ART AUCTION:
### SIGN EXCHANGE AND SUMPTUARY VALUE

It may seem strange to be analyzing the ideological process somewhere other than in the traditional, political or cultural sanctuaries. But the point is precisely that the market for paintings and the auction sale of the work of art permit us to decipher the articulation, and thus the process, of ideological labor because they are situated in the contexts of economic power and the cultural field. The auction, this crucible of the interchange of values, where economic value, sign value and symbolic value transfuse according to the rules of the game, can be considered as an ideological matrix — one of the shrines of the political economy of the sign.

It is a question of decoding the birth of the sign form in the same way that Marx was able to uncover the birth of the commodity form in the *Critique of Political Economy*. In consumption generally, economic exchange value (money) is converted into sign exchange value (prestige, etc.); but this operation is still sustained by the alibi of use value. By contrast, the auction of the work of art has this notable characteristic: that economic exchange value, in the pure form of its general equivalent, money, is exchanged there for a pure sign, the painting. So it is an experimental terrain, simultaneously collective and institutional, for separating out the operation of this sign value.[1]

The decisive action is one of a simultaneous double reduction — that of exchange value (money) and of symbolic value (the painting as an *oeuvre*) — and of their transmutation into sign value (the signed, appraised painting as a luxury value and rare object) by expenditure and agonistic competition.

### 1. The Other Face of Political Economy

In expenditure, money changes meaning. This fact, established in the auction, can be transferred as a hypothesis to the whole sphere of consumption. The act of consumption is never simply a purchase (reconversion of exchange value into use value); it is also an expenditure (an aspect as radically neglected by political economy as by Marx); that is to say, it is wealth manifested, and a manifest destruction of wealth. It is that value, deployed beyond exchange

---

1.    The very considerable problems posed by the analysis of use value will be taken up later in the chapter, Beyond Use Value.

value and founded upon the latter's destruction, that invests the object purchased, acquired, appropriated, with its differential sign value. It is not the quantity of money that takes on value, as in the economic logic of equivalence, but rather money spent, sacrificed, eaten up according to a logic of difference and challenge. Every act of purchase is thus simultaneously an economic act and a trans-economic act of the production of differential sign value.

Certainly in everyday consumption the specific (and fundamental) aspects of the auction are largely effaced: the direct experience of competition, the challenge, the agonistic community of peers, etc., which make it such a fascinating moment, the equivalent of poker or the *fête*. But behind the purchase (or individual reappropriation of use value) there always remains the moment of expenditure, which even in its banality presupposes something of a competition, a wager, a challenge, a sacrifice and thus a potential community of peers and an *aristocratic measure of value*. Let us not be mistaken: it is this, and not the satisfaction of needs, that occasionally turns con sumption into a passion, a fascinating game, something other than functional economic behavior: it becomes the competitive field of the destruction of economic value for the sake of another type of value.

The process of production and systematization of economic exchange value has been described as essential, and in fact it is: political economy is this immense transmutation of all values (labor, knowledge, social relations, culture, nature) into economic exchange value. Everything is abstracted and reabsorbed into a world market and in the preeminent role of money as a general equivalent. This aspect of the analysis has been privileged (for historical and ideological reasons that have nothing to do with "scientific objectivity," and which should be analyzed more fully, even in Marx). Thus the equally essential, equally generalized process has been largely neglected — a process that is neither the inverse nor the residue nor the relay of production: that immense process of the transmutation of economic exchange value into sign exchange value. This is the process of *consumption* considered *as a system of sign exchange value*: not consumption as traditional political economy defines it (reconversion of economic exchange value into use value, as a moment of the production cycle), but consumption considered as the conversion of economic exchange value into sign exchange value. At this point, the field of political economy, articulated only through exchange value and use value, explodes and must be entirely re-analyzed as *generalized political economy*, which implies the production of sign exchange value in the same way and in the same movement as the production of material goods and of economic exchange value. The analysis of the production of signs and of culture thus does not impose itself as exterior, ulterior, and "superstructural" in relation to that of material production; it imposes itself as *a revolution of political economy* itself, generalized by the theoretical and practical irruption of the political economy of the sign.

All efforts to autonomize this field of consumption (that is, of the systematic production of signs) as an object of analysis are mystifying: they lead directly to culturalism. But it is necessary to see that the same ideological mystification results from autonomizing the field of material production as a determining agency. Those who specify culture (sign production) in order to circumscribe it as superstructure are also culturalists without knowing it: they institute the same split as the cultural idealists, and constrict the field of political economy just as arbitrarily. If culture, consumption and signs must be analyzed as ideology this is not achieved by banishing them, or expelling them to an outer field, but, on the contrary, by integrating them into the very structures of political economy. Yet this implies that the traditional boundaries of political economy, canonized by bourgeois economic science as well as by Marxist analysis, should be disregarded. And the resistances to this are strong, for they are of all orders: theoretical, political, phantasmagorical. Yet today only a generalized political economy can define a revolutionary theory and practice.

Insofar as the market for paintings is specifically concerned, it may be said that it is the appropriation of the paintings as signs which acts as a factor of legitimation of economic and social power. But that gets us almost nowhere. We are still within the political vulgate: culture annexed and manipulated by the dominant class. The same is said of "needs," "consumption," leisure or sex. The dominant class would hold a sort of *jus primae noctis* over culture. Not content to exploit the "reserve of manpower," this class would exploit the reserve of signs, the system of values, in order to confuse the class conflict and mystify proletarian consciousness. But where do these signs originate? Are they already inherent in things, in a social nature, so that it is enough to forcibly appropriate them? Magical vision. And how can signs or myths be articulated upon an objective social and economic condition, in order to confuse its meaning? *There is little use in appealing to the "consciousness" argument!* Moreover, why would the dominant class have need of culture if the economic is truly the determining instance?

More profoundly, what is a signification? In what social relation is it produced? What is the mode of production of significations? The "capitalist" mode of production? Absurd.

Sign values are produced by a certain type of social labor. But the production of differences, of differential hierarchical systems, is not to be confused with the extortion of economic surplus value, nor does it result from it. Between the two, another type of labor intervenes which transforms economic value and surplus value into sign value: it is a *sumptuary* operation, devouring (*consummation*) and surpassing economic value according to a radically different type of exchange. Yet in a certain way it also produces a surplus value: domination, which is not to be confused with economic privilege and profit. The latter are in a way only the primary material and springboard for a *political* operation involving the transfiguration of power by signs. Domination is thus linked to economic power, but it does not "emanate" from it automatically and mysteriously; it issues from it through a reworking of economic value. As a result of having forgotten this very specific labor, Marxist analysis today finds itself in the same position with respect to the field of ideology as the bourgeois economists before (and since) Marx *vis-à-vis* material production: the *real* source of value and the *real* process of production are skipped over. It is from neglect of this social labor of sign production that ideology derives its transcendence; signs and culture appear enveloped in a "fetishism," a mystery equivalent to, and contemporaneous with that of the commodity.

Critical theorists of the political economy of the sign are rare. They are exiled, buried under Marxist (or neo-Marxist) terrorist analysis. Veblen and Goblot [2] are the great precursors of a cultural analysis of class which, beyond the "dialectical materialism" of productive forces, examines the *logic of sumptuary values* which assures and perpetuates through its code the hegemony of the dominant class, and, in a way, shelters the latter, through its "transsubstantiation" of values, from economic revolutions and their social repercussions.

In the economic order it is the mastery of *accumulation*, of the appropriation of surplus value, which is essential. In the order of signs (of culture), it is mastery of *expenditure* that is decisive, that is, a mastery of the transsubstantiation of economic exchange value into sign exchange value based on a monopoly of the code. Dominant classes have always either assured their domination over sign values from the outset (archaic and traditional societies), or endeavoured

---

2.   Veblen, *Theory of the Leisure Class* and Goblot, *La Barrière et le Niveau.*

(in the capitalist bourgeois order) to surpass, to transcend, and to consecrate their economic privilege in a semiotic privilege, because this later stage represents the ultimate stage of domination. This logic, which comes to relay class logic and which is no longer defined by ownership of the means of production but by the mastery of the process of signification; and which activates a mode of production radically different from that of material production (and which for this reason escapes "Marxist" analysis) is found in its entirety, though microscopically, in the art auction.

## 2. Difference from Economic Exchange

1. Like the game (poker, etc.), the art auction is always both a ritual and a unique event. The rules are arbitrary and fixed, yet one never knows exactly what will take place, nor afterward exactly what has happened, because it involves a dynamic of personal encounter, an algebra of individuals, as opposed to the economic operation where values are exchanged impersonally, arithmetically.

2. This personal character of the exchange implies the insularity (*unicité*) of the place (one cannot participate without being present), and above all, the concrete integrality (*unicité*) of the process (the time, order, rhythm, tempo are essential elements of the bidding). In the altercation and the out-bidding, each moment depends on the previous one and on the reciprocal relation of partners. Hence there is a specific development, which is different from the abstract time of economic exchange.

3. There is no interplay of supply and demand, as in the market, with a maximal approximation of the exchange value offered and the use value anticipated. The mercantile auction that reaches a point of equilibrium of supply and demand is found, for example, in a fish auction. But in the art auction, at the moment of bidding, exchange value and use value are no longer correlated according to an economic calculus. The anticipated use value (if there is one) does not increase during the auction. In fact, the particular activity of the auction institutes a specific relation and occurs outside use value. Once the latter has been put out of play, exchange value is no longer offered (in exchange for); it is wagered (*mise en jeu*). At once, it ceases to be exchange value and the whole situation is transferred out of the realm of the economic. It does not, however, cease to be an exchange, although it no longer takes the form of supply and demand, but of *reciprocal wager*. Thus the auction simultaneously institutes:

— a transmutation of value and of the economic coordinates;
— another type of social relation.

*Transmutation of Value*

In the crucial moment of the auction, money is nullified as a divisible exchange value and is transsubstantiated by its expenditure into an indivisible sumptuary value. Thus it becomes the homolog of the painting as a sign, a unique and indivisible object. There is no longer an equivalence, but an aristocratic *parity* [3] established between money, which has become a suptuary material through the loss of its economic exchange value, and the canvas, which has become a sign of prestige (hence an element of the restricted corpus that we call "painting") through the loss of its symbolic value. [4]

*Social Relation*

In the sumptuary act, money is nullified as a general equivalent, as form and so as a specific (capitalist) social relation regulated by this form. The social relation instituted in this act by the auction is still one of aristocratic parity (among partners). Contrary to commercial operations, which institute a relation of economic *rivalry* between individuals on the footing of formal *equality*, with each one guiding his own calculation of individual appropriation, the auction, like the fête or the game, institutes a concrete community of exchange among peers. Whoever the vanquisher in the challenge, the essential function of the auction is the institution of a community of the privileged who define themselves as such by agonistic speculation upon a restricted corpus of signs. Competition of the aristocratic sort seals their *parity* (which has nothing to do with the formal equality of economic competition), and thus their collective caste privilege with respect to all others, from whom they are no longer separated merely by their purchasing power, but by the sumptuary and collective act of the production and exchange of sign values. [5]

Here is the matrix of ideology — in the coherent logic of a system

3. Cf. the chapter below on Symbolic Value and Aesthetic Function.

4. "The price at which a canvas is sold is not the *measure* of its value in the same way as for an article of consumption. The price only has meaning at the very instant of sale, by the game of competition in which it is the relative equivalent of the absolute values and significations to which the painting refers." P. Dard and J. Michner, *Etude sur l'Exchange de Valeur*. In fact, it is no longer a price but a wager (*enjeu*). Moreover, for real players, money won in the game remains marked by it and cannot be spent for useful economic purposes: it must be put back into the game, poured back into it, "burned" — in a way, it is the *part maudite* of Bataille.

5. "Within this community there is a traffic of paintings on the basis of a *competition* among peers, while from the point of view of the global society, paintings are *retained* in and by this community — that is, the latter functions on the basis of a *social discrimination*. Yet this community presents itself as open by the competitive aspect of acquisition.... There we are at the frontiers of *strategies* of domination, where the possibility of individual mobility masks social discrimination." P. Dard and J. Michner, *Etude sur l'Echange de Valeur*.

of production, exchange and social relations that is radically different from the system of production, exchange and social relations based on the economic. Ideology is not a mysterious duping (*trucage*) of consciousness; it is a social logic that is substituted for another (and which resolves the latter's contradictions), thus changing the very definition of value. In our failure to recognize this, we have always reverted back to the rather embarrassing psychology of "interiorization." But whence arises this strange perversion of "consciousness" — mystifying itself, and abandoning itself of "ideological values" — when the social actors who are the subjects of this consciousness continue to produce their "objective" social relations? Indeed, when consciousness decides to flip over to the "objective" side, it becomes revolutionary, and we call it the *prise de conscience!* What a strange bourgeois novel psychology is — yet it profoundly infects revolutionary theory.

In fact, what is called the "psychology" of the art lover is also in its entirety a reduction from the system of exchange. The singularity that he asserts — that fetishist passion for the object lived as an elective affinity — is established on his recognition as peer, by virtue of a competitive act, in a community of the privileged. He is the equal of the canvas itself, whose unique value resides in the relation of parity, of statutory privilege, which, as a sign, it maintains with the other terms of the limited corpus of paintings. Hence, the "élitist" affinity between the amateur and the canvas that psychologically connotes the very sort of value, of exchange and of aristocratic social relation that is instituted by the auction. The passion of the amateur is ignited by the latent summation, by the exalting and continual obsession of all other amateurs, just as the fetishized value of the canvas, his *mana* is made from:

— its differential reference to all the other canvases in the same sublime sphere of status;

— its pedigree, its genealogy, that is, its signature and the cycles of its successive owners.

Thus, it is not the psychological relation of the individual to the object that gives birth to fetishism and that sustains the principle of exchange. "Object Fetishism" never supports exchange in its principle, but *the social principle of exchange supports the fetishized value of the object.*

### 3. Economic Power and Domination

There is another ideological reduction: that which makes the painting a commodity pure and simple. No, here it is not a question of the expanded reproduction of capital and of the capitalist class; it is a question of the production of a caste by the collective grace of a play of signs, and of the production of these signs by the destruction of economic value. Something similar to this sumptuary exchange and this aristocratic model, but weakened and geared down, diffuses through the whole system of consumption and provides its ideological efficacy. It seems absurd to speak of a "democratized" logic of caste. Yet consumption is instituted on the basis of the exchange of differences, of a distinctive material and thus of a potential community, which, however little remains of it — and precisely because nothing of it remains — is nevertheless articulated upon a fiction of aristocratic parity. The difference — a major one — between the aristocratic potlatch and consumption is that today differences are produced industrially, they are bureaucratically programmed in the form of collective models. They no longer arise in the personal reciprocity of challenge and exchange. Only the mass-mediatized simulacra (*simulacre*) of competition operate in the statutory rivalry. This latter no longer has the real, distinctive function that it still had in Veblen: the great dinosaurs of "*wasteful expenditure*" are changed into innumerable individuals pledged to a parody of sacrificial consumption, mobilized as consumers by the order of production. Expenditure has thus radically changed its meaning. The fact remains that it is because the collective phantom of lost (sumptuary) values is reactivated in expenditure and in mass-mediatized consumption, that this practice can be lived individually as gratification, as liberty, as fulfillment — and so act as ideology. Even the simulation model of a differential aristocratic code still acts as a powerful factor of integration and of control, as participation in the same "rule of the game." Everywhere prestige haunts our industrial societies, whose bourgeois culture is never more than the phantom of aristocratic values. Everywhere the magic of the code, the magic of an elective and selective community, fused together by the same rules of the game and the same system of signs, is collectively reproduced, beyond economic value and on the basis of it. Everywhere this process comes to penetrate class conflicts, everywhere — diluted over the entire extent of the society, whatever the economic status and class condition — it acts to the advantage of the dominant class. It is the keystone of domination. It is not automatically dismantled by the revolutionary logic of productive forces, by the "dialectical" process of capital or by the traditional critique of political economy.

Only a critique of the political economy of the sign can analyze how the present *mode of domination* is able to regain, integrate and simultaneously take advantage of all the modes of production — not only of the capitalist mode of production, but of all "previous," "archaic" modes of production and exchange, infra- or trans-economic. Only such a critique can analyze how at the very heart of the economic the mode of domination reinvents (or reproduces) the logic and the strategy of signs, of castes, of segregation, and of discrimination; how it reinstates the feudal logic of personal relations or even that of the gift exchange and of reciprocity, or of agonistic exchange — in order simultaneously to thwart and crown the "modern" socio-economic logic of class. But perhaps economic exploitation and "class" domination are at bottom only a "historic" variant and a detour in the immense genealogy of the forms of social domination. Perhaps contemporary society is once again becoming primarily a society of domination by signs, hence giving rise to the total demand for a "cultural revolution," which implies the whole process of ideological production — the theoretical basis of which can only be given by a political economy of the sign.

## 4. Symbolic Value and the Aesthetic Function

What happens to symbolic value in this whole operation, to the value peculiar to the "work of art"? It does not appear anywhere. It is repudiated, absent. Parallel to the ascension of economic exchange value into sign value, there is a reduction of symbolic value into sign value. On either side, economic exchange value and symbolic value lose their own status and become *satellites* of sign value. At the level of paintings, manipulated as supersigns, symbolic value is resolved into an *aesthetic function*, that is, it only operates *inter linea*, behind the operation of the sign, as a reference-alibi, as a sublime rationalization of the sumptuary operation.[6]

Repudiated as symbolic labor, the painting acts as:

— distinctive material, the foundation of the "noble" and of restrained exchange;

— and as universal "aesthetic" value — it doubles itself as *an idea* of painting serving to legitimize the operation in the absolute.

But this absolute is an alibi. We have seen that the true value of the painting is its genealogical value (its "birth": the signature and the aura of its successive transactions: its pedigree). Just as the cycle

---

6. From that moment on, the economic can also serve as rationalization. The market for paintings is sometimes placed under the rubric of "love of art," sometimes under that of "good investment."

of successive gifts in primitive societies charges the object with more and more value, so the painting circulates from inheritor to inheritor as a title of nobility, being charged with prestige throughout its history. Here, by the very circulation of signs a sort of surplus value is produced which must be radically distinguished from economic surplus value. It does not create profit, but *legitimacy* and it is with this that the art lover identifies himself by his economic sacrifice in the auction. Thus for caste members the only real values are those produced and exchanged within the caste (similarly for Goblot's bourgeoisie, for whom originality, virtue, genius, etc., all the "universal" values, do not compare with regard to "distinction," the specific value of class — or of caste).

The caste of partners knows at bottom that the veritable status, the veritable legitimacy, the reproduction of the social relation, and so the perpetuation of the dominant class "in its essence," is enacted in the aristocratic manipulation of works as the material of sign exchange. At bottom it disdains the "aesthetic," "art," the symbolic, and "culture" which, as "universal" values, are barely good for collective consumption. Aesthetic enjoyment, spiritual commerce with the works, and the values labelled "absolute" are all that is left to those who cannot aspire to the privileged potlatch.[7]

The process of ideology in its totality thus acts on the simultaneous operation:

— of a system of restricted exchange upon a limited corpus and in the mode of aristocratic parity competition;

— of a system of exchange of "universal" values for the use of all, in the mode of formal equality.

Still in the realm of painting, it is interesting in this sense to confront the reciprocal function of the institution of the market and of the auction with the institution of the museum. One might believe that, by removing the works from this private parallel market to "nationalize" them, the museum returns them to a sort of collective ownership and so to their "authentic" aesthetic function. In fact, the museum acts as a *guarantee* for the aristocratic exchange. It is a double guarantee:

— just as a gold bank, the public backing of the Bank of France, is necessary in order that the circulation of capital and private speculation be organized, so the fixed reserve of the museum is necessary for the functioning of the sign exchange of paintings.

7.   All else being equal, it is the same discrimination that dedicates the immense majority to use value in consumption, and to the functional enjoyment of products — the dominant class strategically reserves for itself the manipulation of exchange value, of capital and of surplus value.

Museums play the role of banks in the political economy of paintings: — not content to act as an organic guarantee of speculation in art, the museum acts as an agency guaranteeing the universality of painting and so also the aesthetic enjoyment (a socially inessential value, it has been seen) of all others.

## 5. Conclusion

In the auction and the art market we wished to comprehend a sort of *nucleum* of the strategy of values, a sort of concrete space-time, strategic moment and matrix in the process of ideology, which latter is always the production of sign value and of coded exchange. This economy of values is a *political* economy. It goes well beyond economic calculation and concerns all the processes of the transmutation of values, all those socially produced transitions from one value to another, from one logic to another logic of value which may be noted in determinate places and institutions — and so it also concerns the connection and implication of different systems of exchange and modes of production. The critique of this general political economy of value is the only one which today can recapture Marx's analysis on a global level. And it is the only one which can make this "beyond value" (*au-dela de la valeur*) appear theoretically as a basis for the practical overthrow of political economy.

## NB

Objects other than paintings, of course, could be analyzed in the same terms: for example, knowledge. The institutional space-time of the competitive community is then the examination, better yet the national entrance examination. It is there that the "transsubstantiation of profane knowledge into sacred knowledge" operates, that "bureaucratic baptism of knowledge" (Marx), whose function with respect to the baccalauréat, the social threshold of the caste, has been well analyzed by Goblot. The same operation of transmutation of knowledge as a universal value into knowledge as sign value, as a title of nobility, is accompanied by the same legitimation, the same discrimination of all the peers who participate in the white mass, in this *sacrament*. One could also analyze the academic congress (of scholars, of intellectuals, of sociologists) as places of transmission, of hereditary reproduction of the intelligentsia and of a privileged community on the basis of an agonistic debauch of signs. Conferences are almost as useful to the advancement of knowledge as horse races and parimutuels to the advancement of the equine race (horses and races, moreover, as well as the parallel market of sumptuary values, would be an excellent object for study).

# CHAPTER SIX

# FOR A GENERAL THEORY

## I

"The Ideological Genesis of Needs" postulated four different logics of value:
— the functional logic of use value
— the economic logic of exchange value
— the differential logic of sign value
— the logic of symbolic exchange
with, for their respective principles: utility, equivalence, difference, ambivalence.

The study of "The Art Auction" explored a particular case of the strategy of values in the passage from economic exchange value to sign exchange value. Continuing from that point, it is tempting to lay out a hypothetical general conversion table of all values that could serve as an orientation table for a general anthropology.

*Use Value* (UV):
1. UV — EcEV
2. UV — SgEV
3. UV — SbE

*Economic Exchange Value* (EcEV)
1. EcEV — UV
2. EcEV — SgEV
3. EcEV — SbE

*Sign Exchange Value* (SgEV)
1. SgEV — UV
2. SgEV — EcEV
3. SgEV — SbE

*Symbolic Exchange* (SbE)
1. SbE — UV
2. SbE — EcEV
3. SbE — SgEV

Here there is no attempt at a theoretical articulation of these various logics. There is simply an attempt to mark out the respective fields and the transit from one to the other.

1. *UV — EcEV*: The field of the process of production of exchange value, of the commodity form (*forme-marchandise*) etc., described by political economy. Productive consumption.

2. *UV — SgEV*: The field of the production of signs originating in

the destruction of utility ("conspicuous consumption," sumptuary value). "Unproductive" consumption (of time as well, in conspicuous idleness and leisure), in fact productive of differences: it is functional difference playing as a statutory difference (semi-automatic vs. entirely automatic washing machine). Here, the advertising process of conferring value transmutes use goods (*biens d'usage*) into sign values. Here technique and knowledge are divorced from their objective practice and recovered by the "cultural" system of differentiation. It is thus the extended field of *consumption*, in the sense we have given it of production, systems and interplay of signs. Of course, this field also includes the production of signs originating from economic exchange value (see 5 below).

3. *UV — SbE*: The field of consumption (*consumation* as opposed to the usual French, *consommation*), that is, of the destruction of use value (or of economic exchange value, cf. 6), no longer, however, in order to produce sign values, but in the mode of a *transgression* of the economic, reinstating symbolic exchange. The presentation, the gift, the festival (*fête*).

4. *EcEV — UV:* This is the process of "consumption" in the traditional economic sense of the term, that is, the reconversion of exchange value into use value (by private individuals in the act of purchase or by production in the productive consumption). 4 and 1 are the two moments of the cycle of classical (and Marxist) political economy, which does not take into account the political economy of the sign. It is also the field of the consecration of exchange value by use value, of the transfiguration of the commodity form into the object form (cf. below, "Beyond Use Value").

5. *EcEV — SgEV:* The process of *consumption* according to its redefinition in the political economy of the sign. It includes the act of spending as production of sign value and, conjointly with 2, it comprises the field of sumptuary value. But here more accurately, we have the ascension of the commodity form into the sign form, the transfiguration of the economic into sign systems and the transmutation of economic power into domination and social caste privilege.

6. *EcEV — SbE:* While 2 and 5 describe the *transfiguration* of use value and exchange value into sign value (or again: of the object form and commodity form into sign form), 3 and 6 mark the *transgression* of these two forms (that is, of the economic) in symbolic exchange. According to our reformulation which implicates the sign form in the field of general political economy, 9 completes 3 and 6 as transgression of the sign form towards symbolic exchange.

There is no articulation between these three forms (which describe general political economy) and symbolic exchange. There is, on the contrary, a radical separation and transgression, an eventual deconstruction of these forms, which are *codes of value*. Accurately speaking, there is no symbolic "value," there is only symbolic "exchange," which defines itself precisely as something distinct from, and beyond value and code. All forms of value (object, commodity or sign) must be negated in order to inaugurate symbolic exchange. This is the radical rupture of the field of value.

7. $SgEv - UV$: Signs, like commodities, are at once use value and exchange value. The social hierarchies, the invidious differences, the privileges of caste and culture which they support, are accounted as profit, as personal satisfaction, and lived as "need" (need of social value-generation to which corresponds the "utility" of differential signs and their "consumption").

8. $SgEV - EcEV$: This involves the reconversion of cultural privilege, of the monopoly of signs, etc., into economic privilege. Coupled with 5, this reconversion describes the total cycle of a political economy in which economic exploitation based on the monopoly of capital and "cultural" domination based on the monopoly of the code engender one another ceaselessly.

9. $SgEV - SbE$: The deconstruction and transgression of the sign form towards symbolic exchange (cf. 3 and 6).

10, 11, and 12. $SbE - UV, EcEV, SgEV$: All three describe a single process, the inverse of the transgression described in 3, 6, and 9 — the process of breaking and reducing symbolic exchange, and the inauguration of the economic. Taken together, they amount to a kind of "cost analysis" of symbolic exchange under the abstract and rational jurisdiction of the various codes of value (use value, exchange value, sign value). For example: the objects involved in reciprocal exchange, whose uninterrupted circulation establishes social relationships, i.e., social *meaning*, annihilate themselves in this continual exchange without assuming any value of their own (that is, any appropriable value). Once symbolic exchange is broken, this same material is abstracted into utility value, commercial value, statutory value. The symbolic is transformed into the instrumental, either commodity or sign. Any one of the various codes may be specifically involved, but they are all joined in the single form of political economy which is opposed, as a whole, to symbolic exchange.

This "combined" interpretation of the matrix (*grille*) of values is only a first approach. It appears that certain correlations group together naturally, that certain are reversible, that certain values are convertible into one another, that certain are exclusive of each other. Some function term by term, others in a more complex cycle. Their general principles — utility, equivalence, difference, and ambivalence — are difficult to articulate clearly. And above all, it should be borne in mind that this remains a combinatory exploration, with its merely formal symmetries. There is no organizing theory behind it.

## II

A second phase consists in extracting some dominant articulation from this moving ensemble of production and reproduction, of conversion, transgression and reduction of values. The first that presents itself can be formulated thus:

$$\frac{SgEV}{SbE} = \frac{EcEV}{UV}$$

or: sign value is to symbolic exchange what exchange value (economic) is to use value.

That is to say that between symbolic exchange and sign value there is the same reduction, the same process of abstraction and rationalization (cf. "Fetishism and Ideology" concerning the body, the unconscious, etc.) as between the multiple "concrete" use values and the abstraction of exchange value in the commodity. Consequently, the form of the equation, if it is accepted, implies that an identical process is at work on both sides of the equation. This process is none other than that of political economy (traditionally directed upon the second relation: $\frac{EcEV}{UV}$). This implies analyzing the first relation in terms of a *political economy of the sign*, which is articulated in the political economy of material production and *countersigns* it in the process of ideological labor. This sign economy exists, more or less, in the form of theoretical linguistics and, more generally, semiology. But these latter carefully avoid placing their analyses under the rubric of *political* economy (which implies a *critique* of the political economy of the sign, following the same theoretical procedure as Marx). This, however, is what they amount to without knowing it: they are simply the equivalent, in the domain of signs and meaning, of classical bourgeois political economy *prior* to its critique by Marx.

If the political economy of the sign (semiology) is susceptible to a critique in the same way as classical political economy, it is because their form is the same, not their content: sign form and commodity form.

This second phase has moved from a matrix (*grille*) and from a more or less mechanical combinatory of values to a relation of forms and to an homology of the ensemble: it is a considerable advance, but not decisive. This relation effectively articulates the various logics of value; but if the homology is to be fully coherent, there must be a horizontal relation to reinforce the vertical one. Not only must sign value be to symbolic exchange what exchange value is to use value (the relation posited above), but also sign value must be to exchange value what symbolic exchange is to use value. That is:

$$\frac{SgEV}{EcEV} = \frac{SbE}{UV}$$

Now, if sign value and exchange value (sign form and commodity form) really are implicated, by reason of their logical form, in the framework of a general political economy, we can claim no affinity of the same order linking symbolic exchange and use value — quite the contrary, because the former implies the *transgression* of the latter, the latter the *reduction* of the former (cf. in 1, 3 and 10-12). The formula then is not coherent, so much the more so in that the integration of symbolic exchange as a factor homogeneous to the others in the relation does not take into account what has been posited: that the symbolic is not a value (i.e., not positive, autono-misable, measurable or codifiable). It is the ambivalence (positive and negative) of personal exchange — and as such it is radically opposed to all values.

## II

These incoherencies finaly result in bursting the formula and in a general restructuring.

1. In place of the sign as global value, it is necessary to make its constituent elements, the signifier and the signified, appear.

2. Then, the definitive correlation between sign form and commodity form is established thus:

$$\frac{EcEV}{UV} = \frac{Sr}{Sd}$$

or: exchange value is to use value what the signifier is to the signified.

The horizontal implication — exchange value is to the signifier what use value is to the signified (i.e., the logical affinity of exchange value and the signifier on the one hand, and of use value and the signified on the other) — will emerge from the analysis of the respective vertical implications. On this basis, we will say that this homologous relation (this time coherent) describes the field of general political economy.

3. The homologous relation being saturated, symbolic exchange finds itself expelled from the field of value (or the field of general political economy). This corresponds to the radical definition as the alternative to and transgression of value.

4. The bar marking the process of reduction, or of rational abstraction, which (it is believed) separates use value from exchange value, and signified from signifier, is displaced. The fundamental reduction no longer takes place between UV and EV, or between signifier and signified.[1] It takes place between the system as a whole and symbolic exchange.

The bar which separates use value from exchange value, and that which separates the signified from the signifier is a line of formal logical implication. It does not radically separate these respective terms; rather, it establishes a structural relation between them (and similarly between exchange value and signifier, between use value and signified). In fact, *all these relations form a system in the framework of political economy.* And the logical organization of this entire system denies, represses and reduces symbolic exchange. The bar that separates all these terms from symbolic exchange is not a bar of structural implication, it is a line of radical exclusion (which presupposes the radical alternative of transgression). Thus we arrive at the following general distribution of terms:

$$\frac{EcEV}{UV} = \frac{Sr}{Sd} \Big/ SbE \ (symbolic \ exchange)$$

that is to say, a single great opposition between the whole field of value (where the process of material production [commodity form] and the process of sign production [sign form] are articulated through the same systematic logic) and the field of non-value, of symbolic exchange.

### General Political Economy $\Big/$ Symbolic Exchange

A critique of general political economy (or a critical theory of value) and a theory of symbolic exchange are one and the same thing. It is the basis of a revolutionary anthropology. Certain elements of this anthropology have been elaborated by Marxist analysis, but it has since proved unable to develop them to the critical point of departure.

The present theory posits three essential tasks, beginning from and going beyond Marxist analysis.

1. The extension of the critique of political economy to *a radical*

---

1. We will return (in Towards a Critique of the Political Economy of the Sign) to the problem of the referent, which only exists in an integrated relation to the signified (such that they are often confused).

*critique of use value,* in order to reduce the idealist anthropology which it still subtends, even in Marx (whether at the level of "needs" of individuals or at the level of the "use value of labor"). A critique of use value fetishism is necessary — an analysis of the object form in its relations to the commodity form.

2. The extension of the critique of political economy to the sign and to systems of signs is required in order to show how the logic, free play and circulation of signifiers is organized like the logic of the exchange value system; and how the logic of signifieds is subordinated to it tactically, as that of use value is subordinated to that of exchange value. Finally, we need a critique of signifier-fetishism — an analysis of the sign form in its relation to the commodity form. In the global relation

$$\frac{EcEV}{UV} = \frac{Sr}{Sd}$$

these two initial points aim towards a critical theory of the three terms which Marxist analysis has not yet mastered. In fact, strictly speaking, Marx offers only a critical theory of exchange value. The *critical* theory of use value, signifier, and signified remains to be developed.

3. A theory of symbolic exchange.

# CHAPTER SEVEN

# BEYOND USE VALUE

The status of use value in Marxian theory is ambiguous. We know that the commodity is both exchange value and use value. But the latter is always concrete and particular, contingent on its own destiny, whether this be in the process of individual consumption or in the labor process. (In this case, lard is valued as lard, cotton as cotton: they cannot be substituted for each other, nor thus "exchanged.") Exchange value, on the other hand, is abstract and general. To be sure, there could be no exchange value without use value — the two are coupled; but neither is strongly implied by the other: "In order to define the notion of commodity, it is not important to know its particular content and its exact destination. It suffices that before it is a commodity — in other words, the vehicle (support) of exchange value — the article satisfy a given social need by possessing the corresponding useful property. That is all."[1] Thus, use value is not implicated in the logic peculiar to exchange value, which is a logic of equivalence. Besides, there can be use value without exchange value (equally for labor power as for products, in the sphere outside the market). Even if it is continually reclaimed by the process of production and exchange, use value is never truly inscribed in the field of the market economy: it has its own finality, albeit restricted. And within it is contained, from this standpoint, the promise of a resurgence beyond the market economy, money and exchange value, in the glorious autonomy of man's simple relation to his work and his products.

So it appears that commodity fetishism (that is, where social relations are disguised in the qualities and attributes of the commodity itself) is not a function of the commodity defined *simultaneously* as exchange value and use value, but of exchange value alone. Use value, in this restrictive analysis of fetishism, appears neither as a social relation nor hence as the locus of fetishization. Utility as such escapes the historical determination of class. It represents an objective, final relation of intrinsic purpose (*destination propre*), which does not mask itself and whose transparency, as form, defies history (even if its content changes continually with respect to social and cultural determinations). It is

---

1. Marx, *Capital*, Vol. I. I have been unable to find this passage in the exact form Baudrillard cites it. But see Marx's *Grundrisse* (New York: Vintage, 1973), for example, at the bottom of p. 404. — *Trans.*

here that Marxian idealism goes to work; it is here that we have to be more logical than Marx himself — and more radical, in the true sense of the word. For use value — indeed, utility itself — is a fetishized social relation, just like the abstract equivalence of commodities. Use value is an abstraction. It is an abstraction of the *system of needs* cloaked in the false evidence of a concrete destination and purpose, an intrinsic finality of goods and products. It is just like the abstraction of social labor, which is the basis for the logic of equivalence (exchange value), hiding beneath the "innate" value of commodities.

In effect, our hypothesis is that needs (i.e., the system of needs) are the *equivalent of abstract social labor:* on them is erected the system of use value, just as abstract social labor is the basis for the system of exchange value. This hypothesis also implies that, for there to be a system at all, use value and exchange value must be regulated by an identical abstract logic of equivalence, an identical code. The code of utility is also a code of abstract equivalence of objects and subjects (for each category in itself and for the two taken together in their relation); hence, it is a combinatory code involving potential calculation (we will return to this point). Furthermore, it is in itself, as system, that use value can be "fetishized," and certainly not as a practical operation. It is always the systematic abstraction that is fetishized. The same goes for exchange value. And it is the *two* fetishizations, reunited — that of use value and that of exchange value — that constitute commodity fetishism.

Marx defines the form of exchange value and of the commodity by the fact that they can be equated on the basis of abstract social labor. Inversely, he posits the "incomparability" of use values. Now, it must be seen that:

1. For there to be economic exchange and exchange value, it is also necessary that the principle of utility has already become the reality principle of the object or product. To be abstractly and generally exchangeable, products must also be thought and rationalized in terms of utility. Where they are not (as in primitive symbolic exchange), they can have no exchange value. The reduction to the status of utility is the basis of (economic) exchangeability.

2. If the exchange principle and the utility principle have such an affinity (and do not merely coexist in the commodity), it is because utility is already entirely infused with the logic of equivalence, contrary to what Marx says about the "incomparability" of use values. If use value is not quantitative in the strictly arithmetical sense, it still involves equivalence. Considered as useful values, all

goods are already comparable among themselves, because they are assigned to the same rational-functional common denominator, the same abstract determination. Only objects or categories of goods cathected in the singular and personal act of symbolic exchange (the gift, the present) are strictly incomparable. The personal relation (non-economic exchange) renders them absolutely unique. On the other hand, as a useful value, the object attains an abstract universality, an "objectivity" (through the reduction of every symbolic function).

3. What is involved here, then, is an object form whose general equivalent is utility. And this is no mere "analogy" with the formulas of exchange value. The same logical form is involved. Every object is translatable into the general abstract code of equivalence, which is its rationale, its objective law, its meaning — and this is achieved independently of who makes use of it and what purpose it serves. It is functionality which supports it and carries it along as code; and this code, founded on the mere adequation of an object to its (useful) end, subordinates all real or potential objects to itself, without taking any one into account at all. Here, the economic is born: the economic calculus. The commodity form is only its developed form, and returns to it continually.

4. Now, contrary to the anthropological illusion that claims to exhaust the idea of utility in the simple relation of a human need to a useful property of the object, use value is very much a social relation. Just as, in terms of exchange value, the producer does not appear as a creator, but as abstract social labor power, so in the system of use value, the consumer never appears as desire and enjoyment, but as abstract social need power (one could say *Bedürfniskraft, Bedürfnisvermögen,* by analogy with *Arbeitskraft, Arbeitsvermögen*).

The abstract social producer is man conceived in terms of exchange value. The abstract social individual (the person with "needs") is man thought of in terms of use value. There is a homology between the "emancipation" in the bourgeois era of the private individual given final form by his needs and the functional emancipation of objects as use values. This results from an objective rationalization, the surpassing of old ritual and symbolic constraints. In a radically different type of exchange, objects did not have the status of "objectivity" that we give them at all. But henceforward secularized, functionalized and rationalized in purpose, objects become the promise of an ideal (and idealist) political economy, with its watchword "to each according to his needs."

At the same time, the individual, now disengaged from all

collective obligations of a magical or religious order, "liberated" from his archaic, symbolic or personal ties, at last private and autonomous, defines himself through an "objective" activity of transforming nature — labor — *and* through the destruction of utility for his benefit: needs, satisfactions, use value.

Utility, needs, use value: none of this ever comes to grips with the finality of a subject up against his ambivalent object relations, or with symbolic exchange between subjects. Rather, it describes the relation of the individual to himself conceived in economic terms — better still, the relation of the subject to the economic system. Far from the individual expressing his needs in the economic system, it is the economic system that induces the individual function and the parallel functionality of objects and needs.[2] The individual is an ideological structure, a historical form correlative with the commodity form (exchange value), and the object form (use value). The individual is nothing but the subject thought in economic terms, rethought, simplified, and abstracted by the economy. The entire history of consciousness and ethics (all the categories of occidental psycho-metaphysics) is only the history of the political economy of the subject.

Use value is the expression of a whole metaphysic: that of utility. It registers itself as a kind of *moral law* at the heart of the object — and it is inscribed there as the finality of the "need" of the subject. It is the transcription at the heart of things of the same moral law (Kantian and Christian) inscribed on the heart of the subject, positivizing it in its essence and instituting it in a *final* relation (with God, or to some transcendent reality). In both cases, the circulation of value is regulated by a providential code that watches over the correlation of the object with the needs of the subject, under the rubric of functionality — as it assures, incidentally, the coincidence of the subject with divine law, under the sign of morality.

This is the same teleology that seals the essence of the subject (his self-identity through the recognition of this transcendent finality). It establishes the object in its truth, as an essence called use value, transparent to itself and to the subject, under the rational banner of utility. And this moral law effects the same fundamental reduction of all the symbolic virtualities of the subject and the object. A simple

---

2. By the same token, there is no fundamental difference between "productive" consumption (direct destruction of utility during the process of production) and consumption by persons in general. The individual and his "needs" are produced by the economic system like unit cells of its reproduction. We repeat that "needs" are a *social labor*, a productive discipline. Neither the actual subject nor his desire is addressed in this scheme. It follows that there is only productive consumption at this level.

finality is substituted for a multiplicity of meanings. And it is still the principle of equivalence that functions here as the reducer of symbolic ambivalence:

1. It establishes the object in a functional equivalence to itself in the single framework of this determined valence: utility. This absolute signification, this rationalization by identity (its equivalence to itself) permits the object to enter the field of political economy as a positive value.

2. The same absolute simplification of the subject as the subject of moral consciousness and needs permits him to enter the system of values and practices of political economy as an abstract individual (defined by identity, equivalence to himself).

Thus the functionality of objects, their moral code of utility, is as entirely governed by the logic of equivalence as is their exchange value status. Hence, functionality falls just as squarely under the jurisdiction of political economy. And if we call this abstract equivalence of utilities the object form, we can say that *the object form is only the completed form of the commodity form.* In other words, the same logic (and the same fetishism) plays on the two sides of the commodity specified by Marx: use value and exchange value.

By not submitting use value to this logic of equivalence in radical fashion, by maintaining use value as the category of "incomparability," Marxist analysis has contributed to the mythology (a veritable rationalist mystique) that allows the relation of the individual to objects conceived as use values to pass for a concrete and objective — in sum, "natural" — relation between man's needs and the function proper to the object. This is all seen as the opposite of the abstract, reified "alienated" relation the subject would have toward products as exchange values. The truth of the subject would lie here, in usage, as a concrete sphere of the private relation, as opposed to the social and abstract sphere of the market.[3] (Marx does provide a radical

---

3. Consumption itself is only apparently a concrete operation (in opposition to the abstraction of exchange). For what is consumed isn't the product itself, but its utility. Here the economists are right: consumption is not the destruction of products, but the destruction of utility. In the economic cycle, at any rate, it is an abstraction that is produced or consumed as *value* (exchangeable in one case, useful in another). No where is the "concrete" object or the "concrete" product concerned in the matter (what do these terms mean, anyway?): but, rather, an abstract cycle, a value system engaged in its own production and expanded reproduction. Nor does consumption make sense as a *destruction* (of "concrete" use value). Consumption is a labor of expanded reproduction of use value as an abstraction, a system, a universal code of utility — just as production is no longer in its present finality the production of "concrete" goods, but the expanded reproduction of the exchange value system. Only consumation (*consummation*) escapes recycling in the expanded reproduction of the value system — not because it is the destruction of substance, but because it is a transgression of the law and finality of objects — the abolition of their abstract

analysis of the abstraction of the private individual as a social relation in another connection, however.) Against all this seething metaphysic of needs and use values, it must be said that abstraction, reduction, rationalization and systematization are as profound and as generalized at the level of "needs" as at the level of commodities. Perhaps this was not yet very clear at an anterior stage of political economy, when one could imagine that if the individual was alienated by the system of exchange value, at least he would return to himself, become himself again in his needs and in the moment of use value. But it has become possible today, at the present stage of consummative mobilization,[4] to see that needs, far from being articulated around the desire or the demand of the subject, find their coherence elsewhere: in a generalized system that is to desire what the system of exchange value is to concrete labor, the source of value. All the drives, symbolic relations, object relations and even perversions — in short, all the subject's *labor* of cathexis — are abstracted and given their general equivalent in utility and the system of needs, as all values and real social labor find their general equivalent in money and in coin. Everything surging from the subject, his body and his desire, is dissociated and catalyzed in terms of needs, more or less specified in advance by objects. All instincts are rationalized, finalized and objectified in needs — hence symbolically cancelled. *All ambivalence is reduced by equivalence.* And to say that the system of needs is a system of general equivalence is no metaphor: it means that we are completely immersed in political economy. This is why we have spoken of *fetishism of use value.* If needs were the singular, concrete expression of the subject, it would be absurd to speak of fetishism. But when needs erect themselves more and more into an abstract system, regulated by a principal of equivalence and general combinative, then certainly the same fetishism is in play. For this system is not only homologous to that of exchange value and the commodity; *it expresses the latter in all its depth and perfection.*

Indeed, just as exchange value is not a substantial aspect of the product, but a form that expresses a social relation, so use value can

---

finality. Where it appears to consume (destroy) products, consumption only consummates their utility. Consumption destroys objects as substance the better to perpetuate this substance as a universal, abstract form — hence, the better to reproduce the value code. *Consumation* (play, gift, destruction as pure loss, symbolic reciprocity) attacks the code itself, breaks it, deconstructs it. The symbolic act is the destruction of the value code (exchange and use), not the destruction of objects in themselves. Only this act can be termed "concrete," since it alone breaks and transgresses the abstraction of value.

4. See the chapter above on The Ideological Genesis of Needs.

no longer be viewed as an innate function of the object, but as a social determination (at once of the subject, the object, and their relation). In other words, just as the logic of the commodity extends itself indifferently to men and things and makes men (all obedient to the same law) appear only as exchange value — thus the restricted finality of utility imposes itself on men as surely as on the world of objects. It is illogical and naive to hope that, through objects conceived in terms of exchange value, that is, in his needs, man can fulfill himself *otherwise than as use value.* However, such is the modern humanist vulgate: through the functionality, the domestic finality of the exterior world, man is supposed to fulfill himself *qua man.* The truth is something else entirely. In an environment of commodities and exchange value, man is no more himself than he is exchange value and commodity. Encompassed by objects that function and serve, man is not so much himself as the most beautiful of these functional and servile objects. It is not only *Homo oeconomicus* who is turned entirely into use value during the process of capitalist production. This utilitarian imperative even structures the relation of the individual to himself. In the *process of satisfaction,* he valorizes and makes fruitful his own potentialities for pleasure; he "realizes" and manages, to the best of his ability, his own "faculty" of pleasure, treated literally like a productive force. Isn't this what all of humanist ethics is based on — the "proper use" of oneself?

In substance, Marx says: "Production not only produces goods; it produces people to consume them, and the corresponding needs." This proposition is most often twisted in such a way as to yield simplistic ideas like "the manipulation of needs" and denunciations of "artificial needs."[5] It is necessary to grasp that what produces the commodity system in its general form is the *concept* of need itself, as constitutive of the very structure of the individual — that is, the historical concept of a social being who, in the rupture of symbolic exchange, autonomizes himself and rationalizes his desire, his relation to others and to objects, in terms of needs, utility, satisfaction and use value.

Thus, it is not merely such and such a value that reduces symbolic

---

5. It should be pointed out that Marx's formulations in this domain (and the anthropology that they imply) are so vague as to permit culturalist interpretations of the type: "Needs are functions of the historical and social context." Or in its more radical version: "Needs are produced by the system in order to assure its own expanded reproduction" — that is, the sort of interpretation that takes into account only the multiple *content* of needs, without submitting the concept of need itself and the system of needs as form to a radical critique. [As in Marx's *Grundrisse*, p. 527, where both the "culturalist" and "more radical" position are mixed. — *Trans.*]

exchange, or emerges from its rupture; it is first the structural opposition of two values: exchange value and use value, whose logical form is the same, and whose dual organization punctuates the economic. We are faced here at a global anthropological level with the same schema of "semiological reduction" analyzed above in the section on "Fetishism and Ideology." In that study, we demonstrated the way in which this binary oppositive structuration constituted the very matrix of ideological functioning — from the fact that this structuration is never purely structural: it always plays to the advantage of one of the two terms. *Structural logic* always redoubles in a strategy (thus masculine-feminine, to the profit of the former, conscious-unconscious, to the advantage of consciousness, etc.).

Precisely the same thing is going on here. In the correlation:

$$\frac{EV}{UV} = \frac{Sr}{Sd}$$

use value and signified do not have the same weight as exchange value and signifier respectively. Let us say that they have a tactical value — whereas exchange value and signifier have strategic value. The system is organized along the lines of a functional but hierarchized bipolarity. Absolute preeminence redounds to exchange value and the signifier. Use value and needs are only an effect of exchange value. Signified (and referent) are only an effect of the signifier (we will return to this point later).[6] Neither is an autonomous reality that either exchange value or the signifier would express or translate in their code. At bottom, they are only simulation models, produced by the play of exchange value and of signifiers. They provide the latter with the guarantee of the real, the lived, the concrete; they are the guarantee of an objective reality for which, however, in the same moment, these systems qua systems substitute their own total logic. (Even the term "substitute" is misleading, in this context. It implies the existence somewhere of a fundamental reality that the system appropriates or distorts. In fact, there is no reality or principle of reality other than that directly produced by the system as its ideal reference.) Use value and the signified do not constitute an *elsewhere* with respect to the systems of the other two; they are only their alibis.

We have seen, in a first approximation, that the field of political economy generalizes and saturates itself through the system of use value (that is, the extension of the process of abstraction and productive rationality to the entire domain of consumption through the system of needs as system of values and productive forces). In this

---

6. In Toward a Critique of the Political Economy of the Sign.

sense, use value appears as the completion and fulfillment of exchange value (of political economy in general). The fetishism of use value redoubles and deepens the fetishism of exchange value.

That is a starting point. But it is necessary to see that the system of use value is *not only* the double, transposition or extension of that of exchange value. It functions simultaneously as the latter's ideological guarantee (and once again, if this is so, it is because it is logically structured in the same way). It is understood, of course, that it is a naturalizing ideology we are concerned with here. Use value is given fundamentally as the instance (i.e., tribunal) before which all men are equal. On this view, need, leaving aside any variation in the means of satisfying it, would be the most equally distributed thing in the world.[7] Men are not equal with respect to goods taken as exchange value, but they would be equal as regards goods taken as use value. One may dispose of them or not, according to one's class, income, or disposition; but the *potentiality* for availing oneself of them nevertheless exists for all. Everyone is equally rich in *possibilities* for happiness and satisfaction. This is the secularization of the potential equality of all men before God: the democracy of "needs." Thus use value, reflected back to the anthropological sphere, reconciles in the universal those who are divided socially by exchange value.

Exchange value erases the real labor process at the level of the commodity, such that the latter appears as an autonomous value. Use value fares even better: it provides the commodity, inhuman as it is in its abstraction, with a "human" finality. In exchange value, social labor disappears. The system of use value, on the other hand, involves the resorption without trace of the entire ideological and historical labor process that leads the subject in the first place to think of himself as an individual, defined by his needs and satisfaction, and thus ideally to integrate himself into the structure of the commodity.

Thus, without ceasing to be a system in historical and logical solidarity with the system of exchange value, that of use value succeeds in naturalizing the latter and offers it that universal and atemporal guarantee without which the exchange value system simply couldn't reproduce itself (or doubtless even be produced in its general form).

Use value is thus the crown and scepter of political economy:
— In its lived reality: it is the immanence of political economy in

---

7. Here Baudrillard alludes to the rationalist lineage of anthropological substantialism. See the first paragraph of Descartes' *Discourse on Method*, which Baudrillard parodies here. — *Trans.*

everyday life, down to the very act in which man believes he has rediscovered himself. He does not rediscover his objects except in what they serve; and he does not rediscover himself except through the expression and satisfaction of his needs — in what he serves.

— In its strategic value: ideologically, it seals off the system of production and exchange, thanks to the institution of an idealist anthropology that screens use value and needs from their historical logic in order to inscribe them in a formal eternity: that of utility for objects, that of the useful appropriation of objects by man in need.

This is why use value fetishism is indeed more profound, more "mysterious" than the fetishism of exchange value. The mystery of exchange value and the commodity can be unmasked, relatively — it has been since Marx — and raised to consciousness as a social relation. But value in the case of use value is enveloped in total mystery, for it is grounded anthropologically in the (self-) "evidence" of a naturalness, in an unsurpassable original reference. This is where we discover the real "theology" of value — in the order of finalities: in the "ideal" relation of equivalence, harmony, economy and equilibrium that the concept of utility implies. It operates at all levels: between man and nature, man and objects, man and his body, the self and others. Value becomes absolutely self-evident, "la chose la plus simple." Here the mystery and cunning (of history and of reason) are at their most profound and tenacious.

If the system of use value is produced by the system of exchange value as its own ideology — if use value has no autonomy, if it is only the *satellite* and *alibi* of exchange value, though systematically combining with it in the framework of political economy — then it is no longer possible to posit use value as an alternative to exchange value. Nor, therefore, is it possible to posit the "restitution" of use value, at the end of political economy, under the sign of the "liberation of needs" and the "administration of things" as a revolutionary perspective.

Every revolutionary perspective today stands or falls on its ability to reinterrogate radically the repressive, reductive, rationalizing metaphysic of utility. All critical theory depends on the analysis of the object form.[8] This has been absent from Marxist analysis. With all the political and ideological consequences that this implies, the result has been that all illusions converged on use value, idealized by opposition to exchange value, when it was in fact only the latter's naturalized form.

8. Critical theory must also take the sign form into account. We shall observe that an identical logic regulates the organization of the sign in the present-day system; it turns the signified (referent) into the *satellite* term, the *alibi* of the signifier, the play of signifiers, and provides the latter with a reality guarantee.

## Marx and Crusoe

Marx says in Volume I of *Capital* (Part 1, Section 4): "So far as (a commodity) is a value in use, there is nothing mysterious about it, whether we consider it from the point of view that by its properties it is capable of satisfying human wants, or from the point that those properties are the product of human labor. It is as clear as noonday that man, by his industry, changes the forms of the materials furnished by Nature, in such a way as to make them useful to him.

"The mystical character of commodities does not originate, therefore, in their use value.

"The categories of bourgeois economy consist of...forms of thought expressing with social validity the conditions and relations of a definite historically determined mode of production, viz., the production of commodities. The whole mystery of commodities, all the magic and necromancy that surrounds the products of labor as long as they take the form of commodities, vanishes therefore, so soon as we come to other forms of production.

"Since Robinson Crusoe's experiences are a favorite theme with political economists, let us take a look at him on his island.... All the relations between Robinson and the objects that form this wealth of his own creation are here so simple and clear as to be intelligible without exertion, even to Mr. Baudrillard.[9] And yet those relations contain all that is essential to the determination of value."

Having quite justifiably played his joke at the expense of the bourgeois economists and their interminable Robinsonnades, Marx would have done well to examine his own use of the Crusoe myth. For by opposing the obscure mysticism of commodity value to the simplicity and transparency of Crusoe's relation to his wealth, he fell into a trap. If one hypothesizes (as Marxists do) that all the ideology of bourgeois political economy is summed up in the myth of Robinson Crusoe, then it must be admitted that everything in the novel itself agrees with the mystical theology and metaphysics of bourgeois thought, including (and above all) this "transparency" in man's relation to the instruments and products of his labor.

This ideal confrontation of man with his labor capacity (*Arbeitsvermögen*) and with his needs is not only abstract because it is separated out from the sphere of political economy and commercial social relations; it is abstract *in itself*: not abstracted from political economy, but abstract because it epitomizes the abstraction of political economy itself, that is, the ascension of exchange value via use value, the apotheosis of the economic in the providential finality of utility.

---

9.    Any resemblance to a living person is purely coincidental.

Robinson Crusoe is the outcome of a total mutation that has been in progress since the dawn of bourgeois society (though truly theorized only since the 18th century). Man was transformed simultaneously into a productive force and a "man with needs." The manufacturers and the ideologues of Nature divided him between themselves. In his labor, he became a use value for a system of production. Simultaneously, goods and products became use values for him, taking on a meaning as functions of his needs, which were henceforth legalized as "nature." He entered the regime of use value, which was also that of "Nature." But this was by no means according to an original finality rediscovered: All these concepts (needs, nature, utility) were born together, in the historical phase that saw the systematization of both political economy and the ideology that sanctions it.

The myth of Robinson Crusoe is the bourgeois avatar of the myth of Terrestrial Paradise. Every great social order of production (bourgeois or feudal) maintains an ideal myth, at once a myth of culmination and a myth of origin. Theology supported itself on the myth of the fulfillment of man in the Divine Law; political economy is sustained on the great myth of human fulfillment according to the natural law of needs. Both deal in the same finality: an ideal relation of man to the world through his needs and the rule of Nature; and an ideal relationship with God through faith and the divine rule of Providence. Of course, this ideal vocation is lived from the outset as lost or compromised. But the finality tarries, and use value, entombed beneath exchange value, like the natural harmony of Earthly Paradise broken by sin and suffering, remains inscribed as an invulnerable essence to be disinterred at the last stage of History, in a promised future redemption. The logic and ideology are the same: under the sign of a bountiful nature, where the primitive hunting and gathering mode of production, anterior to the feudal mode, is highlighted, and from which serfdom and labor are made to disappear, the myth of Earthly Paradise describes the ideality of feudal relations (suzerainty and fealty of vassals). Likewise, the Crusoe myth describes, in a "transparent" isolation (where the anterior mode of agriculture and craftsmanship reappears, and the laws of the market and exchange disappear), the ideality of bourgeois relations: individual autonomy, to each according to his labor and his needs, moral consciousness bound to nature — and, if possible, some Man Friday, some aboriginal servant. (But if Crusoe's relations to his labor and his wealth are so "clear," as Marx insists, what on earth has Friday got to do with this setup?)

In fact, nothing is clear about this fable. Its evidence of simplicity and transparency is, as that of the commodity for Marx, "abounding in metaphysical subtleties and theological niceties." There is nothing clear and natural in the fact of "transforming nature according to one's needs" or in "rendering oneself useful" as well as things. And there was no need for this moral law of use value to have escaped the critique of political economy: the whole system and its "mystery" were already there with Robinson on his island, and in the trumped-up immediacy of his relation to things.

# CHAPTER EIGHT

## TOWARD A CRITIQUE OF THE POLITICAL ECONOMY OF THE SIGN

The critique of the political economy of the sign proposes to develop the analysis of the sign form, just as the critique of political economy once set out to analyze the commodity form.

Since the commodity comprises simultaneously exchange value and use value, its total analysis must encompass the two sides of the system. Similarly, the sign is at once signifier and signified; and so the analysis of the sign form must be established on two levels. Concurrently, of course, the logical and strategic analysis of the relation between the two terms is pressed upon us, thus:

1. Between the system of exchange value (EV) and that of use value (UV), or between the commodity form and the object form: this was the attempt in the preceding article.

2. Between the systems of the signifier and the signified (or between their respective codes, which define the articulation of sign value and the sign form).

In both cases, this (internal) relation is established as a hierarchical function between a dominant form and an alibi (or satellite) form, which is the logical crowning and ideological completion of the first.

### 1. The Magical Thinking of Ideology

The effect of this homological structuration of values in what can conveniently be called the fields of economy and of signification is to displace the whole process of ideology and to theorize it in radically different terms. Ideology can no longer be understood as an infra-superstructural relation between a material production (system and relations of production) and a production of signs (culture, etc.), which expresses and masks the contradictions at the "base." Henceforth, all of this comprises, with the same degree of objectivity, a general political economy (its critique), which is traversed throughout by the same form and administered by the same logic.

It should be recalled that the traditional vision of ideology still proves incapable of grasping the "ideological" function of culture and of signs — except at the level of the signified. This follows inevitably from its separation of culture (and signs) in the artificial distinction between the economic and the ideological, not to mention the desperate contortions ("superstructure," "dialectic," "structure in dominance") that this entails. Thus, ideology (of such-and-such a group, or the dominant class) always appears as the overblown discourse of some great theme, content, or value (patriotism, morality, humanism, happiness, consumption, the family) whose *allegorical* power somehow insinuates itself into consciousnesses (this has never been explained) in order to integrate them. These become, in turn, the *contents of thought* that come into play in real situations. In sum, ideology appears as a sort of cultural surf frothing on the beachhead of the economy.

So it is clear that ideology is actually *that very form* that traverses both the production of signs and material production — or rather, it is the logical bifurcation of this form into two terms:

$$\frac{EV}{Sr} \Big/ \frac{UV}{Sd}$$

This is the functional, strategic split through which the form reproduces itself. It signifies that ideology lies *already whole in the relation of EV to UV, that is, in the logic of the commodity*, as is so in the relation of Sr to Sd, i.e., in the internal logic of the sign.

Marx demonstrated that the objectivity of material production did not reside in its materiality, but in its *form*. In fact, this is the point of departure for all critical theory. The same analytical reduction must be applied to ideology: its objectivity does not reside in its "ideality," that is, in a realist metaphysic of thought contents, but in its form.

The "critique" (not excluding here the Marxist critique of ideology) feeds off a magical conception of its object. It does not unravel ideology as form, but as content, as given, transcendent value — a sort of *mana* that attaches itself to several global representations that magically impregnate those floating and mystified subjectivities called "consciousnesses." Like the concept of need, which is presented as the link between the utility of an object and the demand of a subject, ideology appears as the relation between the projection of a consciousness and the ideality of — vaguely — an idea, or a value. Transposed from the analysis of material goods to collective representations and values, the same little magic footbridge is suspended between artificial, even metaphysical, concepts.[1]

In fact, ideology is the process of reducing and abstracting

---

1. ·It should be noted here that alienation itself is one of these magical concepts devoted to sealing up an artificial disjunction — here, the disjunction between the consciousness of the subject and his own ideal content (his rediscovered totality).

symbolic material into a form. But this reductive abstraction is given immediately as value (autonomous), as content (transcendent), and as a representation of consciousness (signified). It is the same process that lends the commodity an appearance of autonomous value and transcendent reality — a process that involves the misunderstanding of the form of the commodity and of the abstraction of social labor that it operates. In bourgeois (or, alas, Marxist) thought, culture is defined as a *transcendence of contents* correlated with consciousnesses by means of a "representation" that circulates among them like positive values, just as the fetishized commodity appears as a real and immediate value, correlated with individual subjects through "need" and use value, and circulating according to the rules of exchange value.

It is the cunning of form to veil itself continually in the evidence of content. It is the cunning of the code to veil itself and to produce itself in the obviousness of value. It is in the "materiality" of content that form consumes its abstraction and reproduces itself as form. That is its peculiar magic. It simultaneously produces the content and the consciousness to receive it (just as production produces the product and its corresponding need). Thus, it installs culture in a dual transcendence of values (of contents) and consciousness, and in a metaphysic of exchange between the two terms. And if the bourgeois vulgate enshrines it in this transcendence precisely in order to exalt it as *culture*, the Marxist vulgate embalms it in the very same transcendence in order to denounce it as *ideology*. But the two scriptures rejoin in the same magical thinking.[2]

Just about all contemporary thought in this area confounds itself on false problems and in endless controversies ensuing from artificial disjunctions:

1. The subject-object dichotomy, bridged by the magical concept of need. Things might run quite smoothly here if the general system of production-consumption were not disrupted by the insoluble problem of supply and demand. Can one still speak of autonomy of choice, or is it a question of manipulation? Perhaps the two perspectives can be synthesized? — mere pseudo-dialectic. It is all an eternal litany — and over a false problem anyway.

2. The infrastructure-superstructure dichotomy, which, as we have seen, covers over again the implacable disjunction between the materiality of contents and the ideality of consciousness, reuniting

---

2. Thus the "critical" denunciation of artificial needs and the manipulation of needs converges in the same mystification the unconditional exaltation of consumption.

the two thereby separated poles with the magical conception of ideology. Even here, matters would run more smoothly if the problem of the "determinant instance" were not held eternally in suspense (since it is usually "in the last instance" — it never actually appears on the stage), with all the acrobatics of "interaction," "dialectic," "relative autonomy" and "overdetermination" that follow in its wake (and whose interminable careers have redounded to the glory of generations of intellectuals).

3. The exploitation-alienation distinction, which reiterates this false problem at the level of political analysis. The infinite debate over whether exploitation is the ground of alienation or vice versa; or whether the second succeeds the first as "the most advanced stage of capitalism" — all this is absurd. Not for the first time, the confusion arises from an artificial separation — this time of the sign and the commodity, which are not analyzed in their form, but posed instead as contents (the one of signification, the other of production). Whence emerges the distinction between an "exploitation" of labor power and an "alienation by signs." As if the commodity and the system of material production "signified" nothing! As if signs and culture were not immediately abstract social production at the level of the code and models, in a generalized exchange system of values.

Ideology is thus properly situated on neither side of this split. Rather, it is the one and only form that traverses all the fields of social production. Ideology seizes all production, material or symbolic, in the same process of abstraction, reduction, general equivalence and exploitation.

1. It is because *the logic of the commodity and of political economy is at the very heart of the sign*, in the abstract equation of signifier and signified, in the differential combinatory of signs, that signs can function as exchange value (the discourse of communication) and as use value (rational decoding and distinctive social use).

2. It is because *the structure of the sign is at the very heart of the commodity form* that the commodity can take on, immediately, the effect of signification — not epiphenomenally, in excess of itself, as "message" or connotation — but because its very form establishes it as a total *medium,* as a *system of communication* administering all social exchange. Like the sign form, the commodity is a code managing the exchange of values. It makes little difference whether the contents of material production or the immaterial contents of signification are involved; it is the code that is determinant: the rules of the interplay of signifiers and exchange value. Generalized in

the system of political economy, it is the code which, in both cases, reduces all symbolic *ambivalence* in order to ground the "rational" circulation of values and their play of exchange in the regulated equivalence of values.

It is here that the concept of alienation proves useless, by dint of its association with the metaphysic of the subject of consciousness. The code of political economy, which is the fundamental code of our society, does not operate by alienating consciousness from contents. A parallel confusion arises in the view of "primitive" myths as false stories or histories that consciousnesses recount to themselves. Here the pregnant effects of mythic contents are held to bind society together (through the "cohesion" of belief systems). But actually, these myths make up a code of signs that exchange among themselves, integrating the group through the very process of their circulation. Likewise, the fundamental code of our societies, the code of political economy (both commodity form and sign form) does not operate through the alienation of consciousness and contents. It rationalizes and regulates exchange, makes things communicate, but only under the law of the code and through the control of meaning.

The division of labor, the functional division of the terms of discourse, does not mystify people; it socializes them and informs their exchange according to a general, abstract model. The very concept of the individual is the product of this general system of exchange. And the idea of "totality" under which the subject (either that of consciousness or that of History) thinks itself in its ideal reference is nothing but the effect and the symptom of the system — the shadow that it wears. The concept of alienation involves a kind of wizardry in which consciousness thinks itself as its own ideal content (its rediscovered totality): it is an ideological concept. And ideology, in its version as a superstructure of contents of consciousness, is, in these terms, an alienated concept.

Today consumption — if this term as a meaning other than that given it by vulgar economics — defines precisely *the stage where the commodity is immediately produced as a sign, as sign value, and where signs (culture) are produced as commodities.* But this whole area of study is still occupied, "critically" or otherwise, by specialists of production (economy, infrastructure), or ideology specialists (signs, culture), or even by a kind of seamless dialectician of the totality. This partitioning of the object domain obscures even the simplest realities. If any progress is to be made at this point, "research" — especially Marxist research — must come to terms with the fact that nothing produced or exchanged today (objects, services, bodies, sex, culture, knowledge, etc.) can be decoded exclusively as a sign, nor solely measured as a commodity; that everything appears in the context of a general political economy in which the determining instance is neither the commodity nor culture (not even the updated commodity, revised and reinterpreted in its signifying function, with its message, its connotations, but always as if there still existed an objective substrate to it, the potential objectivity of the *product* as such; nor culture in its "critical" version, where signs, values, ideas are seen as everywhere commercialized or recuperated by the dominant system, but again, as if there subsisted through all this something whose transcendence could have been rationalized and simply compromised — a kind of sublime use value of culture distorted in exchange value). The object of this political economy, that is, its simplest component, its nuclear element — that which precisely the commodity was for Marx — is no longer today properly either commodity or sign, but indissolubly both, and *both only in the sense that they are abolished as specific determinations, but not as form.* Rather, this object is perhaps quite simply the *object*,[3] the object form, on which use value, exchange value and sign value converge in a complex mode that describes the most general form of political economy.

## 2. The Metaphysics of the Sign

The meaning value of the sign asserts itself with the same apparent obviousness as the natural evidence of the value of the commodity to the predecessors of Marx. These, as they say, are "the simplest of matters," and yet they are the most mysterious. Like political economy before it, semiology accomplishes little more than a description of their circulation and structural functioning.[4]

We have seen, in the preceding study, that the abstraction of the exchange value system is sustained by the effect of concrete reality and of objective purpose exhaled by use value and needs. This is the strategic logic of the commodity; its second term acts as the satellite and alibi for the first. The present hypothesis is that the same analysis holds true for the logic and strategy of the sign, thus exploding the "scientific postulates" of semio-linguistics — the arbitrary character of the sign in particular, as originally defined by

3. For the specialized sense in which Baudrillard uses the term "object" here, see the penultimate discussion in this volume: Design and Environment: The Blitz of Political Economy.  — *Trans.*

4. Two types of analysis have grappled with this parallel fetishism of the commodity and the sign: the critique of political economy, or theory of material production, inaugurated by Marx, and critical semiology, or the theory of textual production, led more recently by the Tel Quel group.

Saussure and modified by Benveniste.

The arbitrariness of the sign does not reside in its non-motivation — in the commonplace that the signifier "table" has no "natural" vocation to signify the concept or the reality of the table (any more than *Tisch* in German, etc.); it is rooted in the very fact of positing an equivalence between such and such an Sr and such and such an Sd. In this sense, arbitrariness is total even in the case of the symbol,[5] where the principle of equivalence between signifier and signified is fully retained in their analogy. Arbitrariness arises from the fundamental institution of an exact correlation between a given "discrete" Sr and an equally discrete Sd. In other words, arbitrariness lies in the "discretion" which alone grounds the possibility of the equational relation of the sign, so that This equals this, and nothing else. This discretion is thus the very principle of the sign's rationality; it functions as the agent of abstraction and universal reduction of all potentialities and qualities of meaning (*sens*) that do not depend on or derive from the respective framing, equivalence, and specular relation of a signifier and a signified. This is the directive and reductive rationalization transacted by the sign — not in relation to an exterior, immanent "concrete reality" that signs would supposedly recapture abstractly in order to express, but in relation to all that which overflows the schema of equivalence and signification; and which the sign reduces, represses and annihilates in the very operation that constitutes it (the sudden crystallization of an Sr and an Sd). The rationality of the sign is rooted in its exclusion and annihilation of all symbolic ambivalence on behalf of a fixed and equational structure. The sign is a discriminant: it structures itself through exclusion. Once crystallized on this exclusive structure, the sign aligns its fixed field, resigns the differential, and assigns Sr and Sd each its sphere of systemic control. Thus, the sign proffers itself as full value: positive, rational, exchangeable value. All virtualities of meaning are shorn in the cut of structure.

This one-to-one assignation of Sr to Sd can be complicated quite easily into an equivocal or multivocal relation without violating the logic of the sign. A signifier may refer to many signifieds, or vice versa: the principle of equivalence, ergo of exclusion and reduction, which roots the arbitrariness of the sign, remains untouched. While still opposing itself as radically as ever to *ambivalence, equivalence*

---

5.   The term "symbol" is here intended in the classic semio-linguistic sense of an analogical variant of the sign. In contrast, we will always use the term symbol (the symbolic, symbolic exchange) in opposition to and as a radical alternative to the concept of the sign and of signification.

has simply transmuted into *polyvalence*. Ambiguity itself is only the vacillation of a principle which, for all intents and purposes, rests intact. Nor does the "dissolve" effect (of signification) jeopardize the principle of the rationality of the sign — i.e., its reality principle. While retaining their discreteness, Sr and Sd are capable of multiple connections. But (through all these combinatory possibilities) the code of signification never ceases to monitor and systematically control meaning.

Only ambivalence (as a *rupture* of value, of another side or beyond of sign value, and as the *emergence of the symbolic*) sustains a challenge to the legibility, the false transparency of the sign; only ambivalence questions the evidence of the use value of the sign (rational decoding) and of its exchange value (the discourse of communication). *It brings the political economy of the sign to a standstill;* it dissolves the respective definitions of Sr and Sd — concepts emblazoned with the seal of signification; and since they assume their meaning through the process of signification in the classical sense, Sr and Sd would be doomed by the shattering of the semiologic. In the logic of ambivalence and of the symbolic, we are dealing with a process of the resolution of the sign, a resolution of the equation on which the sign is articulated, and which, in communicative discourse, *is never resolved:* integrated, opaque, never elucidated, the sign gives rise, in communicative discourse, to the same type of social mystery as that other medium, the commodity, which also depends on an abstract equation of all values.[6]

The critique of political economy, worked out by Marx at the level of exchange value, but whose total scope implies also that of use value, is quite precisely this *resolution* of the commodity and of its implicit equation — a resolution of the commodity as the form and code of general equivalence. It is this same critical resolution that must be extended to the field of signification, in a critique of the political economy of the sign.

### 3. The Mirage of the Referent

Where the sign presents itself as a unity of discrete and functional meaning, the Sr refers to an Sd, and the ensemble to a referent. The sign as abstract structure refers to a fragment of objective reality. It

---

6.  The resolution of the sign entails the abolition of the Sr and the Sd as such, but not the abolition, toward some mystical nothingness, of the material and operation of meaning. The symbolic operation of meaning is also exercised upon phonic, visual, gestural (and social) material, but according to an entirely different logic, to the question of which we shall return later.

is, moreover, between these two terms that Benveniste, modifying Saussure, relocates the arbitrariness of the sign — which is between the sign and that which it designates, and not between the Sr and the Sd, which are both of a psychic nature and necessarily associated in the mind of the subject by a veritable consubstantiality. Thus: "What is arbitrary is that a certain sign, and not another, is applied to a certain element of reality, and not to any other. In this sense, and only in this sense, it is permissible to speak of contingency, and even in so doing we would seek less to solve the problem than simply to pinpoint it in order to set it aside provisionally. . . . The domain of arbitrariness is thus left outside the comprehension (logical intention) of the linguistic sign." [7]

But banishing arbitrariness to the exterior of the sign does no more than displace the problem; and to believe in the possibility of deferring it is here only another way of providing a solution which, far from being merely provisional and methodological, risks reviving its eternal metaphysical formulation.

For Saussure the internal contingency of the sign was an obstacle that always threatened the reciprocal coherence of the Sr and the Sd. Through the expulsion of the arbitrary, Benveniste attempts to rescue the inner organization and logical necessity of the sign (not to mention that of semio-linguistics). But this adjustment is only possible on the basis of a separation between the sign and reality (the referent). As we have seen, Benveniste seems quite content to refer the solution to the problem that this creates back to philosophy; but in fact he responds to the question himself, and very metaphysically, like all linguists and semiologists — with the concepts of "motivation" and of "arbitrariness."

In the end, the difficulty with Benveniste's analysis (and the analyses of others) comes down to the fact that things are just not cut out according to his idealist scheme. The scission (*coupure*) does not occur between a sign and a "real" referent. It occurs between the Sr as form and, on the other side, the Sd and the Rft, which are registered together as content — the one of thought, the other of reality (or rather, of perception) — under the aegis of the Sr. The referent in question here is no moral external to the sign than is the Sd: indeed, it is governed by the sign. It is carved out and projected as its function; its only reality is of that which is *ornamentally inscribed on the sign itself*. In a profound sense, the referent is the reflection of the sign, and this profound collusion, which depends on

7. Emile Benveniste, *Problems in General Linguistics* (Miami, 1971).

form, is "instinctively" translated at the level of contents by the speaking subject. Benveniste declares: "For the speaking subject, there is complete adequation between language and reality. The sign recovers and commands reality; better still, it *is* that reality...."[8] The poor speaker evidently knows nothing of the arbitrary character of the sign (but then, he probably isn't a semiologist)! Yet there is a certain truth to his naive metaphysic, for Benveniste's "arbitrary" link between the sign and reality has no more existence than the one postulated by Saussure between Sr and Sd.

So Benveniste's argument ultimately turns back on itself. For if one admits, with him, and against Saussure, that the Sd is consubstantial with the Sr, then so must be the referent (reality), since the Sd and Rft are both cut from the same cloth (as assigned to them by the Sr). The process of carving out and separation, of abstract formalization, is continuous from one end to the other of the chain — from Sr to Rft inclusive. In fact, it makes little difference whether one claims either:

1. That *motivation* is general throughout the chain: But then it is no longer the substantial motivation of the psychologistic type (that of content) that emanates somehow from the Rft toward the Sr; it is a kind of formal motivation "from on high" — it is the law of the code and the signifier that informs and determines (to the point of) "reality." The code becomes a veritable reality principle.

2. Or that it is *arbitrariness*, the conventionality of the sign, that reigns over the entire chain. Then the concrete ceases to exist, and the very perception of it hinges on the abstraction and the "discretion" of the Sr. The *spectre* of the Sr extends onto the world (in two senses: it "analyzes" it spectrally, and it haunts it).

The crucial thing is to see that the separation of the sign and the world is a fiction, and leads to a science fiction. The logic of equivalence, abstraction, discreteness and projection of the sign engulfs the Rft as surely as it does the Sd. This "world" that the sign "evokes" (the better to distance itself from it) is nothing but the effect of the sign, the shadow that it carries about, its "pantographic" extension. Even better: this world is quite simply the Sd-Rft. As we have seen, the Sd-Rft is a single and compact thing, an identity of content that acts as the moving shadow of the Sr. It is the reality effect in which the play of signifiers comes to fruition and deludes the world.

And now the homology between the logic of signification and the

---

8.   *Ibid.*

logic of political economy begins to emerge. For the latter exploits its reference to needs and the actualization of use value as an anthropological horizon while precluding their real intervention in its actual functioning and operative structure. Or so it appears. Similarly, the referent is maintained as exterior to the comprehension of the sign: the sign alludes to it, but its internal organization excludes it. In fact, it is now clear that the system of needs and of use value is thoroughly implicated in the form of political economy as its completion. And likewise for the referent, this "substance of reality," in that it is entirely bound up in the logic of the sign. Thus, in each field, the dominant form (system of exchange value and combinatory of the Sr respectively) provides itself with a referential rationale (*raison*), a content, an alibi, and, significantly, in each this articulation is made *under the same metaphysical "sign," i.e., need or motivation.*

All of this venerable old psychology nourishes the semiological organism:

1. The referent, the "real" object, is the phenomenal object, the perceptual contents and lived experience of the subject — situated half way between phenomenology and Bergsonian substance opposed to form.

2. In a manner of speaking, this perceptual content emerges flush; it is shifted to the level of the sign by the signified, the content of thought. Between the two, one is supposed to glide in a kind of frictionless space from the perceptual to the conceptual, in accordance with the old recipes of philosophical idealism and the abstract associationism that was already stale in the 19th century.

And how is the articulation established between the sign and referent (or between the Sr and the Sd), subtly differentiated as they are (so subtly, in fact, as to preserve them in each other's image!)? We have already broached the term: it is by *motivation*. Whether it is in order to deny motivation, according to the Saussurian theory of the sign (to relativize it, to proportion it in the definition of the symbol), or simply to affirm it, like Benveniste in his critique of the Saussurian theory (justified, to be sure, but only from the internal perspective of semio-linguistics) — the only relation thinkable, the only concept under which the articulation of the phenomenal (psychological) and the sign can be thought is that of motivation. It is a hollow and somewhat supernatural concept. But it can hardly be otherwise, once one has granted this metaphysical representation of the referent, this abstract separation between the sign and the world. *Some* form of wizardry is required to rejoin them: and — what a coincidence! — it is with this very term that political economy attempts to reunite the subject and the object it posits as separate: need. *Need, motivation:* one never escapes this circle. Each term conceals the same metaphysical wile. In the latter version, the term as a rather more logical resonance, in the other, a more psychological one; but let us not be mistaken here. The logical and the psychological are here indissolubly mixed: semiological motivation has all of psychology behind it. As to economic need, it is much more than a question of the "demand" of the subject: the entire logical articulation of economic science demands it as a functional postulate.

These concepts are not accidentally nebulous. Concepts are quite meaningless when they are busy bridging non-existent gaps. There is no distinction between the sign and the phenomenal referent, except from the metaphysical perspective that simultaneously idealizes and abstracts the sign and the *Lebenswelt,* the one as form, the other as content, in their formal opposition. Having provided itself with false distinctions, it cannot be expected to resolve them except with false concepts. But such distinctions are strategic and operational — that is the point. To resolve them (and to rupture the conceptual unreality, which would be the only means of resolving the false problem of the arbitrariness and motivation of the sign) would amount to shattering the possibility of all semiology.

The emptiness of the concepts in question evidently hides a strategy that can be analyzed simultaneously in the field of signification and of the economy. Motivation (need) only describes, behind the formal opposition between two terms, a kind of circuit, a sort of specular and tautological process between two modalities of the same form, via the *detour* of a self-proclaimed content; and the reproduction of a systematic abstraction (whether it be that of the exchange value or of the code of the signifier) via the detour of the real. We have seen that needs (UV system) do not constitute a qualitative, incommensurable concrete reality exterior to political economy, but rather a system that is itself induced by the EV system and which functions according to the same logic. If the two systems are in some way matched up in an identical form, then it is evident that the concept of need (like motivation) analyzes nothing at all. It only describes, through an illusory articulation, the general circulation of the same model and its internal operation. A typical rendition of this (necessarily) tautological definition of need might read: People appropriate a given object for themselves as use value "because they need it."

Benveniste's motivation partakes of the same circularity, the same psychological tautology.

1. The sign derives its necessity from a psychological consensus that inescapably binds a given Sr to a given Sd (some fraction of the "real" of thought).

2. But: the objectivity of this "denoted" fraction of the real is evidently the perceptive consensus of (speaking) subjects.

3. And this is supported no less evidently by the psychological consensus that links any given Sr to a given Sd.

The circle that legitimates the sign by the real and which founds the real by the sign is strictly vicious; but this circularity is the very secret of all metaphysical (ideological) operationality.

Needs are not the actuating (*mouvante*) and original expression of a subject, but the functional reduction of the subject by the system of use value in solidarity with that of exchange value. Similarly, the referent does not constitute an autonomous concrete reality at all; it is only the extrapolation of the excision (*decoupage*) established by the logic of the sign onto the world of things (onto the phenomenological universe of perception). It is the world such as it is seen and interpreted through the sign — that is, *virtually excised and excisable* at pleasure. The "real" table does not exist. If it can be registered in its identity (if it exists), this is because it has already been *designated*, abstracted and rationalized by the separation (*decoupage*) which establishes it in this equivalence to itself. Once again, given this line of reasoning, there is no fundamental difference between the referent and the signified, and the spontaneous confusion which so often arises here can only be symptomatic: the referent has no other value than that of the signified, of which it wants to be the substantial reference *in vivo*, and which it only succeeds in extending *in abstracto*.[9] Thus the strategy repeats itself: the double aspect of the

---

9. This facsimile of the concrete concept (concept "en dur") only transliterates the fetish of realism, and of substance, the last stage of idealism fantasizing matter. (For more on "en dur," cf. J.-M. Lefebvre, *N.R.F.*, February 1970, No. 1: "The referent is not truly reality. . . it is the image we make of reality. It is a signified determined by an intention carried toward things (!) and not considered in its simple relation to the Sr, as is usual in linguistics. From the Sd-concept, I pass to the referent as a concrete approach to the world.") It is, however, on these intermingled vestiges of idealism and materialism, deriving from all the confines of Western metaphysics, that semiology is based. The position of Lefebvre is moreover characteristic of the cunning with which "reality" succeeds in resurrecting itself surreptitiously behind all semiological thought, however critical, in order to establish more firmly the strategy of the sign. It thus gives witness to the impossibility of escaping the metaphysical problems posed by the sign without radically challenging semiological articulation itself. In effect, Lefebvre says: "The referent is not reality (i.e., an object whose existence I can test, or control): we relate to it as real, but this intentionality is precisely an act of mind that belies its reality, which makes a fiction, an artificial construction out of it." Thus, in a kind of

commodity (UV/EV) in fact conceals a formal homogeneity in which use value, regulated by the system of exchange value, confers on the latter its "naturalist" guarantee. And the double face of the sign (Sr/ Sd, generalizable into Sr/Sd — Rft) obscures a formal homogeneity in which Sd and Rft (administered by the same logical form, which is none other than that of the Sr), serve together as the reference-alibi — precisely the guarantee of "substance" for the Sr.

Saussure's sheet of paper theory of language (the double face of the sign one "cuts up") is thus perfectly idealist.[10] By giving the Sr and the Sd "in equivalence" as constitutive agencies (instances) of the sign, it veils the strategic apparatus of the sign, which rests precisely on the disparity of the two terms and on the fundamental circularity of the dominant term:

1. To summarize what we have so far, there is a metaphysic of the Sd -Rft, homologous with that of needs and use value. The Sd -Rft is taken for an original reality, a substance of value and recurring finality through the supporting play of signifiers (cf. the analysis of *Tel Quel*, in particular Derrida). Similarly, use value is given as origin and purpose (*finalité*), and needs as the basic motor of the economic — the cycle of exchange value appearing here as a necessary detour, but incompatible with true finalities.

2. In reality, this moral and metaphysical privilege of contents (UV and Sd-Rft) only masks the decisive privilege of form (EV and Sr). These two terms are respectively the last "Reason," the structural principle of the entire system, of which the former terms are only the detour. It is the rational abstraction of the system of exchange value and of the play of signifiers which commands the whole. But this fundamental strategy (of which it is impossible [11] here to demonstrate the operational repercussions at every level of contemporary society — from cybernetic programming to bureaucratic systems,

---

flight in advance, the referent is drained of its reality, becomes again a simulacrum, behind which, however, the tangible object immediately re-emerges. Thus, the articulation of the sign can gear down in infinite regress, while continually reinventing the real as its beyond and its consecration. At bottom, the sign is haunted by the nostalgia of transcending its own convention, its arbitrariness; in a way, it is obsessed with the idea of *total motivation*. Thus it alludes to the real as its beyond and its abolition. But it can't "jump outside its own shadow": for it is the sign itself that produces and reproduces this real, which is only its *horizon* — not its transcendence. Reality is the phantasm by means of which the sign is indefinitely preserved from the symbolic deconstruction that haunts it.

10.   Ferdinand de Saussure, *Course in General Linguistics* (New York, 1959), p. 113.

11.   Of course, it is not impossible at all. But such an analysis would depend for its full impact on our grasp of the whole process of development of the political economy of the sign. To this we shall return later.

and to the system of "consumption") is carefully hidden by the spreading out of the signification process over the two (or three) agencies (Sr, Sd, Rft), and the play of their distinction and of their equivalence.

## 4. Denotation and Connotation

The entire conceptual battery of semio-linguistics must be subjected to the same radical analysis as Marx applied to the concepts of classical political economy. And so we shift to the level of the message, where, as we shall see, the by now familiar metaphysics reappears in the concepts of denotation and connotation.

Denotation maintains itself entirely on the basis of the myth of "objectivity" (whether the denotation is that of the linguistic sign, the photographic analagon, iconic, etc.). Objectivity in this case is the direct adequation of an Sr to a precise reality. Even the difficulty which arises in the case of the image (i.e., its nondiscreteness, the fact that its Sr and Sd form a continuum, etc.) poses no fundamental challenge to the rule of the equivalence of the sign, i.e., that assignation of two terms which makes possible the further assignation of a fictive real to the contoured image (*decoupé*) of the sign — and thus to the rationalization and general control of meaning.

The Sd of connotation [12] is quite certainly amenable to the same analysis, since it also re-emerges as a "denotation effect" of the *new* process of "staggered" signification. Barthes' analysis of the advertisement for Panzani pasta, with its connotation of "Italianity" is an example. [13] "Italianity" is only apparently of the Sd, conceptual content, etc. In fact, it constitutes a code unto itself — a myth, if you wish. But myths are not comprised of content. They are a process of exchange and circulation of a code whose *form* is determinant. And so it is for the role of connotation here. And if it is the locus of ideology, this is not a question of its having grafted annex and parasitical significations onto an "objective" denotative process; nor that it has smuggled in parallel contents, foreign to the infrastructure of the sign that would otherwise constitute the process of denotation: [14]

12. In the "staggered scheme of connotation, the entire sign is transformed into the signifier of another signified: $\dfrac{\dfrac{Sr/Sd}{Sr}}{Sd}$

[See Part IV of "Elements of Semiology," in Roland Barthes, *Writing Degree Zero and Elements of Semiology* (Boston, 1968), p. 89, and also his discussion of "Myth as a Semiological System," in *Mythologies* (Frogmore: St. Albans, 1973), esp. P. 115. — *Trans.*]

13. Roland Barthes, "Rhetorique de l'Image," in *Communications* 4 (1964).

14. It is no accident here if the mythical scheme of infrastructure and

what is involved here is precisely a free play of concatenation and exchange of Srs — a process of indefinite reproduction of the code (cf. "Fetishism and Ideology": ideology is bound to form, not content: it is the passion of the code).

Having said this, we can return to the process of denotation in order to show that it differs in no way from connotation: the denoted Sd, this objective "reality," is itself nothing more than a coded form (code of perception, "psychological" code, code of "realistic" values, etc.). In other words, ideology is as rife with the denotative as with the connotative process and, in sum, denotation is never really anything more than the most attractive and subtle of connotations.

As Barthes says in *S/Z:* "Denotation is not the first among meanings, but pretends to be so; under this illusion, it is ultimately no more than the *last* of the connotations (the one that seems both to establish and to close the reading), the superior myth by which the text pretends to return to the nature of language, to language as nature: doesn't a sentence, whatever meaning it releases, subsequent to its utterance, it would seem, appear to be telling us something simple, literal, primitive: something *true*, in relation to which all the rest is literature?" [15]

So it all parallels use value as the "denotative" function of objects. Indeed, doesn't the object have that air, in its "being serviceable," of having said something objective? This manifest discourse is the subtlest of its mythologies. A false ingenuity, and a perversion of objectivity is involved. Utility, like the literality of which Barthes speaks, is not a nature; it is a code of natural evidence which has the privilege over many other possible codes (the moral, the aesthetic, etc.) of appearing *rational*, while the others seem like mere rationalizations of more or less "ideological" purposes. Denotation or use value; objectivity or utility: it is always the complicity of the real with the code under the sign of evidence which generates these categories. And just as use value, the "literal" and ideal finality of the object, resurges continually from the system of exchange value, the effect of concreteness, reality and denotation results from the complex play of interference of networks and codes — just as white light results from the interference of the colors of the spectrum. So the white light of denotation is only the play of the spectrum — the chromatic ghost — of connotations.

Thus the denotation-connotation distinction appears unreal and

superstructure resurfaces at least implicitly in the field of signification: *denotative* infrastructure and *ideological* superstructure.

15.    Roland Barthes, *S/Z* (New York, 1974), p. 9.

itself ideological. It could, however, be restored in a paradoxical sense, exactly opposed to the current accepted use. For denotation distinguishes itself from other significations (connoted) by its singular function of effacing the traces of the ideological process by restoring its universality and "objective" innocence. Far from being the objective term to which connotation is opposed as an ideological term, denotation is thus (since it naturalizes the very process of ideology) *the most ideological term* — ideological to the second degree. It is the "superior myth" of which Barthes speaks. This is exactly the same ideological function we have discerned of use value in its relation to exchange value. Hence, the two fields reciprocally illuminate each other in the totality of the ideological process.[16]

## 5. Beyond the Sign: The Symbolic

A critique of the political economy of the sign implies certain perspectives of transcendence — a "beyond" of the signification process through which sign exchange value organizes itself; and thus also a "beyond" of semiology which, in its quite "objective innocence," simply details the functioning of sign exchange value.

In general, the critical perspectives of transcendence of the sign (of its abstract rationality, its "arbitrariness") are generated in the spirit of one of the two terms that comprise it: that is, either in the name of the Sd (of the Rft: same thing), which it is then necessary to liberate from the stranglehold of the code (of the Sr) — or in the name of the Sr, which must be liberated from that of the Sd.

The first perspective — the party of the Sd — is to be analyzed in

---

16.   The analysis could be extended to the level of metalanguage (a system of signification staggered in reverse):

$$\frac{\frac{Sr / Sd}{Sd}}{Sr}$$

where the entire sign is transformed into the Sd of a new Sr. In the end, the signified of metalinguistic denotation is only an effect of the Sr, only a simulation model whose coherence derives from the regulated exchange of signifiers. It would be interesting to push, to the verge of paradox:

—The hypothesis (though it is scarcely even that) that the historical event is volatilized in its successive coding by the media; that it is invented and manipulated by the simple operation of the code. The historical event then appears as a combinatory effect of discourse;

—The hypothesis, in the same mode, at the metalinguistic level, that the object of a (given) science is only the effect of its discourse. In the carving out and separation of the field of knowledge the rationality of a science is established through its exclusion of the remainder (the same process, as we have seen, is involved in the institution of the sign itself): or, to take this even further, that this (scientific) discourse posits its object as a simulation model, purely and simply. It is known, after all, that a science is established in the last instance as the language-consensus of a scientific community.

the framework of Derrida's (and *Tel Quel's*) critique of the primacy
of the signified in the occidental process of meaning, which moralizes
the sign in its content (of thought or of reality) at the expense of
form, and confers an ethical and metaphysical status to meaning
itself. This "natural philosophy" of signification implies an "idealism
of the referent." It is a critique of the abstraction and arbitrariness of
the sign in the name of "concrete" reality. Its phantasm is that of a
total resurrection of the "real" in an immediate and transparent
intuition, which establishes the economy of the sign (of the Sr) and of
the code in order to release the Signifieds (subjects, history, nature,
contradictions) in their actuating, dialectical, authentic truth.
Today, this vision is developed largely in the critique of the
abstraction of systems and codes in the name of authentic values
(which are largely derived from the bourgeois system of individualist
values). It amounts to a long sermon denouncing the alienation of
the system, which becomes, with the expansion of this very system, a
kind of universal discourse.

The temptation to criticize the Sr in the name of the Sd (Rft), to
make of the "real" the ideal alternative to the formal play of signs, is
congruent with what we have analyzed as the idealism of use value. [17]
The salvation of UV from the system of EV, without realizing that
UV is a satellite system in solidarity with that of EV: this is precisely
the idealism and transcendental humanism of contents which we
discover again in the attempt to rescue the Sd (Rft) from the
terrorism of the Sr. The velleity of emancipating and liberating the
"real" leaves intact the entire ideology of signification — just as the
ideology of political economy is preserved *in toto* in the ideal
autonomization of use value.

Because it confirms the separation which establishes the logic of
the sign, every attempt to surpass the political economy of the sign
which takes its support from one of its constituent elements is
condemned to reproduce its arbitrary character (ergo, ideology) in
the alternated mode of Sd or Sr. [18] Any basis for a crucial interrogation of the sign must be situated from the perspective of what it
expels and annihilates in its very institution, in the respective
emergence and structural assignation of the Sr and the Sd. The
process of signification is, at bottom, nothing but a gigantic
*simulation model of meaning.* Clearly, neither the real, the referent,
nor some substance of value banished to the exterior shadow of the

---

17. See Beyond Use Value, in this volume.
18.   The impasse is much more subtle in the case of the "liberation of the signifier."
We shall return to this problem.

sign can abolish this process. It is the symbolic that continues to haunt the sign, for in its total exclusion it never ceases to dismantle the formal correlation of Sr and Sd. But the symbolic, whose virtuality of meaning is so subversive of the sign, cannot, for this very reason, be named except by allusion, by infraction (*effraction*). For signification, which names everything in terms of itself, can only speak the language of values and of the *positivity* of the sign.

Indeed, in the final analysis, the whole problem revolves around the question of the positivity of the sign, its "assumption of value" (*prise de valeur*). Of what is outside the sign, of what is other than the sign, *we can say nothing*, really, except that it is ambivalent, that is, it is impossible to distinguish respective separated terms and to positivize them as such. And we can say that in this ambivalence is rooted a type of exchange that is radically different from the exchange of values (exchange values or sign values). But this (symbolic) exchange is foreclosed and abolished by the sign in its simultaneous institution of: (1) a separation, a distinctive structure; and (2) a positive relation, a sort of structural copulation between the two terms, which clearly only eternalizes their separation. This copulation is objectified in the bar of structural inclusion between Sr and Sd (Sr/ Sd).[19] It is then even further objectified and

19.   All the arbitrariness and positivity of the sign is amassed on this line separating the two levels of the sign. This structural-inclusive copula establishes the process of signification as *positive* and occults its prior function — the process of reducing and abolishing meaning (or non-meaning: ambivalence); the process of misunderstanding and denegation with which, moreover, the sign never finishes. This line is in fact the barrier whose raising would signify the deconstruction of the sign, its resolution, and the dissolution of its constituent elements, Sr and Sd, as such. Lacan's formulation of the linguistic sign reveals the true meaning of this line: $\frac{S}{s}$ . It becomes the line (barrier) of repression itself — no longer that which articulates, but that which censors — and thus the locus of transgression. This line highlights what the sign denies, that upon which the sign establishes itself negatively, and of which it is only, in its positive institution, the symptom.

However, Lacan's formula introduces this radically new line in terms of the *traditional* schema of the sign, maintaining the usual place of the Signified. This Signified is not the Sd-Rft of linguistics. It is the repressed. It still retains a sort of content, and its representation is always that of a substance, though no longer assigned term for term, but only coinciding at certain points with the metaphoric chain of Srs ("anchoring points" — *points de capiton*). [On "points de capiton" and other matters concerning Lacan, see Anthony Wilden, *The Language of the Self* (New York: Delta, 1968): "Perhaps language is in fact totally tautologous in the sense that it can only in the end talk about itself, but in any event, Lacan has suggested that there must be some privileged 'anchoring points,' points like the buttons on a mattress or the intersections of quilting, where there is a 'pinning down' (*capitonnage*) of meaning, not to an object, but rather by 'reference back' to a symbolic function" (p. 273). For Lacan's version of the Saussurian formula, see Jacques Lacan, "The Insistence of the Letter in the Unconscious," in Jacques Ehrmann, ed., *Structuralism* (New York, 1970). — *Trans.*]

positivized in the "R" of Hjemslev's formula: E R C.[20] It is this positive relation that makes a value of the sign. Whether it is understood to be arbitrary or motivated makes little difference. These terms divert the problem by inscribing it in an already established logic of the sign. Its true arbitrariness, or true motivation, is its positivization, which creates its rationality. And this is nothing other than the radical *reduction* of all ambivalence, through its dual abstraction. The motivation of the sign is thus purely and simply its strategy: structural crystallization and the liquidation of ambivalence by the "solidification" of value. And this motivation evidently functions by means of the arbitrariness of its form: foreclosure and reduction. The concepts of arbitrariness and motivation are thus hardly contradictory from a strategic (political) perspective.

Still, the arbitrariness of the sign is at bottom untenable. The sign value cannot admit to its own deductive abstraction any more than exchange value can. Whatever it denies and represses, it will attempt to exorcise and integrate into its own operation: such is the status of the "real," of the referent, which are only the simulacrum of the symbolic, its form reduced and intercepted by the sign. Through this mirage of the referent, which is nothing but the phantasm of what the sign itself represses during its operation,[21] the sign attempts to mislead: it permits itself to appear as totality, to efface the traces of its abstract transcendence, and parades about as the reality principle of meaning.[22]

---

According to the very different logic of linguistics, it is a question of the partition of two agencies (instances), where the *reference* is only representative of one. It appears on the contrary that to conceive the sign as censor, as a barrier of exclusion, is not to wish to retain for the repressed its position as signifiable, its position of latent value. Rather, it is to conceive it as that which, denied by the sign, in turn denies the sign's form, and can never have any place within it. It is a non-place and non-value in opposition to the sign. Barred (*barrée*) and deleted (*rayée*) by the sign, it is a symbolic ambivalence that only re-emerges fully in the total resolution of the sign, in the explosion of the sign and of value. The symbolic is not inscribed anywhere. It is not what comes to be registered beneath the repression barrier (line), the Lacanian Sd. It is rather what tears all Srs and Sds to pieces, since it is what dismantles their pairing off (*appareillage*) and their simultaneous carving out (*découpe*). See note 6 above.

20. See Roland Barthes, "Elements of Semiology," *op. cit.* ["It will be remembered that any system of signification comprises a plane of expression (E) and a plane of content (C) and that the signification coincides with the relation (R) of the two planes: E R C." — *Trans.*]

21. One could say that the referent becomes "symbolic" again, by a curious inversion — not in the radical sense of the term, but in the sense of a "symbolic" gesture, that is, its meager reality. Here the referent is *only* "symbolic," the principle of reality having passed over into the code.

22. Even exchange value could not exist in its pure state, in its total abstraction. It can only function under the cover of use value, where a simulacrum of totality is

As the functional and terrorist organization of the control of meaning under the sign of the positivity of value, signification is in some ways kin to the notion of reification. It is the locus of an elemental objectification that reverberates through the amplified systems of signs up to the level of the social and political terrorism of the bracketing (*encadrement*) of meaning. All the repressive and reductive strategies of power systems are already present in the internal logic of the sign, as well as those of exchange value and political economy. Only total revolution, theoretical and practical, can restore the symbolic in the demise of the sign and of value. Even signs must burn.

---

restored at the horizon of political economy, and where it resuscitates, in the functionality of needs, the phantom of precisely what it abolishes: the symbolic (*le symbolique*) of desire.

# CHAPTER NINE

## REQUIEM FOR THE MEDIA

*Introit*

There is no theory of the media. The "media revolution" has remained empirical and mystical, as much in the work of McLuhan as with his opponents. McLuhan has said, with his usual Canadian-Texan brutalness, that Marx, the spiritual contemporary of the steam engine and railroads, was already obsolete in his lifetime with the appearance of the telegraph.[1] In his candid fashion, he is saying that Marx, in his materialist analysis of production, had virtually circumscribed productive forces as a privileged domain from which language, signs and communication in general found themselves excluded. In fact, Marx does not even provide for a genuine theory of railroads as "media," as modes of communication: they hardly enter into consideration. And he certainly established no theory of technical evolution in general, except from the point of view of production — primary, material, infrastructural production as the almost exclusive determinant of social relations. Dedicated to an intermediate ideality and a blind social practice, the "mode of communication" has had the leisure for an entire century of "making revolution" without changing the theory of the mode of production one iota in the process.

Having admitted this much, and on condition (which is already a revolution by comparison to orthodox Marxism) that the exchange of signs is not treated as a marginal, superstructural dimension in relation to those beings whom the only "true" theory (materialist) defines as "producers of their real life" (i.e., of goods destined to satisfy their needs), it is possible to imagine two perspectives:

1. One retains the general form of Marxist analysis (dialectical contradiction between forces and relations of production), but admits that the classical definition of productive forces is too restricted, so one expands the analysis in terms of productive forces to the whole murky field of signification and communication. This involves setting loose in all their originality the contradictions born from this theoretical and practical extension of the field of political economy. Such a hypothesis is the point of departure for Enzensberger: "Monopoly capitalism develops the consciousness shaping industry more quickly and more extensively than other

---

1. Marshall McLuhan, *War and Peace in the Global Village* (New York, 1968), p. 5.

sectors of production; it must at the same time fetter it. A socialist media theory has to work at this contradiction."[2] But this hypothesis does little more than signal the virtual extension of the commodity form to all the domains of social life (and tardily, at that). It recognizes the existence, here and now, of a classical communication theory, a bourgeois political economy of signs and of their production (just as there existed one of material production as early as the 18th century). It is a class-bound theoretical discipline.[3] It has not been answered by any fundamental critique that could be seen as the logical extension of Marx's. Since the entire domain was relegated to the superstructure, this *critique of the political economy of the sign* was rendered unthinkable. Thus, at best, Enzensberger's hypothesis can do little more than try to vitiate the immense retardation of classical Marxist theory. It is only radical in the eyes of official Marxism, which is totally submerged in the dominant models, and would risk its own survival if it went even that far. *The radical alternative lies elsewhere.*

2. The production of meaning, messages and signs poses a crucial problem to revolutionary theory. Instead of reinterpreting it in terms of classical forces of production — that is, instead of merely generalizing an analysis that is considered final and stamped with the seal of approval by the "spokesmen of the revolution" — the alternative is to thoroughly disrupt the latter in the light of the eruption of this new problem into the theoretical field (an approach no self-respecting Marxist would take, even under the guise of a hypothesis).

In other words: perhaps the Marxist theory of production is irredeemably partial, and cannot be generalized. Or again: the theory of production (the dialectical chaining of contradictions linked to the development of productive forces) is strictly homogeneous with its object — *material* production — and is nontransferable, as a postulate or theoretical framework, to contents that were never given for it in the first place.[4] The dialectical form is

2.  Hans Magnus Enzensberger, "Constituents of a Theory of the Media," *The Consciousness Industry* (New York: The Seabury Press, 1974), pp. 96-128.

3.  This political economy of the sign is structural linguistics (together with semiology, to be sure, and all its derivatives, of which communication theory will be discussed below). It is apparent that within the general ideological framework, structural linguistics is the contemporary master discipline, inspiring anthropology, the human sciences, etc., just as, in its time, did political economy, whose postulates profoundly informed all of psychology, sociology and the "moral and political" sciences.

4.  In this case, the expression "consciousness industry" which Enzensberger uses to characterize the existing media is a dangerous metaphor. Unfortunately, it underlies his entire analytic hypothesis, which is to extend the Marxist analysis of the capitalist

adequate to certain contents, those of material production: it exhausts them of meaning, but unlike an archetype, it does not exceed the definition of this object. The dialectic lies in ashes because it offered itself as a system of interpreting the *separated* order of material production.

All in all, this point of view is quite logical. It accords a global coherence to Marxist analysis — an internal homogeneity that prevents certain elements from being retained and others from being excluded, according to a technique of *bricolage* of which the Althusserians are the most subtle artificers. On the other hand, we credit Marxism with a maximum coherence. And so we demand that this coherence be breached, for it is incapable of responding to a social process that far exceeds material production.[5]

### Enzensberger: A "Socialist" Strategy

In the absence of a theory and a positive strategy, argues Enzensberger, the Left remains disarmed. It is content to denounce mass-media culture as an ideological manipulation. The Left dreams of a media takeover, sometimes as a *means* of nudging the revolutionary *prise de conscience* of the masses, sometimes as a *consequence* of radical change in social structures. But this is a contradictory velleity, reflecting quite straightforwardly the impossibility of integrating the media into a theory of infra- and superstructure. The media (and the entire domain of signs and communication, it should be added) remain a social mystery for the Left, according to Enzens-

---

mode of production to the media, to the point of discovering a structural analogy between the following relations:

> dominant class / dominated class
> producer-entrepreneur / consumer
> transmitter-broadcaster / receiver

5.   In fact, Marxist analysis can be questioned at two very different levels of radicality: either as a system for interpreting the separated order of *material* production, or else as that of the separated order of *production* (in general). In the first case, the hypothesis of the non-relevance of the dialectic outside its field of "origin" must be logically pushed further: if "dialectical" contradictions between the productive forces and the relations of production largely vanish in the field of language, signs and ideology, *perhaps they were never really operative in the field of material production either,* since a certain capitalist development of productive forces has been able to absorb — not all conflict, to be sure — but revolutionary antagonisms at the level of social relations. Wherein lies the validity of these concepts, then, aside from a purely conceptual coherence?

In the second case, the concept of production must be interrogated at its very root (and not in its diverse contents), along with the separated form which it establishes and the representational and rationalizing schema it imposes. Undoubtedly it is here, at the extreme, that the real work needs to be done. [See Baudrillard's *Mirror of Production,* translated by Mark Poster (St. Louis: Telos Press, 1975). — *Trans.*]

berger, because the Left has failed to conceive of them as a new and gigantic potential of productive forces. The Left is divided between fascination and practice before this sorcery to which it also falls victim, but which it reproves morally and intellectually (here is that Left intellectual speaking through Enzensberger himself, making his autocritique). This ambivalence only reflects the ambivalence of the media themselves, without going beyond it or reducing it.[6] With a bold stroke of Marxist sociology, Enzensberger imputes this "phobia" of intellectuals and Left movements to their bourgeois or petty bourgeois origins: they defend themselves instinctively from mass culture because it snaps their cultural privilege.[7] True or false, perhaps it would be more valuable to ask, with respect to this mesmerized distrust, this tactical disarray and the Left intelligentsia's refusal to get involved with the media, precisely how much are Marxist preconceptions themselves to blame? The nostalgic idealism of the infrastructure? The theoretical allergy to everything that isn't "material" production and "productive labor"? "Revolutionary" doctrine has never come to terms with the exchange of signs other than as pragmatically functional use: information, broadcasting, and propaganda. The contemporary new look of left-wing public relations, and the whole modernist party subculture, are hardly designed to transform this tendency. They demonstrate quite sufficiently how bourgeois ideology can be generated independently of "social origin."

All of this, Enzensberger continues, results in a political schizophrenia of the Left. On one side, a whole (subversive) revolutionary faction abandons itself to apolitical exploration of new media (subculture, underground); on the other, militant political groups still live essentially through archaic modes of communication, refusing to "play the game," or to exploit the immense possibilities of the electronic media. Thus, he reproaches the students of May '68 for having regressed to artisanal means (referring to the hand presses of the Ecole des Beaux Arts) for spreading their slogans and for having occupied the Odéon, "steeped in tradition," instead of the ORTF.[8,9]

---

6.Enzensberger, *ibid.,* p. 96.

7.    This genre of reductive determinism may be found in the works of Bourdieu and in the phraseology of the Communist Party. It is theoretically worthless. It turns the *mechanism* of democratization into a revolutionary value per se. That intellectuals may find mass culture repugnant hardly suffices to make it a revolutionary alternative. Aristocrats used to make sour faces at bourgeois culture, but no one ever said the latter was anything more than a class culture.

8.    Most of the above references are to Enzensberger, *op.cit.,* pp. 102-103.

9.    French radio-TV headquarters. The ORTF is a highly centralized state-run monopoly.

Enzensberger attempts to develop an optimistic and offensive
position. The media are monopolized by the dominant classes, which
*divert* them to their own advantage. But the structure of the media
remains "fundamentally egalitarian," and it is up to revolutionary
praxis to disengage this potentiality inscribed in the media, but
perverted by the capitalist order. Let us say the word: to liberate the
media, to return them to their social vocation of open communication and unlimited democratic exchange, their true socialist
destiny.

Clearly what we have here is an extension of the same schema
assigned, since time immemorial, from Marx to Marcuse, to
productive forces and technology: they are the promise of human
fulfillment, but capitalism freezes or confiscates them. They are
liberatory, but it is necessary to liberate them.[10] The media, as we
can see, do not escape this fantastic logic of inscribing the revolution
*inter alia* onto things. To set the media back to the logic of
productive forces no longer qualifies as a critical act, for it only locks
them more firmly into the revolutionary metaphysic.

As usual, this position bogs down in contradictions. Through their
own (capitalist) development, the media assure that socialization is
pushed to more and more advanced stages. Even though it is technically quite imaginable, there is no closed-circuit television for the
happy few who could afford it, "because this would go against the
grain of the structure" of the medium.[11] "For the first time in
history, the media make possible the participation of the masses in a
collective process that is social and socialized, participation in which
the practical means are in the hands of the masses themselves."[12] But
the "socialist movements must fight and will fight for their own wavelengths."[13] Why fight (above all for wavelengths), if the media
realize themselves in socialism? If such is their structural vocation?

The existing order, says Enzensberger following Brecht (*Theory of
Radio,* 1932), reduces the media to a simple "medium of
distribution."[14] So they must be revamped into a true medium of
communication (always the same dream haunts the Marxist
imaginary: strip objects of their exchange value in order to restore
their use value); and this transformation, he adds, "is not technically

10.   Thus we find authority, the state and other institutions either devoid or full up
with revolutionary content, depending on whether they are still in the grip of capital
or the people have taken them over. Their form is rarely questioned.
11.   Enzensberger, *op.cit.,* pp. 105, 108.
12.   *Ibid.,* p. 97.
13.   *Ibid.,* p. 107.
14.   *Ibid.,* pp. 97-98.

a problem." But:

1. It is false that in the present order the media are "purely and simply means of distribution." Once again, that is to treat them as the relay of an ideology that would find its determinations elsewhere (in the mode of material production); in other words, the media as marketing and merchandizing of the dominant ideology. It is from this perspective that the relation media producer-transmitter *versus* irresponsible, receptive masses is assimilated to that of capitalist versus salaried worker. But it is not as vehicles of content, but in their form and very operation, that media induce a social relation; and this is not an exploitative relation: it involves the abstraction, separation and abolition of exchange itself. The media are not *co-efficients,* but *effectors* of ideology. Not only is their destiny far from revolutionary; the media are not even, somewhere else or potentially, neutral or non-ideological (the phantasm of their technical status or of their social use value). Reciprocally, ideology does not exist in some place apart, as the discourse of the dominant class, *before* it is channeled through the media. The same applies to the sphere of commodities: nowhere do the latter possess ontological status independently of the form they take in the operation of the exchange value system. Nor is ideology some Imaginary floating in the wake of exchange value: it is the very operation of exchange value itself. After the *Requiem* for the dialectic, it is necessary to toll the *Requiem* of the infra- and superstructure.

2. It follows that when Brecht and Enzensberger assert that the transformation of the media into a true medium of communication is not technically a problem ("it is nothing more," says Brecht, "than the natural consequence of their technical development"), it is necessary to understand (but, contrarily, and without playing on words) that in effect it is quite correctly *not a technical problem,* since media ideology functions at the level of *form,* at the level of the separation it establishes, which is a *social* division.

## Speech Without Response

The mass media are anti-mediatory and intransitive. They fabricate non-communication — this is what characterizes them, if one agrees to define communication as an exchange, as a reciprocal space of a speech and a response, and thus of a *responsibility* (not a psychological or moral responsibility, but a personal, mutual correlation in exchange). We must understand communication as something other than the simple transmission-reception of a message, whether or not the latter is considered reversible through feedback. Now, the totality of the existing architecture of the media founds itself on this latter definition: *they are what always prevents response*, making all processes of exchange impossible (except in the various forms of response *simulation*, themselves integrated in the transmission process, thus leaving the unilateral nature of the communication intact). This is the real abstraction of the media. And the system of social control and power is rooted in it.

To understand the term *response* properly, we must take it in an emphatic sense, by referring to an equivalent in "primitive" societies: power belongs to the one who can give and *cannot be repaid*. To give, and to do it in such a way that one is unable to repay, is to disrupt the exchange to your profit and to institute a monopoly. The social process is thus thrown out of equilibrium, whereas repaying disrupts this power relationship and institutes (or reinstitutes), on the basis of an antagonistic reciprocity, the circuit of symbolic exchange. The same goes for the media: they speak, or something is spoken there, but in such a way as *to exclude any response anywhere*. This is why the only revolution in this domain — indeed, the revolution everywhere: the revolution *tout court* — lies in restoring this possibility of response. But such a simple possibility presupposes an upheaval in the entire existing structure of the media.

No other theory or strategy is possible. All vague impulses to democratize content, subvert it, restore the "transparency of the code," control the information process, contrive a reversibility of circuits, or take power over media are hopeless — unless the monopoly of speech is broken; and one cannot break the monopoly of speech if one's goal is simply to distribute it equally to everyone. Speech must be able to exchange, give and repay itself [15] as is occasionally the case with looks and smiles. It cannot simply be interrupted, congealed, stockpiled, and redistributed in some corner of the social process. [16]

For the time being, we live in the era of non-response — of irresponsibility. "Minimal autonomous activity on the part of the spectator and voter," says Enzensberger. The mass medium *par excellence,* and the most beautiful of them all, is the electoral system: its crowning achievement is the referendum, where the

---

15.   It is not a question of "dialogue," which is only the functional adjustment of two abstract speeches without response, where the "interlocutors" are never mutually present, but only their stylized discourses.

16.   The occupation of the ORTF changed nothing in itself, even if subversive "contents" were "broadcast." If only those involved had scuttled the ORTF as such, for its entire technical and functional structure reflects the monopolistic use of speech.

response is implied in the question itself, as in the polls. It is a speech that answers itself via the simulated detour of a response, and here as well, the absolutization of speech under the formal guise of exchange is *the* definition of power. Roland Barthes has made note of the same non-reciprocity in literature: "Our literature is characterized by the pitiless divorce which the literary institution maintains between the producer of the text and its user, between its owner and customer, between its author and its reader. This reader is thereby plunged into a kind of idleness — he is intransitive; he is, in short, *serious*: instead of functioning himself, instead of gaining access to the magic of the signifier, to the pleasure of writing, he is left with no more than the poor freedom either to accept or reject the text: reading is nothing more than a *referendum*."[17]

Today, the status of the *consumer* defines this banishment. The generalized order of consumption is nothing other than that sphere where it is no longer permitted to give, to reimburse or to exchange, but only to take and to make use of (appropriation, individualized use value). In this case, consumption goods also constitute a mass medium: they answer to the general state of affairs we have described. Their specific function is of little import: the consumption of products and messages is the abstract social relation that they establish, the ban raised against all forms of response and reciprocity.

Thus, it is far from true that, as Enzensberger affirms, "for the first time in history, the media make possible a mass participation in a productive social process;" nor that "the practical means of this participation are in the hands of the masses themselves." As if owning a TV set or a camera inaugurated a new possibility of relationship and exchange. Strictly speaking, such cases are no more significant than the possession of a refrigerator or a toaster. There is no *response* to a functional object: its function is already there, an integrated speech to which it has already responded, leaving no room for play, or reciprocal *putting in play* (unless one destroys the object, or turns its function inside out).[18] So the functionalized object, like all messages functionalized by the media, like the operation of a referendum, controls rupture, the emergence of meaning, and censorship. As an extreme case, authority would provide every citizen

---

17. Roland Barthes, *S/Z* (New York, 1974), p. 4.
18. Multifunctionality evidently changes nothing on this score. Multifunctionality, multidisciplinarity — polyvalence in all its forms — are just the system's response to its own obsession with centrality and standardization (uni-équivalence). It is the system's reaction to its own pathology, glossing over the underlying logic.

with a TV set without preoccupying itself with programming (assuming an authority that was not also obsessed by content and convinced of the ideological force of media "persuasion," and thus of the need to control the message). It is useless to fantasize about state projection of police control through TV (as Enzensberger has remarked of Orwell's *1984*): TV, by virtue of its mere presence, is a social control in itself. There is no need to imagine it as a state periscope spying on everyone's private life — the situation as it stands is more efficient than that: it is the *certainty that people are no longer speaking to each other*, that they are definitively isolated in the face of a speech without response.

From this perspective, McLuhan, whom Enzensberger scorns as a kind of ventriloquist, is much closer to a theory when he declares that "the medium is the message" (save that, in his total blindness to the social forms discussed here, he exalts the media and their global message with a delirious tribal optimism). *The medium is the message* is not a critical proposition. But in its paradoxical form, it has analytic value,[19] whereas the ingenuity of Enzensberger with regard to the "structural properties of the media" such that "no power can permit the liberation of their potentiality" turns out to be mysticism, although it wants to be revolutionary. The mystique of the socialist predestination of the media is opposite but complementary to the Orwellian myth of their terrorist manipulation by authority. Even God would approve of socialism: Christians say it all the time.

### Subversive Strategy and "Symbolic Action"

It could be objected that the media did, after all, play a significant role in the events of May '68 in France, by spontaneously playing up the revolutionary movement. During at least one moment of the action, they were turned against the power structure. It is through this breach and on the possibility of this reversal that the subversive strategy of the American Yippies (e.g., Hoffman, Rubin) is founded, and on which a theory of "symbolic action" is elaborated in the world revolutionary movements: co-opt the media through their power to chain react; use their power to generalize information instantaneously. The assumption here of course is that the impact of the media

---

19. Enzensberger (pp. 118-119) interprets it this way: "The medium is the message" is a bourgeois proposition. It signifies that the bourgeoisie has nothing left to say. Having no further message to transmit, it plays the card of medium for medium's sake. — If the bourgeoisie has nothing left to say, "socialism" would do better to keep quiet.

is reversible, a variable in the class struggle that one must learn to appropriate. But this position should be questioned, for it is perhaps another rather large strategic illusion.

May '68 will serve well enough as an example. Everything would lead us to believe in the subversive impact of the media during this period. Suburban radio stations and newspapers spread the student action everywhere. If the students were the detonators, the media were the resonators. Furthermore, the authorities quite openly accused the media of "playing the revolutionary game." But this sort of argument has been constructed in the absence of analysis. I would say to the contrary that the media have never discharged their responsibilities with more efficiency, and that, indeed, in their function of *habitual* social control, they were right on top of the action. This is because, beneath the disarray of their routine content, they preserved their form; and this form, regardless of the context, is what inexorably connects them with the system of power. By broadcasting the events in the *abstract universality* of public opinion, they imposed a sudden and inordinate development on the movement of events; and through this forced and anticipated extension, they deprived the original movement of its own rhythm and of its meaning. In a word: they short-circuited it.

In the sphere of traditional politics (left- or right-wing),[20] where sanctified models and a kind of canonical speech are exchanged, the media are able to transmit without distorting the meanings intended. They are homogeneous with this kind of speech, as they are with the circulation of the commodity. But transgression and subversion never get "on the air" without being subtly negated as they are: transformed into models, neutralized into signs, they are eviscerated of their meaning.[21] There is no model of transgression, prototypical or serial. Hence, there is no better way to reduce it than to administer

---

20. This left-right distinction is just about meaningless from the point of view of the media. We should give credit where credit is due and grant them the honor of having contributed largely to its elimination. The distinction is interconnected with an order characterized by the *transcendence* of politics, and has nothing to do with what has announced itself in all sorts of forms as the *transversality* of politics. But let us not mistake ourselves, here: the media only help to liquidate this transcendence of politics in order to substitute their own transcendence, abstracted from the mass media form, which is thoroughly integrated and no longer even offers a conflictive structure (left-right). Mass media transcendence is thus reductive of the traditional transcendence of politics, but it is even more reductive of the new transversality of politics.

21. This form of so-called "disclosure" or "propagation" can be analyzed readily in the fields of science or art. Generalized reproducibility obliterates the processes of work and meaning so as to leave nothing but modelized contents (cf. Raoul Ergmann, "Le miroir en miettes," *Diogene*, no. 68, 1969; Baudouin Jurdant, "La vulgarisation scientifique," *Communications*, no. 14).

it a mortal dose of publicity. Originally, this process might have left
one impressed with the possibility of "spectacular" results. In fact, it
was tantamount to dismantling the movement by depriving it of its
own momentum. The act of rupture was transformed into a
bureaucratic model at a distance — and such, in fact, is the ordinary
labor of the media.[22]

All of this can be read from the derivation and distortion of the
term "symbolic" itself. The action of March 22 at Nanterre was
symbolic because it was transgressive: at a given time in a given
place, an act of radical rupture was invented — or, to resume the
analysis proposed above, a particular response was invented there,
where the institutions of administrative and pedagogical power were
engaged in a private *oratoria* and functioned precisely to interdict
any answer. The fact of mass media diffusion and contagion had
nothing to do with the symbolic quality of the action. However,
today it is precisely this interpretation, stressing the imapct of
disclosure, which suffices to define symbolic action. At the extreme,
the subversive act is no longer produced *except as a function of its
reproducibility.*[23] It is no longer created, it is produced directly as a
*model,* like a gesture. The symbolic has slipped from the order of the
very production of meaning to that of its *re*production, which is
always the order of power. The symbolic becomes its own coefficient,
pure and simple, and transgression is turned into exchange value.

---

22.   It should be pointed out that this labor is always accompanied by one of selection and reinterpretation at the level of the membership group (Lazarsfeld's *two-step
flow of communication*). This accounts for the highly relative impact of media contents, and the many kinds of resistance they provoke. (However we should ask ourselves
whether these resistances are not aimed at the abstraction of the medium itself, rather
than its contents: Lazarsfeld's double articulation would lead us to this conclusion,
since the second articulation belongs to the network of *personal* relations, opposed to
the generality of media messages.) Still, this "second" reading, where the membership
group opposes its own code to the transmitter's (cf. my discussion of Umberto Eco's
thesis towards the end of this article) certainly doesn't neutralize or "reduce" the
dominant ideological contents of the media in the same way as it does the critical or
subversive contents. To the extent that the dominant ideological contents (cultural
models, value systems, imposed without alternative or response; bureaucratic contents) are homogeneous with the general form of the mass media (non-reciprocity, irresponsibility), and are integrated with this form in reduplicating it, they are, so to
speak, overdetermined, and have greater impact. They "go over" better than subversive *contents.* But this is not the essence of the problem. It is more important to recognize that the *form* of transgression never "comes off" more or less well on the media: it
is radically denied by the mass media form.

23.   Thus, for Walter Benjamin, the reproduced work becomes more and more the
work "designed" *for reproducibility.* In this way, according to him, the work of art
graduates from ritual to politics. "Exhibition value" revolutionizes the work of art
and its functions.  Walter Benjamin, "The Work of Art in the Age of Mechanical Reproduction," *Illuminations* (New York: Schocken, 1968).

Rationalist critical thought (i.e., Benjamin, Brecht, Enzens-berger) sees this as a sign of decisive progress. The media simply actualize and reinforce the "demonstrative nature of no matter which political act" (Enzensberger). This evidently conforms with the *didactic* conception of the revolution and further with the "dialectic of coming to consciousness," etc. This tradition has yet to renounce the bourgeois Enlightenment. It has inherited all its ideas about the democratic (here revolutionary) virtues of spreading light (broad-casting). The pedagogical illusion of this position overlooks that — in aiming its own political acts at the media, and awaiting the moment to assume the media's mantle of power — the media themselves are in deliberate pursuit of the political act, in order to depoliticize it.

An interesting fact might be cited here as support: the contemporary eruption of tabloid trivia and natural disaster in the political sphere (which converges with Benjamin's notion of the graduation of the art object to the political stage by virtue of its reproducibility). There is a tidal wave in Pakistan, a black title fight in the U.S.; a youth is shot by a bistro owner, etc. These sorts of events, once minor and apolitical, suddenly find themselves invested with a power of diffusion that lends them a social and "historic" aura. New forms of political action have crystallized around this conflictualization of incidents that were hitherto consigned to the social columns. There is no doubt that, to a large extent, the new meanings they have taken on are largely the doing of the media. Such *faits divers* are like undeliberated "symbolic actions," but they take part in the same process of political signification. Doubtless, their reception is ambiguous and mixed; and if, thanks to the media, the political re-emerges under the category of *faits divers*, thanks to the same media the category of *faits divers* has totally invaded politics. Furthermore, it has changed status with the extension of the mass media: from a parallel category (descended from almanacs and popular chronicles), it has evolved into a total system of mythological interpretation, a closed system of models of signification from which no event escapes. Mass mediatization: that is its quintessence. It is no ensemble of techniques for broadcasting messages; it is the *imposition of models*. McLuhan's formula is worth re-examining here: "The medium is the message" operates a transfer of meaning onto the medium itself qua technological structure. Again we are confronted with technological idealism. In fact, the essential Medium is the Model. What is mediatized is not what comes off the daily press, out of the tube, or on the radio: it is what is reinterpreted by the sign form, articulated into models, and administered by the code (just as the commodity is not what is produced industrially, but what is mediatized by the exchange value system of abstraction). At best, what can occur under the aegis of the media is a formal surpassing of the categories of *faits divers* and politics, and of their traditional separation, but only the better to assign them together to the same general code. It is strange that no one has tried to measure the strategic import of this forced socialization as a system of social control. Once again, the first great historical example of this was the electoral system. And it has never lacked revolutionaries (formerly among the greatest, today the least significant) who believed they could "do it" within the system. The general strike itself, this insurrectional myth of so many generations, has become a schematic reducing agent. That of May '68, to which the media significantly contributed by exporting the strike to all corners of France, was in appearance the culminating point of the crisis. In fact, it was the moment of its decompression, of its asphyxiation by extension, and of its defeat. To be sure, millions of workers went on strike. But no one knew what to do with this "mediatized" strike, transmitted and received as a model of action (whether via the media or the unions). Reduced to a single meaning, it neutralized the local, transversal, spontaneous forms of action (though not all). The Grenelle accords[24] hardly betrayed this tendency. They sanctioned *this passage to the generality of political action, which puts an end to the singularity of revolutionary action.* Today it has become (in the form of the calculated extension of the strike) the absolute weapon of the unions against wildcat strikes.

So far the electoral system and the general strike are also media, after a fashion. Playing on extensive formal socialization, they are the subtlest and stealthiest institutions of filtration, dismantling and censorship. They are neither exceptions, nor miracles.

The real revolutionary media during May were the walls and their speech, the silk-screen posters and the hand-painted notices, the street where speech began and was exchanged — everything that was an *immediate* inscription, given and returned, spoken and answered, mobile in the same space and time, reciprocal and antagonistic. The street is, in this sense, the alternative and subversive form of the mass media, since it isn't, like the latter, an objectified support for answerless messages, a transmission system at a distance. It is the

---

24.    The Grenelle accords were worked out between Georges Séguy of the CGT and Georges Pompidou during the May '68 general strike. Although the monetary concessions involved were fairly broad, they missed the point, and were massively rejected by workers.   — *Trans.*

frayed space of the symbolic exchange of speech — ephemeral, mortal: a speech that is not reflected on the Platonic screen of the media. Institutionalized by reproduction, reduced to a spectacle, this speech is expiring.

It is a strategic illusion to have any faith in the critical reversal of the media. A comparable speech can emerge only from the destruction of the media such as they are — through their deconstruction as systems of non-communication. Their liquidation does not follow from this, any more than the radical critique of discourse implies the negation of language as signifying material. But it certainly does imply the liquidation of the existing functional and technical structure of the media — of their operational form, so to speak — which *in toto* reflects their social form. At the limit, to be sure, it is the very concept of medium that disappears — and must disappear: speech exchanged dissolves the idea and function of the medium, and of the intermediary, as does symbolic land reciprocal exchange. It can involve a technical apparatus (sound, image, waves, energy, etc.) as well as a corporeal one (gestures, language, sexuality), but in this case, it no longer acts as a *medium*, as an autonomous system administered by the code. Reciprocity comes into being through the destruction of mediums per se. "People meet their neighbors for the first time while watching their apartment houses burn down."[25]

## The Theoretical Model of Communication

Let us summarize the various hypotheses:

1. McLuhan (for memory's sake): The media make — indeed, they are — the revolution, independently of their content, by virtue of their technological structure alone. After the phonetic alphabet and the printed book comes the radio and the cinema. After radio, television. We live, here and now, in the age of instantaneous, global communication.

2. The media are controlled by power. The imperative is to strip them of it, whether by taking the media over, or reversing them by outbidding the spectacle with subversive content. Here, the media are envisioned as pure message. Their form is never called into question (any more than it is, in fact, by McLuhan, who views the medium only in its aspect as medium).

3. Enzensberger: the present form of the media induces a certain type of social relation (assimilative to that of the capitalist mode of production). But the media contain, by virtue of their structure and

---

25. Jerry Rubin, *Do It* (New York: Simon and Schuster), p. 234.

development, an immanent socialist and democratic mode of communication, an immanent rationality and universality of information. It suffices to liberate this potential.

We are only interested in Enzensberger's hypothesis (enlightened Marxist) and that of the radical American Left (leftists of the spectacle). The practice of the official Left, Marxist or otherwise, which is confounded with that of the bourgeoisie, will be left out of account here. We have analyzed these positions as *strategic illusions*. The cause of this failure is that both share with the dom nant ideology the implicit reference to the same *communication theory*. This theory is accepted practically everywhere, strengthened by received evidence and a (highly scientific) formalization by one discipline, the semio-linguistics of communication, supported on one side by structural linguistics, by information theory on the other, swallowed whole by the universities and by mass culture in general (the mass mediators are its connoisseurs). The entire conceptual infrastructure of this theory is ideologically connected with dominant practice, as was and still is that of classical political economy. It *is* the equivalent of this political economy in the field of communications. And I think that if revolutionary practice has bogged down in this strategic illusion *vis-à-vis* the media, it is because critical analyses have been superficial and fallen short of radically identifying the ideological matrix that communication theory embraces.

Formalized most notably by Roman Jakobsen, its underlying unity is based on the following sequence:

TRANSMITTER — MESSAGE — RECEIVER
(ENCODER — MESSAGE — DECODER)

The message itself is structured by the code and determined by the context. A specific function corresponds to each of these "concepts": the referential, poetic, phatic, etc. [26] Each communication process is thus vectorized into a single meaning, from the transmitter to the receiver: the latter can become transmitter in its turn, and the same schema is reproduced. Thus communication can always be reduced to this simple unity in which the two polar terms are mutually exclusive. This structure is given as objective and scientific, since it follows the methodological rule of decomposing its object into simple elements. In fact, it is satisfied with an empirical given, an abstraction from lived experience and reality: that is, the ideological categories that express a certain type of social relation, namely, in

---

26. See Roman Jakobsen, "Closing Statement: Linguistics and Poetics," in T.A. Sebeok, ed., *Style in Language* (Cambridge, Mass: M.I.T. Press, 1960), pp. 350-377.

which one speaks and the other doesn't, where one has the choice of the code, and the other only liberty to acquiesce or abstain. This structure is based on the same arbitrariness as that of signification (i.e., the arbitrariness of the sign): two terms are artificially isolated and artificially reunited by an objectified content called a message. There is neither reciprocal relation nor simultaneous mutual presence of the two terms, [27] since each determines itself in its relation to the message or code, the "intermedium" that maintains both in a respective situation (it is the code that holds both in "respect"), at a distance from one another, a distance that seals the full and autonomized "value" of the message (in fact, its exchange value). This "scientific" construction is rooted in a *simulation model* of communication. It excludes, from its inception, the reciprocity and antagonism of interlocutors, and the ambivalence of their exchange. What really circulates is information, a semantic content that is assumed to be legible and univocal. The agency of the code guarantees this univocality, and by the same token the respective positions of encoder and decoder. So far so good: the formula has a formal coherence that assures it as the only *possible* schema of communication. But as soon as one posits ambivalent relations, it all collapses. There is no code for ambivalence; and without a code, no more encoder, no more decoder: the extras flee the stage. Even a message becomes impossible, since it would, after all, have to be defined as "emitted" and "received." It is as if the entire formalization exists only to avert this catastrophe. And therein resides its "scientific" status. What it underpins, in fact, is the terrorism of the code. In this guiding schema, the code becomes the only agency that speaks, that exchanges itself and reproduces through the dissociation of the two terms and the univocality (or equivocality, or multivocality — it hardly matters: through the non-ambivalence) of the message. (Likewise, in the process of economic exchange, it is no longer people who exchange; the system of exchange value reproduces itself through them). So, this basic communication formula succeeds in giving us, as a reduced model, a perfect epitome of social exchange *such as it is* — such as, at any rate, the abstraction of the code, the forced rationality and terrorism of separation regulate it. So much for scientific objectivity.

The schema of separation and closure already operates, as we have noted, at the level of the sign, in linguistic theory. Each sign is

---

27. The two terms are so faintly present to each other that it has proven necessary to create a "contact" category to reconstitute the totality theoretically!

divided into a signifier and a signified, which are mutually appointed, but held in "respective" position: and from the depths of its arbitrary isolation, each sign "communicates" with all the others through a code called a language. Even here, a scientific injunction is invoked against the immanent possibility of the terms exchanging amongst each other symbolically, beyond the signifier-signified distinction — in poetic language, for example. In the latter, as in symbolic exchange, the terms *respond* to each other beyond the code. It is this response that we have marked out during the entire essay as ultimately deconstructive of all codes, of all control and power, which always base themselves on the separation of terms and their abstract articulation.

Thus the theory of signification serves as a nuclear model for communication theory, and the arbitrariness of the sign (that theoretical schema for the repression of meaning) takes on its political and ideological scope in the arbitrariness of the theoretical schema of communication and information. As we have seen, all of this is echoed, not only in the dominant social practice (characterized by the virtual monopoly of the transmission pole and the, irresponsibility of the receiving pole, the discrimination between the terms of the exchange and the *diktat* of the code), but also in all the velleities of revolutionary media practice. For example, it is clear that those who aim to subvert media content only reinforce the autonomy of the message as a separated notion, and thus the abstract bipolarity of the term(inal)s of communication.

## The Cybernetic Illusion

Sensible of the non-reciprocity of the existing process, Enzensberger believes that the situation can be mitigated by insisting that the same revolution intervene at the level of the media that once disoriented the exact sciences and the epistemological subject-object relation, which has been engaged in continuous "dialectical" interreaction ever since. The media would have to take into account all the consequences of interreaction, whose effect is to breach monopoly and permit everyone's integration in an open process. "The programs of the consciousness industry must subsume into themselves their own results, the reactions and the corrections that they call forth. . . . They are therefore to be thought of not as means of consumption but as means of their own production."[28] Now, this seductive perspective leaves the separated agency of the code and the message intact while it attempts, instead, to break down the

---

28.   Enzensberger, *op.cit.*, pp. 119, 127.

discrimination of the two poles of communication toward a more supple structure of role exchange and feedbac ("reversibility of circuits"). "In its present form, equipment like television or film does not serve communication but prevents it. It allows no reciprocal action between transmitter and receiver; technically speaking, it reduces feedback to the lowest point compatible with the system."[29] Again, we fail to get beyond the categories of receiver and transmitter, whatever may be the effort to mobilize them through "switching." *Reversibility* has nothing to do with reciprocity. Doubtless it is for this deeper reason that cybernetic systems today understand perfectly well how to put this complex regulation and feedback to work without affecting the abstraction of the process as a whole or allowing any real "responsibility" in exchange. This is indeed the system's surest line of defense, since it thus integrates the contingency of any such response in advance.

As Enzensberger has demonstrated in his critique of the Orwellian myth, it no longer makes sense to conceive a megasystem of centralized control (a monitoring system for the telephone network would have to exceed it $n$ times in size and complexity; hence, it is practically excluded). But it is a little naive to assume that the fact of media extension thus eliminates censorship. Even over the long haul, the impracticality of police megasystems simply means that present systems will integrate these otherwise useless metasystems of control by means of feedback and autoregulation. They know how to introduce what negates them *as supplementary variables*. Their very operation is censorship: megasystems are hardly required. Hence they do not cease to be totalitarian: in a way, they realize the ideal one might refer to as decentralized totalitarianism.

On a more practical level, the media are quite aware how to set up formal "reversibility" of circuits (letters to the editor, phone-in programs, polls, etc.), without conceding any response or abandoning in any way the discrimination of roles.[30] This is the social and political form of feedback. Thus, Enzensberger's "dialectization" of communication is oddly related to cybernetic regulation. Ultimately, he is the victim, though in a more subtle

29. *Ibid.*, p. 97.
30. Once again Enzensberger, who analyses and denounces these control circuits, nevertheless links up with idealism: "Naturally [!] such tendencies go against the grain of the structure, and the new productive forces not only permit, but indeed demand [!] their reversal." (*Ibid,* p. 108.) Feedback and interaction are the very logic of cybernetics. Underestimating the ability of the system to integrate its own revolutionary innovations is as delusory as underestimating the capacity of capitalism to develop the productive forces.

fashion, of the ideological model we have been discussing.

From the same perspective, Enzensberger would break down the unilateral character of communication, which translates simultaneously into the monopoly of specialists and professionals and that of the class enemy over the media, by proposing, as a revolutionary solution, that *everyone become a manipulator,* in the sense of active operator, producer, etc., in brief, move from receiver status to that of producer-transmitter. Here is a sort of critical reversal of the ideological concept of manipulation. But again, because this "revolution" at bottom conserves the category of transmitter, which it is content to generalize as separated, transforming everyone into his own transmitter, it fails to place the mass media system in check. We know the results of such phenomena as mass ownership of walkie-talkies, or everyone making their own cinema: a kind of personalized amateurism, the equivalent of Sunday tinkering on the periphery of the system.[31]

Of course, this isn't at all what Enzensberger has in mind. He is thinking of a press edited, distributed and worked by its own readers (as is the underground press, in part), of video systems at the disposal of political groups, and so on.

This would be the only way to unfreeze a blocked situation: "In the socialist movements the dialectic of discipline and spontaneity, centralism and decentralization, authoritarian leadership and anti-authoritarian disintegration has long ago reached a deadlock. Networklike communications models built on the principle of reversibility of circuits might give new indications of how to overcome this situation."[32] Thus it is a question of reconstituting a dialectical practice. But can the problem continue to be posed in dialectical terms? Isn't it the dialectic itself which has reached the moment of deadlock?

The examples Enzensberger gives are interesting precisely in that they go beyond a "dialectic" of transmitter and receiver. In effect, an immediate communication process is rediscovered, one not filtered through bureaucratic models — an original form of exchange, in fact, because there are *neither transmitters, nor receivers,* but only people responding to each other. The problem of spontaneity and organization is not overcome dialectically here: its terms are *transgressed.*

---

31.   Evoking the possibility of an open free press, Enzensberger points to the Xerox monopoly and their exorbitant rental rates. But if everyone had his own Xerox — or even his own wavelength — the problem would remain. The real monopoly is never that of technical means, but of speech.

32.   Enzensberger, *op. cit.,* p. 110.

There is the essential difference: the other hypotheses allow the dichotomized categories to subsist. In the first case (media on the private scale), transmitter and receiver are simply reunited in a single individual: manipulation is, after a fashion, "interiorized."[33] In the other case (the "dialectic of circuits"), transmitter and receiver are simultaneously on both sides: manipulation becomes reciprocal (hermaphroditic grouping). The system can play these two variations as easily as it can the classic bureaucratic model. It can play on all their possible combinations. The only essential is that these two ideological categories be safe, and with them the fundamental structure of the political economy of communication.

To repeat, in the symbolic exchange relation, there is a simultaneous response. There is no transmitter or receiver on both sides of a message: nor, for that matter, is there any longer any "message," any corpus of information to decode univocally under the aegis of a code. The symbolic consists precisely in breaching the univocality of the "message," in restoring the ambivalence of meaning and in demolishing in the same stroke the agency of the code.

All of this should be helpful in assessing Umberto Eco's hypothesis.[34] To summarize his position: changing the contents of the message serves no purpose; it is necessary to modify the reading codes, to impose other interpretive codes. The receiver (who in fact isn't really one) intervenes here at the most essential level — he opposes his own code to that of the transmitter, he invents a true response by escaping the trap of controlled communication. But what does this "subversive" reading actually amount to? Is it still a reading, that is, a deciphering, a disengaging of a univocal meaning? And what is this code that opposes? Is it a unique minicode (an ideolect, but thus without interest)? Or is it yet another controlling schema of interpretation, rising from the ashes of the previous one? Whatever the case, it is only a question of textual variation. One example can illustrate Eco's perspective: the graffiti reversal of advertising after May '68. Graffiti is transgressive, not because it substitutes another content, another discourse, but simply because it responds, there, on the spot, and breaches the fundamental role of non-response enunciated by all the media. Does it oppose one code to

---

33.   This is why the *individual* amateur cameraman remains within the separated abstraction of *mass* communication: through this internal dissociation of the two agencies (instances), the entire code and all of the dominant models sweep in, and seize his activity from behind.

34.   Umberto Eco, *La Struttura assente* (Milan: Bompiani, 1968).

another? I don't think so: it simply smashes the code. It doesn't lend itself to deciphering as a text rivaling commercial discourse; it presents itself as a transgression. So, for example, the witticism, which is a transgressive reversal of discourse, does not act on the basis of another code as such; it works through the instantaneous deconstruction of the dominant discursive code. It volatilizes the category of the code, and that of the message.

This, then, is the key to the problem: by trying to preserve (even as one "dialectically transcends" them) *any separated instances of the structural communication grid*, one obviates the possibility of fundamental change, and condemns oneself to fragile manipulatory practices that would be dangerous to adopt as a "revolutionary strategy." What is strategic in this sense is only what radically checkmates the dominant form.

# CHAPTER TEN

# DESIGN AND ENVIRONMENT
## or
## HOW POLITICAL ECONOMY
## ESCALATES INTO CYBERBLITZ

Not all cultures produce objects: the concept is peculiar to ours, born of the industrial revolution. Yet even industrial society knows only the *product,* not the *object.* The object only begins truly to exist at the time of its formal liberation as a sign function, and this liberation only results from the mutation of this properly industrial society into what could be called our techno-culture, [1] from the passage out of a *metallurgic* into a *semiurgic* society. That is to say, the object only appears when the problem of its finality of meaning, of its status as message and as sign (of its mode of signification, of communication and of sign exchange) begins to be posed beyond its status as product and as commodity (beyond the mode of production, of circulation and of economic exchange). This mutation is roughed out during the 19th century, but the Bauhaus solidifies is theoretically. So it is from the Bauhaus' inception that we can logically date the "revolution of the object."

It is not a question of simple extension and differentiation, however extraordinary, of the field of products on account of industrial development. It is a question of a mutation of status. Before the Bauhaus there were, properly speaking, no objects; subsequently, and according to an irreversible logic, everything potentially participates in the category of objects and will be produced as such. That is why any empirical classification (Abraham Moles, etc.) is ludicrous. To wonder whether or not a house or a piece of clothing is an object, to wonder where the object begins, where it leaves off in order to become a building, etc. — all this descriptive typology is fruitless. For the object is not a thing, nor even a category; it is a status of meaning and a form. Before the logical advent of this object form, nothing is an object, not even the everyday utensils — thereafter, everything is, the building as well as the coffee spoon or the entire city. It is the Bauhaus that institutes this universal semantization of the environment in which everything becomes the object of a calculus of function and of signification. Total functionality, total semiurgy. It is a "revolution" in relation to

---

1. Echoing Galbraith's "techno-structure." Neo-capitalist, neo-industrialist, post-industrial: many terms can designate this passage from an industrial political economy to a *trans*-political economy (or *meta*-political economy).

the traditional mode, in which objects (for lack of a better word) are bound together and not liberated, have no status of their own and do not form a system among themselves on the basis of a rational finality (functionality).

This functionality inaugurated by the Bauhaus defines itself as a double movement of analysis and rational synthesis of forms (not only industrial, but environmental and social in general). It is a synthesis of form and function, of "beauty and utility," of art and technology. Beyond "style" and its caricatured version in "styling," the commercial kitsch of the 19th century and the modern style, the Bauhaus projects the basis of a rational conception of environmental totality for the first time. Beyond the genres (architecture, painting, furnishings, etc.), beyond "art" and its academic sanction, it extends the aesthetic to the entire everyday world; at the same time it is all of technique in the service of everyday life. The possibility of a "universal semiotic of technological experience"[2] is in effect born of the abolition of the segregation between the beautiful and the useful. Or again from another angle: the Bauhaus tries to reconcile the social and technical infrastructure installed by the industrial revolution with the superstructure of forms and meanings. In wishing to fulfill technology (*la technique*) in the finality of meaning (the aesthetic), the Bauhaus presents itself as a second revolution, the crowning perfection of the industrial revolution, resolving all the contradictions that the latter had left behind it.

The Bauhaus is neither revolutionary nor utopian. Just as the industrial revolution marked the birth of a field of political economy, of a systematic and rational theory of material production, so the Bauhaus marks the *theoretical extension of this field of political economy* and the practical extension of the system of exchange value to the whole domain of signs, forms and objects. At the level of the mode of signification and in the name of *design*, it is a mutation analogous to that which has taken place since the 16th century on the level of the mode of material production and under the aegis of political economy. The Bauhaus marks the point of departure of a veritable *political economy of the sign*.

The same general schema emerges: on the one hand, nature and human labor are disengaged from their archaic constraints, liberated as productive forces and as objects of a *rational calculus of production*. On the other, the whole environment becomes a

---

2. Jeremy J. Schapiro, "One Dimensionality: The Universal Semiotic of Technological Experience," in Paul Breines, ed., *Critical Interruptions* (New York: Herder & Herder, 1970).

signifier, objectified as an element of signification. Functionalized and liberated from all traditional implications (religious, magical, symbolic), it becomes the object of a rational calculus of signification.

## The Operation of the Sign

Behind the transparency of the object in relation to its function, behind that universal moral law imposed upon it in the name of design, behind that functional equation, that new "economy" of the object that immediately adopts aesthetic value, behind the general scheme of synthesis (art-technique, form-function), a whole labor of dissociation and abstract restructuration in fact takes place:

1. The dissociation of every complex subject-object relation into simple, analytic, rational elements that can be recombined in functional ensembles and which then take on status as the environment. For it is only on that basis that man is separated from something he calls the environment, and confronted with the task of controlling it. Ever since the 18th century the concept of nature has emerged as a *productive force to be mastered*. That of the environment only shifts it and intensifies it to mean a *mastery of signs*.

2. A generalized division of labor at the level of objects. Analytic fragmentation into 14 or 97 functions, an identical technical response reuniting several functions of the same object, or the same function in several objects, etc. — in short, the whole analytic grid that permits disassembling and reassembling an ensemble.

3. Even more fundamental is the semiological (dis)articulation of the object, from which the latter takes on the force of a sign. And when we say that it becomes a sign, it is according to the strictest definition; it is articulated into a "signifier" and a "signified," it becomes the signifier of a rational, objectifiable "signified" that is its function. This differs sharply from the traditional symbolic relation, where things have meaning, but a meaning that does not come to them from an objective "signified" to which they refer as "signifier." Such, in contrast, is the modern status of the sign-object, which in this respect obeys the linguistic schema: "functionalized" means also "structuralized," that is to say, split into two terms. Design emerges simultaneously as the project of their ideal articulation and the aesthetic of resolution of their equation. For aesthetic is nothing other than that which, as if by excess, seals this *operational semiology*.

In fact, aesthetics in the modern sense of the term no longer has anything to do with the categories of beauty and ugliness. Critics, the public and designers all mix up the two terms beauty and aesthetic value indiscriminately, but they are logically incompatible (the confusion is strategic: in a system dominated by fashion, that is, by sign exchange value, it allows the conservation of the aura of a pre-industrial value, that of style).

A thousand contradictory definitions of beauty and of style are possible. One thing is certain: they are never a calculus of signs. They come to an end with the system of functional aesthetics, as the earlier modes of economic exchange (barter, gift exchange) perished with the rise of capitalism, and with the institution of a rational calculus of production and exchange. The category of the aesthetic succeeds that of beauty (liquidating it) as the semiological order succeeds the symbolic order. Contemporary aesthetics, once the theory of the forms of beauty, has become the theory of a generalized compatibility of signs, of their internal coherence (signifier-signified) and of their syntax. Aesthetic value connotes the internal functionality of an ensemble, it qualifies the (eventually mobile) equilibrium of a system of signs. It simply translates the fact that its elements *communicate* amongst themselves according to the economy of a model, with maximal integration and minimal loss of information (a harmonized interior in the tonality of blue, or "playing" upon the blues and greens; the crystalloid structures of the residential ensemble; the "naturalness" of "green spaces"). The aesthetic is thus no longer a value of style or of content; it no longer refers to anything but to communication and sign exchange. It is an idealized semiology, or a semiological idealism.[3]

In the symbolic order of style frolics a forever unresolved ambivalence — but the semio-aesthetic order is one of operational resolution, of an interplay of referrals, of equivalence and of controlled dissonances. An "aesthetic" ensemble is a mechanism without lapses, without fault, in which nothing compromises the interconnection of the elements and the transparency of the process: that famous absolute *legibility* of signs and messages — the common ideal of all manipulators of codes, whether they be cyberneticians or designers. This aesthetic order is a cold order. Functional perfection exercises a cold seduction, the functional satisfaction of a demonstration and an algebra. It has nothing to do with pleasure, with beauty (or horror), whose nature is conversely to rescue us from the demands of rationality and to plunge us once more into an

3. As early as 1902 Bernadetto Croce was writing an "Aesthetic as Science of Expression and *General Linguistic*".

absolute childhood (not into an ideal transparency, but into the illegible ambivalence of desire).

This operation of the sign, this analytic dissociation into the functional duo signifier-signified, always caught in an ideological scheme of synthesis, is found even in the key concepts of design. It is at the bottom of all the current systems of signification (media, political, etc.), just as the operational bifurcation use value-exchange value is at the foundation of the commodity form and of the whole of political economy.[4] All possible valences of an object, all its ambivalence, which cannot be reduced to any model, are reduced by design to two rational components, two general models — utility and the aesthetic — which design isolates and artificially opposes to one another. It is useless to emphasize the hot-housing (*le forçage*) of meaning, the arbitrariness of circumscribing it by these two restrained finalities. In fact, they form only a single one: they are two dissociated forms of the same rationality, sealed by the same system of values. But this artificial separation then permits evoking their reunification as an ideal scheme. Utility is separated from the aesthetic, they are *named* separately (for neither has any reality other than *being named separately*), then they are ideally reunited and all contradictions are resolved by this magical operation. Now, the two equally arbitrary agencies exist only to mislead. The real problem, the real contradictions are at the level of form, of sign exchange value; but it is precisely these that are obscured by the operation. Such is the ideological function of design: with the concept of the "functional aesthetic," it proposes a model of reconciliation, of formal surpassing of specialization (division of labor at the level of objects) by a universally enveloping value. Thus it imposes a social scheme of integration by the elimination of real structures. The functional aesthetic that conjugates two abstractions is thus itself no more than a superabstraction that consecrates the system of sign exchange value by delineating the utopia behind which the latter dissimulates. The operation of the sign, the separation of signs, is something as fundamental, as profoundly *political,* as the division of labor. Bauhaus theory, like semiology, ratifies this operation and the resultant division of labor of meaning, in the same way that political economy sanctifies economic separation as such, and the material division of labor that flows from it.

The term design must be given all its etymological scope. It can be unfolded in three senses: sketch (*dessin*), plan (*dessein*), and design

---

4.  But this fundamental operation of *form* is what is never mentioned, in either case.

(*design*). In all three cases one finds a scheme of rational abstraction: graphic for the sketch, reflexive and psychological for the plan (conscious projection of an objective) and more generally, for design: passage to sign status, sign-operation, reduction and rationalization into sign elements, transfer to the sign function.

From the beginning, this process of signification is systematic: the sign never exists apart from a code and a language. Thus, the semiotic revolution (as in its time the industrial revolution) concerns virtually all possible practices. Arts and crafts, forms and techniques both plastic and graphic (keeping to domains that have obvious affinity with design, but once again the term goes far beyond the plastic and architectural), which until then were singular and distinct, are synchronized, and homogenized according to the same model. Objects, forms, and materials that until then spoke their own group dialect, which only emerged from a dialectical practice or an original style, now begin to be thought of and written out in the same tongue, the rational esperanto of design.[5] Once functionally liberated, they begin to make signs, in both sense of the phrase (and without a pun): that is, they simultaneously *become* signs and communicate among themselves. Their unity is no longer that of a style or practice, it is that of a system. In other words, as soon as the object is caught up in the structural rationality of the sign (cloven into a signifier and signified), it is simultaneously hooked into a functional syntax (like the morpheme in a syntagm), and assigned to the same general code (like the morpheme in a language). The whole rationality of the linguistic system regains possession of it. On the other hand, if we speak mainly of "structural" linguistics and of the "functionalism" of design, it must be seen that:

1. If the structural vision (signifier-signified, language-speech) is imposed in linguistics it results from, and is contemporaneous with, a purely functionalist vision of language (strictly finalized as a method of communication). The two are the same thing.

2. With "design," objects are also born simultaneously to functionality and to sign status. In the same instant, this restrained and

---

5. In his own way, using Marcusian terms, Schapiro (*op. cit.*) gives a similar analysis, but with more stress on machinery and technology: "The evolution of modern design is an essential component of the process of one-dimensionality (and indeed serves as an index of the latter's temporal development), since it derives from the machine process the forms for creating a total (totalitarian) environment in which technological experience defines and closes the experiential and aesthetic universe" (p. 161). Totalizing abstraction, undimensional homogeneity, certainly, but the machine or technology are neither the *causes* of this process nor its original models. Technological mutation and semio-linguistic mutation (passage to the abstraction of the code) are the two concurrent aspects of the same passage to structural-functional rationality.

rational finality assigns them to structural rationality. Function and structure involve the same "revolution." This means that functional "liberation" amounts to nothing more than being assigned to a code and a system. Once again, the homology is immediately visible in the liberation of labor (or of leisure, or of the body, etc.), which is never more than their assignment to the system of exchange value.

Let us summarize the essential characteristics of the homology (of the same logical process, even if they are separated chronologically) between the emergence of a political economy of the sign and that of political economy (of material production):

1. Political economy: Under the cover of utility (needs, use value, etc., the anthropological reference of all economic rationality), it institutes a coherent logical system, a calculus of productivity in which all production is resolved into simple elements, in which all products are equivalent in their abstraction. This is the logic of the commodity and the system of exchange value.

2. The political economy of the sign: Under the cover of functionality (objective finality, homologous to utility), it institutes a certain mode of signification in which all the surrounding signs act as simple elements in a logical calculus and refer to each other within the framework of the system of sign exchange value.

In the two cases, use value (utility) and functionality, the one given as final reference of political economy, the other of design, serve in fact only as the concrete alibi for the same process of abstraction. Under the pretext of producing maximal utility, the process of political economy generalizes the system of exchange value. Under the pretext of maximizing the functionality of objects (their legibility as meaning and message, that is in the end their use value as sign), design and the Bauhaus generalize the system of sign exchange value.

Just as a product's utility, unattainable when no coherent theory of needs is capable of establishing it, is revealed to be simply its utility for the system of exchange value — so an object's functionality, illegible as a concrete value, no longer qualifies anything other than the coherence of this sign-object with all the others, its commuta-bility and thus its functional adaptation to the system of sign exchange value. Thus the functionality of an object (of a line, of a form) in an oblique architecture is not to be useful or equilibrated, but to be oblique (or vertical by contrast). It is the coherence of the system that defines the aesthetic-functional value of the elements, and this value is an exchange value insofar as it always refers to a model as general equivalent (same abstraction as for economic exchange value).

It is no accident if this homology is even reflected on the ethical level. Like the capitalist revolution that instituted the "spirit of enterprise" and the basis of political economy as early as the 16th century, the Bahaus' revolution is *puritan*. Functionalism is ascetic. This fact is revealed in the sobreity and geometric lines of its models, its phobia of décor and artifice, in short, in the economy of its discourse. But this is only what one might call the writing effect (which moreover has once again become a rhetoric like any other) of the fundamental doctrine: that of rationality in which the functional liberation of the object has the effect of establishing an ethic of objects just as the emancipation of labor as a productive force has the consequence of establishing a work ethic. Three centuries apart [6] an identical morality (and an identical psychology) corresponds to an identical logic. And the terms in which Weber (*The Protestant Ethic and the Spirit of Capitalism*) analyzes the rational economic calculus as worldly asceticism are, *mutatis mutandis*, entirely valid for the rational calculus of signs.

## The Crisis of Functionalism

Before analyzing how this crisis is lived today by designers, it must be seen that its elements have always been present. It is derived from the will of functionalism to impose itself in its order (like political economy in its order) as the *dominant rationality*, susceptible to giving account of everything and to directing all processes. From the outset, this rationality, which is of necessity blind to its own arbitrariness, gives birth to an "irrational" or "fantasy" counter-discourse, which circulates between the two poles of kitsch and surrealism (the one a subtle accomplice of functionality, the other directly antagonistic, while they are not mutually exclusive: surrealism plays very much upon a derision of kitsch and kitsch often adopts surrealist values).

The surrealist object emerges at the same epoch as the functional object, as its derision and transgression. Although they are overtly dys- or para-functional, these phantasmic objects nevertheless presuppose — albeit in a contradictory sense — the advent of functionality as the universal moral law of the object, and the advent of this object itself, separated, autonomous and dedicated to the transparency of its function. When one ponders it, there is something unreal and almost surreal [7] in the fact of reducing an object to its

---

6. Rather, these are *logical* guideposts to mark what in fact was a continuous historical process. However, the moment of formal theorization (which the Bauhaus is for the political economy of the sign) always marks a crucial point in the historical process itself.

7. Similarly, there is something immediately Kafkaesque in the reduction of man

function: and it suffices to push this principle of functionality to the limit to make its absurdity emerge. This is evident in the case of the toaster, iron or "undiscoverable objects" of Carelman.[8] But the calculus of human aspirations in the large ensemble is also stunning and justifies the presence of both sewing machine and umbrella on the dissection table of Lautrémont.

Thus surrealism too is born *a contrario* from the advent of the object and from the extension of the functional (and semantic) calculus to the whole field of everydayness. In this sense, the Bauhaus and surrealism are inseparable, like the monstrous, anomic critical discourse of objects with respect to the rational discourse of objects. (Yet little by little, this subversive discourse grows quickly more customary and will come to be integrated into the functionalized universe as an anomalous variant. In its banal version it enters our whole environment in homeopathic doses.)

Magritte's shoe-foot, his woman in a dress of skin (or nude dress) hung in a closet, men with a chest of drawers, or anthropomorphic machines: everywhere surrealism plays upon the *distance* instituted by the functionalist calculus between the object and itself, or between man and his own body, upon the distance between any term and the abstract finality that is imposed upon it, upon the cleavage that makes men and things suddenly find themselves split apart as signs and confronted with a transcendental "signified": their function. Fusion of the skin of breasts and the folds of a dress, of toes and the leather of a shoe: surrealist imagery plays with this split by denying it, but on the basis of separate terms separately legible in the collage or superimpression. That is to say that it does not restore a symbolic relationship, where there would be no room for the concept of separation, because the relation is integrated in reciprocity and exchange. In surrealism the symbolic relation no longer appears except as the phantasm of subject-object adequation. The surrealist metaphor defines itself as a compromise formation, as a short-circuit between the two orders of functionality (here transgressed and made ridiculous) and the symbolic (distorted and made into a phantasm). It seizes the moment when the object is still stuck in anthropomorphism and has not yet given birth to its pure functionality, that is, the moment when the object is on the way to absorbing man into

to his (bureaucratic) function.

8. Jacques Carelman, *Catalogue a objets introuvables*. [English version: *Catalog of Fantastic Things* (New York: Ballantine Books). In fact these things (like a double-headed hammer which will work in both directions, or for either left- or right-handed carpenters) might be found in joke stores — "gimmick" might be an accurate translation. — *Trans.*]

its functional unreality but has not yet done so. In depicting their contamination to the extreme, surrealism illustrates and denounces the gap between subject and object. It is a revolt against the new reality principle of the object. To the rational calculus, which "liberates" the object in its function, is opposed surrealism, which liberates the object *from* its function, returning it to free associations from which will re-emerge not the symbolic (in which the respective crystallization of subject and object does not take place), but subjectivity itself, "liberated" in the phantasm.

As subjective poetry, where the primary and combinatory processes of dreaming come to upset the functional combinatory, surrealism thus briefly and contradictorily illuminates the growth crisis of the object, which is the generalized abstraction of life under the sign of the functional object. As celebration of the agony of a despairing subjectivity, all nonsense verse (that of Lewis Carroll, for example, a precursor of surrealism) negatively illustrates, through its revolt and parody, the irreversible institution of a political economy of meaning, of a sign form and an object form structurally linked to the commodity form. (In their time, the Romantics represented a similar reaction to the industrial revolution and to the first phase of the development of political economy.)

But the surrealist transgression itself still corresponds to a relative extension of the political economy of the sign. It acts upon figurative, formal objects, upon the contents and the "signifieds" of representation. Today, when functionalism has graduated from the isolated object to the system (hyper-rationality quite as Kafkaesque as the other), when the still almost artisanal functionalism of the Bauhaus is surpassed in the cybernetic and mathematical design of the environment, surrealism can survive only as a folklore. From this moment, we are beyond the object and its function. A "being beyond" the subject in the contemporary systems of relations and information already corresponds to this "being beyond" the object. The hybrid game of the surrealists, legitimate between the face of the object and of man, between function and desire (both instances, separated in reality, still celebrate their impossible conjunction in the surreal) — that subtle mixture of a functional logos with a dismembered, disunited logic of the symbolic that haunts it, resulting in the illogic of a phantasmagoric representation, is resolved when confronted with the cybernetic order. Nothing retains the place of the critical, regressive-transgressive discourse of Dada and of surrealism.

After surrealism, the outburst of abstraction (dreamlike, geometric or expressionist — Klee, Kadinski, Mondrian, Pollock) corresponded to an ever-advancing systematization of the rational order — this was the last critical tirade of art, for where are we today? Presently art limits itself to a kinetic or lumino-dynamic manipulation, or to the psychedelic staging of a flaccid surrealism — in short, to a combinatory, which is the very image of that of real systems, to an aesthetic operationality (whose biblical specimen is the "New Artistic Spirit" of Schoeffer), which is in no way distinguished from that of cybernetic programs. The hyper-reality of systems has absorbed the critical surreality of the phantasm. Art has become, or is on the way to becoming, total design, *metadesign*.

The mortal enemy of design is kitsch. Ostensibly destroyed by the Bauhaus, it always rises again from its ashes. That is because it has the whole "economic system" behind it, say the designers; whereas they have only their virtue. So, in 1967, in an article in *Esthétique Industrielle* [9] Abraham Moles analyzes the crisis of functionalism as the overflowing of the sober rationality of design, and of its strict ethos of function, through the irrational proliferation of consumption goods. The "absolute consumer mentality promoted by the economic machine" progressively buries the functionalist blueprint under a jumble of neo-kitsch. Functionalism suffers from this contradiction and dies.

In fact, this analysis absolves design of any internal contradiction: the fault then lies in an "obsession with status" and a "strategy of desire." But Moles (with many others) forgets that the system (and the whole process of consumption that it implies) is also rational and perfectly consistent with itself. It triumphantly fulfills the claims of functionality. It is precisely through the "anarchic production" denounced by our virtuous functionalist academics that it suffices to its goal, which is its own survival and extended reproduction. So there is no contradiction: the model of rationality was originally and still remains fundamentally economic; it is normal that the functionality of the economic system embody it. Hard and pure design can do nothing, for rationality based on calculation *is precisely the kind that inspires it*. From the very beginning, it rests on the same basis of rational abstraction as the economic system. Undoubtedly this rationality may be potentially absurd, but for both design and consumption in the same way. Their apparent contradiction is only the logical debt of their deep-rooted complicity.

9. This review which originally had the name "Esthétique Industrielle" has changed title several times since its first publication in 1952 and is presently called *Design Industry*. — *Trans.*

So, designers complain of being misunderstood and of their ideal being disfigured by the system? All puritans are hypocrites.

This crisis must in fact be analyzed on an entirely different level, the level of semiology, the elements of which we have explained above. In summary, the formula of the Bauhaus is: for every form and every object there is an objective, determinable *signified* — its function. This is what is called in linguistics the level of *denotation*. The Bauhaus claims to strictly isolate this nucleus, this level of denotation — all the rest is coating, the hell of *connotation*: residue, superfluity, excrescence, eccentricity, ornamentation, uselessness. Kitsch. The thing denoted (functional) is beautiful, the connoted (parasitical) is ugly. Better yet: the thing denoted (objective) is true, the connoted is false (ideological). In effect, behind the concept of objectivity, the whole metaphysical and moral argument of truth is at stake.[10]

Now today this postulate of denotation is in the process of breaking up. It is finally beginning to be seen (in semiology as well) that it is arbitrary, not merely an artifact of a method, but a metaphysical fable. *There is no* truth of the object, and denotation is never more than the most beautiful of connotations. This is not only theoretical: designers, urban technologists and programmers of the environment are confronted daily (if they pose themselves a few questions) with the demise of objectivity. The function(ality) of forms, of objects, becomes more incomprehensible, illegible, incalculable every day. Where is the centrality of the object, its functional equation, today? Where is its directing function, where are the parasitic functions? Who can tell, when now the economic, the social, the psychological and the metapsychological are so inextricably mixed together? Can anyone demonstrate beyond a doubt that a particular "superfluous" form, a given "irrational" trait does not find its echo elsewhere, after all (in the unconscious, for all I know), in some more subtle equilibrium, and thus does not in some way have a functional justification?[11] In this systematic logic (for functionality is nothing

---

10.   The Platonic and Kantian heritage of functionalism is striking: morality, aesthetics and truth are confused in the same ideal. The functional is the synthesis of pure reason and practical reason. Or again: the functional is the beautiful plus the useful. Utility itself is simultaneously that which is moral and that which is true. Stir up the whole thing, and we have the Platonic holy trinity.

11.   In any case, something else radically escapes any calculus of function: ambivalence, which acts such that any positive function is in the same movement denied and decomposed, annulled according to a logic of desire for which a unilateral finality never exists. This level is beyond even functional complexity. Were one to have achieved a perfect computation of even contradictory functions, this ambivalence would forever remain insoluble, irreducible.

other than a *system of interpretation*), everything is potentially functional and nothing is in fact. The guiding utopia turns upon itself. And it is not surprising that, as things gradually lose this quality of objective finality, it is transferred to the system itself which, in its process of reproduction, completes on its own terms what remains. In the end, the system becomes the only bearer of active functionality, which it redistributes to its elements. It alone is admirably "designed," and its own finality envelops it like an egg.[12]

If there is no further absolute utility of the object, it is also the end of the superfluous, and the whole theoretical edifice of functionalism crumbles. This works to the interests of fashion, which plays entirely upon connotation, not encumbering itself with objective denotation (though it claims to). With its unstable, "irrational" rhetoric, and sanctioned only by the *contemporaneity* of signs, fashion appropriates the whole system. And if functionalism defends itself weakly against fashion, it is because the latter expresses the total systematic potential, while functionalism, rooted in the metaphysic of denotation, expresses only a particular case, which it arbitrarily privileges according to a universal ethic. Once a sign calculus has been instituted nothing can oppose its generalization. Neither rational nor irrational any longer exists. The Bauhaus and design claim to control the process by mastery of the signifieds (the objective evaluation of functions), but in fact it is the play of signifiers that carries the process forward (the play of sign exchange value). Now the latter is unlimited, and escapes all control (as in political economy, with respect to the system of exchange value: it invades all spheres, despite any opposition by liberal and pious souls who believe themselves able to circumscribe it).

Such is the crisis of functionalism. Nothing can successfully oppose whatever form enters the unlimited combinatory of fashion — whose only function, therefore, is its sign function. Even the forms created by design do not escape. And if "styling," which the Bauhaus believed it had disqualified, re-emerges through design without the latter ever being truly able to eliminate its traces and regain control of itself in its severity, it is because what appears pathological to it is already contained in the logic of its own design (i.e., plan, project). If our era nostalgically salvages all the kitsch of the 19th century, despite the Bauhaus revolution, it is because in fact this *already*

---

12.   It is known that the egg is one of the ideal tendencies of design — a formal stereotype, as "kitsch" as any other. This means that the finality of the system is quite simply *tautological*. But the completed stage of development of function is tautology — the perfect redundancy of the "signified" succumbing to the vicious circle of the "signifier" — an egg.

belongs to it. The floral motif on the sewing machine or the metro entrance is a regressive compromise, but by its resurgence today it takes on a surrealist value of fashion and it is logical: surrealism in a way only formalizes the hybrid production of commercial kitsch as an artistic transgression. Today, pure design spurns the floral motif but it carries the naturist ideology much deeper: the branching (*étoilé*) structures of organic bodies serve as models for an entire city. There is no radical difference between the two. Everywhere, ever since the concept was born, nature, whether taken as décor or as a structural model, remains as the projection of a *social* model. And the branching structure is always that of capital.

But if design is immersed in fashion, one must not complain, for this is the mark of its triumph. It is the mark of the territorial scope established by the political economy of the sign, whose first rational theorization was design and the Bauhaus. Everything that today wishes to be marginal, irrational, insurrectionary, "anti-art," anti-design, etc., from pop to psychedelic or to street art — everything obeys the same economy of the sign, whether it wants to or not. All of it is design. Nothing escapes design: that is its fate.

So we are discussing much more than a crisis. It is pointless to deplore the fate (*fatalité*) of consumption as Abraham Moles does, and to refer appeals to a neo-functionalism that puts into play "the stimulation of fantasy and of the imagination by a systematic effort"! This neo-functionalism can only be a re-semantization (resurrection of signifieds),[13] and thus a recycling of the same contradictions. More likely, neo-functionalism will be the image of neo-capitalism, that is, an intensification of the play of signifiers, a mathematization and cybernetization of the code. "Humanist" neo-functionalism has no chance when faced with operational metadesign. The era of function and of the signified has revolved, the era of the signifier and the code is beginning.

*The Environment and Cybernetics:*
*The Highest Stage of Political Economy*

This revolution of the sign inaugurated by the Bauhaus was at least foreseen by it and has since been brought relatively to light by the analysts of design. In *Critique* (November 1967), Van Lier sees clearly that "these new forms and their operation...refer gradually to the very extremities of the system," and that functionality is not

---

13.   "Social" design will be redone with human contents, or alternatively the game, playfulness, the "free" combinatory, etc. will be reintroduced. But make no mistake: it is still the "game" which is taken into account, the game as a particular function, a liberal-modernist variant of the same code.

utility but "transforming things into reciprocal information, permitting them to become signs, creating significations," and he adds as if it were self-evident, "food of all culture and of all humanity." The eternal humanist metaphor: the more signs there are, the more messages and information there are, the more one communicates — the better it is. Having revealed the advent of sign value and its indefinite extension on the basis of rational productivity, he sees in it, without hesitation, an absolute progress for humanity. It is an analogous reaction to that which sees the industrial upsurge more or less in the long run as abundance and happiness for all. This was the 19th century illusion with respect to material production. In the 20th century, it takes off again with even more strength in sign productivity. Now we have cybernetic idealism, blind faith in radiating information, mystique of information services and the media.

In both cases the fundamental error is the same: only the *use value* aspect of the product or sign is retained, and the industrial (or semiurgic) mutation is understood exclusively in terms of an infinite multiplication of use values (signs as messages). Profusion of goods and profusion of signs in the interest of maximal consumption and maximal information. Account is never taken of the fact that this mutation institutes first and above all a system of *exchange value*, a generalized abstract social form that is by no means "the food of all culture and all humanity." This idealism of content (of production or of signification) never takes form into account. This idealism of messages forgets that it is the hegemony of the code that is installed behind their accelerated circulation. In fact, the two quite simply forget political economy and its strategic, political social dimension, in order to be situated from the outset in the transparent sphere of value. This optimism can seem to be in good faith, it can take on the benign air of the designer who plans, for his small part, to contribute to increased information by his creativity, or the prophetic air of McLuhan, who exalts the "already present" global communication. Everywhere, this ideology of communication becomes mistress, a myth in which cybernetics presents itself as neo-humanism. The profusion of messages in a way replaces the profusion of goods (the myth of abundance) in the imaginary (*imaginaire*) of the species.

Everywhere the ideologues of use value have been the accomplices and henchmen of the political extension of the system of exchange value. Thus, in the order of material goods, consumption came to perform the function of reviving the system of production, not by being the apotheosis of use value, but as the blind social constraint of satisfaction. Thanks to consumption, the system not only succeeds in exploiting people by force, but in making them *participate* in its multiplied survival. This is a considerable advance. But this participation only takes on its whole fantastic scope at the level of signs. It is there that the entire strategy of "neo-capitalism" is articulated in its originality: in a semiurgy and an operational semiology, which are only the developed form of controlled participation.

From this perspective, in which the production of signs seen as a system of exchange value takes on an entirely different meaning than in the naive utopia of their use value, design and the environmental disciplines can be considered as one of the branches of mass communication, a gigantic ramification of human and social engineering. From this moment on, our true environment is the universe of communication.[14] It is in this that it differs radically from the 19th century concepts of "nature" or of "milieu." While these latter referred to physical, biological (determinism of substance, of heredity and of species) or "socio-cultural" (the "milieu") laws, environment is from the beginning a network of messages and signs, its laws being those of communication.

The environment is the autonomization of the entire universe of practices and forms, from the everyday to the architectural, from the discursive to the gestural and the political, as a sector of operations and calculation, as sending-receiving of messages, as space-time of communication. The practical concept of design — which in the final instance is analyzed as the production of communication (man to signs, signs among themselves, men among themselves) — corresponds to the theoretical concept of environment. Here one must be made to communicate — that is to say, participate — not by the purchase of material goods but in the data-processing mode, by the circulation of signs and messages. That is why the environment, like the market (which is its economic equivalent) is a virtually universal concept. It is the concrete summary of the whole political economy of the sign. Design, which is the corresponding practice of this political economy, is generalized proportionately, and if it began by being applied only to industrial products, today it embraces and logically must embrace all sectors. Nothing is more false than the limits that a "humanistic" design wishes to fix for itself; in fact, everything belongs to design, everything springs from it, whether it says so or not: the body is

---

14.    Paradoxically (and undoubtedly symptomatically) the British Ministry of the Environment presides over almost all sectors, *except* the media.

designed, sexuality is designed, political, social, human relations are
designed, just as are needs and aspirations, etc. This "designed"
universe is what properly constitutes the environment. Like the
market, the environment is in a way only a logic: that of (sign)
exchange value. Design is the imposition of this sign exchange value
at all levels of models and operational practices. Once again it is the
practical triumph of the political economy of the sign and the
theoretical triumph of the Bauhaus.

Like public relations, human relations and the psycho-sociology of
enterprise, like planning and participation, marketing and merchandizing strive to produce a relationship, to restore it where
the social relations of production make it problematic. Similarly, the
task, the strategic function of design in the contemporary system, is
to produce communication between men and an environment which
never exists precisely save as a foreign agency (still like the market).
Like many other ideological concepts, "environment" designates by
antiphrasis that from which one is separated; it designates the end of
the proximate world. Beings and things are held as far away from
one another as possible. And the mystique of the environment is
proportionate to the moat between man and nature which the system
digs deeper every day, whether it likes it or not. This split, this
fundamentally broken and dissociated relationship (in the image of
social relations) between man and his environment is the *raison
d'être* and the site of design. There it tries desperately to restore
meaning, to restore transparency by means of a great deal of information, and "comprehension" by means of a great number of
messages. If one considers it carefully, the philosophy of design,
echoed by the whole theory of the environment, is in the end the
*doctrine of participation and of public relations extended to all of
nature*. Nature (which seems to become hostile, wishing by pollution
to avenge its exploitation) must be made to participate. With nature,
at the same time as with the urban world, it is necessary to recreate
communication by means of a multitude of signs (as it must be
recreated between employers and employees, between the governing
and the governed, by the strength of media and of planning). In
short, it must be offered an industrial contract: protection and
security — incorporating its natural energies, which become
dangerous, in order to regulate them better. For of course all this
only aims at the better and better alignment of this participant
nature (which is contradicted and recycled by intelligent design),
along the norms of a rational hyperproductivity.

Such is the political ideology of design, which attains its global scope today in the discourse of environment. From Gropius to Universitas [15] there is a continuous succession of stages toward what could be termed a metadesign, a meta-political economy which is to neo-capitalism what the classic liberal economy was to capitalism.

If one speaks of environment, it is because it has already ceased to exist. To speak of ecology is to attest to the death and total abstraction of nature. Everywhere the "right" (to nature, to the environment) countersigns the "demise of." This gradual destruction of nature (as vital and as ideal reference) is strictly linked to what we have called the gradual decline of the signified in the analysis of the contemporary sign (of an objective, real referent, of the denoted function, of the truth of the world as the real guarantee of the sign — a little like its gold backing. The gold of the signified-referent has disappeared; it is the end of the gold exchange standard. The sign is no longer convertible into its reference value, as is seen in the trend of the current international situation, where there is no longer anything but the free interrelation of floating currencies). The great signified, the great referent Nature, is dead, replaced by environment, which simultaneously designates and designs its death and the restoration of nature as simulation model (its "reconstitution," as one says of orange juice that has been dehydrated). And what we have said about nature — that it was always the projection of a social model — is of course also valid for the environment. The passage from a concept of nature that is still objectifiable as a reference, to the concept of environment in which the system of circulation of signs (sign exchange value) abolishes all reference, or even becomes its own referent, designs (i.e., sketches) the passage between societies. We pass from a society that is still contradictory, non-homogeneous, and not yet saturated with political economy; from a society in which the refractory models of transcendence, conflict and surpassing still exist; where a human nature is shredded but still present (cf. the affinity of Marxism itself with a substantialist anthropology of needs and nature), and where there is still a history with its revolutionary theory, etc., to a cybernetized society. We enter a social environment of synthesis in which a total abstract communication and an immanent manipulation no longer leave any point exterior to the system. It is the end of traditional political economy, and simultaneously the commencement of the meta-political economy of a society that has become its own pure environment. (It is this that McLuhan has outlined, in the exalted mode.) As Mitscherlich says:

15. An internationally founded project "for a post-technological society" inaugurated by the Museum of Modern Art in New York.

"Insofar as manipulation of the environment succeeds, there simultaneously succeeds a manipulation of man, who has himself become an object of manipulation, that is to say, simple environment."

The social control of air, water, etc., in the name of environmental protection evidently shows men entering the field of social control a little more deeply themselves. That nature, air, water become rare goods entering the field of value after having been simply productive forces, shows men themselves entering a little more deeply into the field of political economy. At the limit of this evolution, after natural parks, there may be an "International Foundation of Man" just as in Brazil there is a "National Indian Foundation": "The National Indian Foundation is in a position to assure the preservation of the indigenous population in the best conditions, as well as (*sic*) the survival of the animal and vegetable species that have lived alongside them for thousands of years." (Of course this institution disguises and sanctions genocide and massacre: one liquidates and reconstitutes — same schema.) Man no longer even confronts his environment: he himself is virtually part of the environment to be protected.

# CHAPTER ELEVEN

## CONCERNING THE FULFILLMENT OF DESIRE
## IN EXCHANGE VALUE

There was a raid on a U.S. department store several years ago. A group occupied and neutralized the store by surprise, and then invited the crowd by loudspeaker to help themselves. A symbolic action! And the result? Nobody could figure out what to take — or else they took insignificant items they could easily have filched on any normal shopping day.

If you had fifty million dollars, what would you do with it? Chaos.

Faced with the disposal of free time at will, the same immediate panic surfaces in us. How do we get rid of it?

And we could adduce further examples, such as the French 400-meter runner in the European championships, who, 100 meters from the finish line, wilts in his final effort and finishes third. "When I sensed I was going to win," he said afterward, "something inside me broke." Or the French tennis player at a tournament in Spain: two sets ahead and the match in hand with an ailing opponent, he blows the match point and goes down to defeat — "irresistibly," one could say -- and to the general amazement of the spectators. Not to mention Poulidor, the eternal runner-up whose fame is derived precisely from this chronic incapacity to wrap up victory.

When we say of someone that he "almost" won, that he fell just short of winning, what is supposed to have been missed? Don't these phrases indicate in a way that victory would have been the worst thing that could have happened to him, that victory would have been failure?

These are just slips of the will, of the drive for appropriation and satisfaction, performance and supremacy, which is supposed to be the deepest of human motivations. Freud advanced the exploration of human psychology immensely, taking such minutiae as his starting point. But the fantastic perspectives thus revealed have scarcely ruffled the composure of general anthropology, economic "science," or the "humanities." Psychoanalysis itself has helped to circumscribe these anomalies with depth psychology ("everybody has his unconscious and its *his* business"). And so, almost miraculously, we find they have no equivalent in social or political practice, where an essentially fail-safe rationality reigns supreme. It is this indefatigability of general postulates about man in economic, social and political matters that we shall interrogate from the categorical perspective of exhaustion and failure.

The more or less experimental and limiting case of the department store shows that once exchange value has been neutralized, use value disappears with it. When the demand for always more utility and satisfaction is confronted with the possibility of its immediate realization, it evaporates. The whole package of motivations, needs and rationality that is so conveniently supposed to constitute human nature simply flies apart. Beyond the transparency of economics, where everything is clear because is suffices to "want something for your money," man apparently no longer knows what he wants.

Some hypotheses:

— Objects, and the needs that they imply, exist precisely in order to resolve the anguish of not knowing what one wants.

— What isn't mediated by the abstraction of exchange value cannot exist as a "spontaneous" and "concrete" value either — such as utility, for example. Both axiological levels are equally abstract and make common sense. There is no use value without exchange value. Once the latter is neutralized in the gift process, or gratuity, prodigality, expenditure, then use value itself becomes unintelligible.

— This idea applies, *mutatis mutandis*, to sign exchange value. What isn't mediated by statutory social competition, the exchange of differential signs, or by *models*, has no value. With respect to signs, the use value-exchange value distinction is virtually obliterated. If "sign use value" is defined as differential satisfaction, a sort of qualitative surplus value anticipated through a choice, a preference, a semiological calculation; and if sign exchange value is defined as the general form (the code) that regulates the interplay of models; then it becomes clear the extent to which use value issues directly from the functioning of the code and exchange value system. The process is the same in the so-called economic order: hence the abstractness of use value, which only appears already mediatized by the exchange value system (as commodity form) and simultaneously by the models and code (where it appears as sign form).

Thus, today exchange value and sign exchange value mingle inextricably.[1] The completed system (at bottom that of "con-

1. The Veblen effect (I am buying this because it is more expensive) is a significant limiting case in which the economic (quantitative) is converted into sign-difference. Here one can conceptualize the emergence of "need" starting from the pure outbidding of exchange value (cf. also the art auction as the locale of transition between spheres of value). In the case of signs, the Veblen effect becomes the absolute rule: fashion knows only pure and ascending differentiation.

sumption" as the ultimate stage of political economy) depends on liberty, not only at the level of production (liberty to buy and sell labor power), but also, in a second moment, which is by now concurrent, at the level of consumption (freedom of choice). The abstraction of the sign exchange system (i.e., models and their internalization in semiological calculation) is necessarily combined with the systematic abstraction of production and economic exchange (i.e., capital, money, exchange value).

The sign is the apogee of the commodity. Fashion and the commodity are a single, identical form. The differentiation of the commodity is inscribed from the outset, in the form of sign exchange value (and not in a quantitative logic of profit). The commodity achieves its apotheosis when it is able to impose itself as a code, that is as the geometric locus of the circulation of models, and hence as the total medium or a culture (and not only of an economy).

Exchange value is realized in sign exchange value. Sign exchange value and exchange value are definitively realized in use value.

This trinomial delineates a total, coherent universe of value where man is supposed to fulfill himself through the final satisfaction of his needs. According to rational calculation, he is reputed to be continuously raising his rate of value production. Relayed from one summit to the other of the great axiological triangle, he can effectively only hope to transcend himself, to positivize himself, in values. His movement traces the boundaries of a value world that has coincided for centuries with the definition of humanism.

This triangulation of value defines a full, positive world, relentlessly completed by the plus sign: the logic of surplus value (inseparable from value). It is a world in which man is incapable of selling himself short. Hence, the value process is equivalent to a *phantasmic organization*, in which desire is fulfilled and lack resolved; in which desire is achieved and performed; and in which the symbolic dimension and all difference are abolished. Value is totalitarian. It excludes ambivalence, as well as any relation in which man would cease to complete himself in value, or index himself according to the law of equivalence and surplus value. But ambivalence haunts the sphere of value everywhere. It is what resurges, though covertly, in failure.

The crowd fails to react positively to the absolute availability of the commodity (that is, by responding with spontaneous appropriation); it fails to obey the categorical imperative of need; it even fails to understand what it wants and simply take what is offered. In fact, gratuity eliminates supply in the economic sense of the term, and abolishes demand in the same stroke. So the latter is based only in the logic of value. Outside this logic, man has "need" of nothing. What we need is what is bought and sold, evaluated and chosen. What is neither sold nor taken, but only given and returned, no one "needs." The exchange of looks, the present which comes and goes, are like the air people breathe in and out. This is the metabolism of exchange, prodigality, festival — and also of destruction (which returns to non-value what production has erected, valorized). In this domain, value isn't even recognized. *And desire is not fulfilled there in the phantasm of value.*

What comes to light in this inability to just grab consumer goods, as in the case of the slackening athlete, is that the official imperative, orchestrated as individual need (the need to win, etc.), has displaced something else, which is precisely the contrary demand: to lose, misplace, dispossess oneself, or give up. And this isn't some masochistic reversal of a more fundamental economy aimed toward value, performance and achievement, but the inverse and radical necessity of lack (*manque*). Every fulfillment of desire in value returns to this contrary extremity, because with the termination of satisfaction, it alone preserves the subject's questioning concerning his own desire. Such is the foundation of ambivalence.

Taking has never been a sufficient condition for enjoyment. It is necessary to be able to receive, to give, to return, to destroy — if possible, all at once. The realization process of value dissolves all this into an impoverished, unilateral and positive modality, dispossessing the subject of his symbolic insistence: (1) the refusal to fulfill desire, or *lack*; and (2) the necessity of a relationship unmediated by the systemic logic of value, or *symbolic exchange*.

Enjoyment is radical, value is sublime; so this radical symbolic insistence is sublimated in value. The commodity is the incarnation of the sublime in the economic order. The radical demand of the subject is sublimated there in the ever renewed positivity of his demand for objects. But behind this sublime realization of value, there lies something else. Something other speaks, something irreducible that can take the form of violent destruction, but most frequently assumes the cloaked form of deficit, of the exhaustion and refusal of cathexis, of resistance to satisfaction and refusal of fulfillment. Viewing the contemporary economic situation as a whole, all this begins to look like a tendency we might want to call the *falling rate of enjoyment*. According to a mysterious counter economy of lost opportunity, it is this lively, basic denial of value, this latent violence toward the principle of identity and equivalence, this vacillation beyond satisfaction which, in the last instance, assures the subject in his being. And this is not metapsychology. Rather, it is on account of having rejected all these considerations *en bloc* as "meta"-psychology that the contemporary human sciences and economics must watch their rational edifice founder without even being able to account for the reversal. [2]

We have been speaking of syndromes of lost opportunity and illusive pleasure: is this the death instinct talking through us? — preserving ubiquitously and perennially a radical difference, against the unitary phantasm of value? Perhaps. But any discourse in terms of a death instinct verges too close on metapsychology of the subject, forgetting that what is preserved in the splitting of the subject, and the subject's failure to satisfy his desire, is, along with the recognition of castration, the symbolic potentiality of exchange. Lack is always that in terms of which we miss others, and through which others miss us. In the value process (whether the investment be commercial or phantasmic), no one misses anyone, nothing is anything, because everything is equivalent to something, and everyone is assured of equalling at least himself. Only value is exchanged (which is to say, transformed into itself) — only value, and individuals and things as terms of value, according to the law of equivalence. Thus one could say that what preserves the potentiality of exchange, of a reciprocity where individuals truly emerge in their difference and their lack, is Eros — the death instinct being, inversely, that which tends to the abolition of the symbolic in the repetitive cycle of value. From this perspective, the sublime and repetitive world of the commodity could well be considered the field in which the death instinct attains its fulfillment.

---

2. The film *The Loneliness of the Long-Distance Runner* is a very fine example, from a social and political point of view, of this ubiquitous counter-economy. The hero is an adolescent in a rehabilitation center who deliberately renounces a decisive victory in a running contest in order to avoid spreading any of the glory to his institutional oppressors. By losing, he preserves his own truth: here, failure merges with class revolt. Admittedly, in this story, the failure is explicitly deliberate, but it is not difficult to see how "accidental" lapses and physical slips may acquire virtually the same meaning of denial and resistance. In his own way, the 400 meter runner mentioned above calls into question the exchange value system — whose forms are not limited to dominating the salaried worker and the consumer. By running to win, athletes reactivate the competitive value system; they work to reproduce it in "exchange" for the satisfactions of personal prestige. Exploitation is as intense here as at the level of selling one's labor power. It is this bogus exchange mechanism that failure unconsciously causes to break down. In this sense, every "psychological dysfunction" *vis-à-vis* "normality" (which is only the law of the capitalist milieu) is open to a *political* reading. Today politics has no particular sphere unto itself, nor any definition. It is time to discover the latent forms, the displacements and condensations — briefly, the "work" (as in "dream-work") of politics.

But we are never going to get very far quibbling over where to pin these labels. The essential is to grasp that what is speaking, beneath the "objective" process of value, does not speak contradictorily (in the sense of a dialectical contradiction). Ambivalence is not the dialectical negation of value: it is the incessant potentiality of its annulment, of the *destruction of the illusion of value*. It is not with an opposing code that the ambivalent and symbolic confront the discourse of value. Against value's positive transcendence, the symbolic opposes its radicality. Against the logic of sublimation and generality (of abstraction) are opposed the radicality of the non-fulfillment of desire and symbolic exchange.

It remains now to analyze the revolutionary illusion of those responsible for "Operation Super Market." Their hypothesis evidently went something like this: "We are going to suspend the rules of the capitalist game by neutralizing exchange value. We are going to return commodities to their pure use value, thus demystifying consciousness and restoring the clarity of people's relationship to their 'real' needs." Revolution, "hic et nunc." Such is the inspired logic of the purest philosophical Marxism: first, the sharp distinction between use value and exchange value (to the greater philosophical and humanist glory of use value); and then the rationalist theory of mystification. Their conclusion: If people can't spontaneously rediscover a liberated use value, it must be because they are so disciplined in self-repression and the *habitus* of capitalism, it must be because they have so completely internalized the law of exchange value that they are unable to desire a thing when it is simply offered to them.

This overlooks the fact that desire has little vocation to fulfillment in "liberty," but rather in the rule — not in the transparency of a value content, but in the opacity of the code of value. This is the desire of the code, and this desire "needs" to rescue the rules of the game — it requires them — in order to fulfill itself. It is with this investment of the rule by desire, with its own fulfillment in view, that the social order makes its pact. It is this desire that the social order exploits in order to reproduce itself. Here, the phantasm and the institution come together — the political order of power and the fetishized order of perversion (the fulfillment of desire). The phantasm of value is also the phantasm of order and the law.

The "rule" mentioned above is, in our society, the law of exchange value. If there is no longer a set of rules to play by, the game is no longer interesting, for then even cheating and stealing are ruled out. (After all, the latter practices are counter-dependent on the straight rules of the economic game.) If, then, consumption is only possible within the rules, and if desire is only fulfilled fetishistically, the suspension of the rules, instead of clearing the way for wild pleasure, simply prohibits it. The price of things becomes, then, essential, though no longer simply in the quantitative sense, as in exchange value, nor only differentially, as in the "Veblen effect," but as law, as *fetishized form* — a crucial feature of the commodity economy and of the psychic economy of value. The price of things then becomes the guarantor of the psychic economy of value. One may well prefer this equilibrium to free and wild consumption. But for this one pays the additional price of pleasure, whose "rate" falls in proportion with the cycle of expanded reproduction of satisfaction.

Likewise, the athlete who can't stop himself from losing is partly doing this to preserve the very possibility of battling, without the rules of which it would be difficult to run competitions at all.[3] Once again, safeguarding the rules turns out to be a more fundamental imperative than winning itself. Each participant implicitly obeys this structure of exchange, this collective and unconscious function.[4]

So the issue is clearly not "mystified consciousness," nor whatever illusion the aforementioned revolutionaries had about the liberatory suspension of exchange value. They failed to see that there is no contradiction between exchange value and the satisfaction of desire — on the contrary. To be sure, such a contradiction would make the thought of revolution much simpler to grasp, but it is only possible from the perspective of an axiological idealism, and the idealization of use value in particular. In effect, this position is betrayed by its own, powerful sublimation, which leads its adherents to under-estimate the radicality of the law of value, and hence the radicality of its transgression. Having approached the problem so gingerly, they have, in effect, proposed a reformist strategy that contests value at only a relatively superficial level. Then, they are taken aback by the lack of "mass" reaction to their initiative. We can be quite sure they impute this to the fact that their action was too radical, and place their hope in the maturation of the people's consciousness. It never occurs to them for an instant that this passivity might have been due to the fact that their action was too reformist — and that instead of

---

3.   The ideology of sports is a mixture of this implicit "law" and the law of the stronger.

4.   A competitor, a runner for example, who won straightaway, every time — such a case would be a serious exception to the law of exchange, something like incest or sacrilege, and, in the extreme, the collectivity would have to suppress it. Another example of the same sort of thing would be the complete collection, to which not a thing remained to be added: this would be a kind of death.

interpreting it as revolutionary passivity, they would do better to understand it as resistance to reformism.

In other words, this negative reaction of the liberated consumers has perhaps less to do with their submission to the system of exchange value, and more with their resistance to use value, insofar as the latter is at bottom only a ruse of exchange value. Through this refusal to play the use value game, everything happens as though the public had already sniffed out this yet more subtle mystification.

In the final analysis, what is this use value that comes unto them, naked? From where does this offertory emanate, and who gives it? What is this gratuitousness of the content of products, and is it enough to establish the transparency and gratuity of a *social relation?* One thinks not. The unilateral gift is as cold as charity. Granted and submitted to, it is one with the deeper logic of the system, which revolutionary symbolic action therefore manages to escape as ineffectively as the zeal of the shopping public. In the blinding light of revealed use value, no one saw that to abolish the commodity form, pricelessness does not suffice. Radically undermining the logic of exchange value requires more than re-establishing the autonomy and gratuity of use value; it is necessary to restore the possibility of returning, that is, to change the form of social relations. If no counter-gift or reciprocal exchange is possible, we remain imprisoned in the structure of power and abstraction.[5] Such was the case in the example under review. By preserving, in the absence of a radical analysis, a certain level of value (use value), and by experimenting at this level, the "liberators" have also preserved a certain level of power and manipulation. Having played with value, they have inevitably extracted a little surplus from it, in the form of domination.

Hence the negative reaction to this sudden *conferred* profusion, the defensive reaction to the form of the instituted relation, to the non-reciprocity of the situation. This is the defensive reaction of those who "prefer to pay and owe nothing to anyone" — a class reaction that is at bottom perhaps more lucid than that of the liberators, in that they may have sensed, quite correctly, in the unilateral form of the gift and in its content (self-proclaimed liberated use value), one of the many avatars of the system.

To break the circuit of exchange value, it is necessary to restore

---

5.  The unilateral gift is the inverse of the exchange gift. The latter is the basis of reciprocity, whereas the former founds superiority. Only the privileged, like the feudal lord, can allow themselves to receive without returning, without providing a counter-gift, because their rank protects them against challenge and loss of prestige.

exchange itself — not value (not even use value). In fact, use value implies the rupture of exchange for the same reason that exchange value does, namely, it entails the object completed as value and the individual objectified in his relation to this value. In symbolic exchange, however, the object, or the full value that it was, returns again to nothing (consider the ambivalence of the Latin term *res*). It is that something which, through being given and returned, is, as such, annulled, and marks in its presence or absence the movement of the relationship. The "object," this *res nulla*, has absolutely no use value, it is good for nothing. Thus, only that which assumes its meaning through continual reciprocal exchange eludes exchange value, in the gift and counter-gift, in the ambivalence of an open relationship, and *never in a final relation of value.*

In the present case, the "negative reaction" is tantamount to a radical demand for a revolution that would liberate — not objects and their value — but the exchange relationship itself, the reciprocity of a speech that everywhere today is being eradicated by the terrorism of value.

# NAME INDEX